IMAGES
of America

GRAYSLAKE AND AVON TOWNSHIP

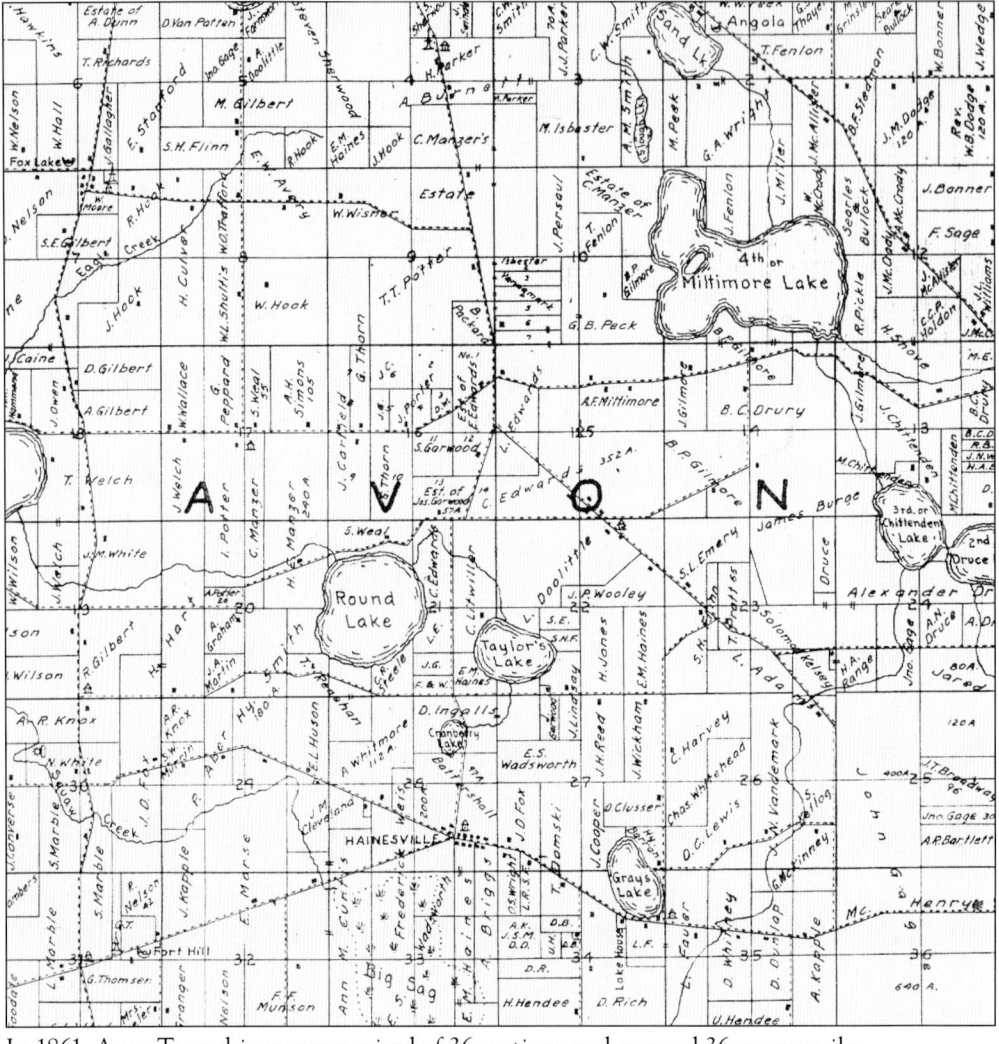

In 1861, Avon Township was comprised of 36 sections and covered 36 square miles.

On the cover: The lakes have not changed, but the land surrounding them has. This is a view of Grays Lake, around 1930. (Courtesy of Grayslake Historical Society.)

IMAGES
of America

GRAYSLAKE AND AVON TOWNSHIP

Charlotte K. Renehan

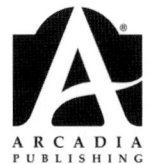

ARCADIA
PUBLISHING

Copyright © 2007 by Charlotte K. Renehan
ISBN 978-0-7385-5097-8

Published by Arcadia Publishing
Charleston SC, Chicago IL, Portsmouth NH, San Francisco CA

Printed in the United States of America

Library of Congress Catalog Card Number: 2007928572

For all general information contact Arcadia Publishing at:
Telephone 843-853-2070
Fax 843-853-0044
E-mail sales@arcadiapublishing.com
For customer service and orders:
Toll-Free 1-888-313-2665

Visit us on the Internet at www.arcadiapublishing.com

This book is dedicated to past, present, and future historians.

CONTENTS

Acknowledgments		6
Introduction		7
1.	Hainesville	9
2.	Grayslake	19
3.	The Round Lake Area	71
4.	Lakes, Resorts, and Recreation	95
5.	The Land	115

ACKNOWLEDGMENTS

Acknowledgments for this work are multifaceted. The first acknowledgment is that this is not a complete history of the Grayslake and Avon Township area. The scope is too large to include all known information. Also, images are not available for many historical scenes and events. It is hoped that following this publication, people with information, including documentation and images, will share with the public by contributing to a historical depository, such as the Grayslake Historical Society. There they will be available for future generations to enjoy.

No work of this sort is possible without using the work of previous authors and editors. It is through their efforts that the history of the area has been preserved thus far. Their writings run the gamut from a few typed pages, as was done by Lonnie Wicks in 1960, to the 500-page hardcover book *Past and Present of Lake County, Illinois* published in 1877 by Wm. LeBaron and Company. Hopefully this book spurs readers to go to other sources to learn more about the area.

Finally, *Grayslake and Avon Township* would not have come to fruition without the helping hands and minds of many. Some furnished pictures, some furnished suggestions, and some located facts. They were all a part of this work. Thanks goes to Pat Anderson, Barbara Bonde, Marie Caviness, the Carl F. Clausen family, College of Lake County public relations office, Winnie Frost Cox, Ann Darrow, Diana Dretske, Connie Dunbar, Greater Round Lake Fire Protection District, Dorothy Groth, Hainesville Village Hall staff, Ed Hall, Penny Heckel, Rich Hermann, Karen Hook, Mary Hook, Joanne Johnson, Rev. Lisle Kaufman, Robert Krause, Lake County Discovery Museum, Lake County Fair Association, Joanne Lawrence, Joe Lodesky, Rudolph Magna, Beverly Millard, Jack Molidor, Marion Doolittle Parker, Nancy Wightman Pease, Kent Rich, Paula Rohrs, Ron Roselli, Round Lake High School Library, Avi Brandstetter Shinners, Kirk Smith, Mary Stang, Cindy Surleta, Bill Thompson, Evie Turner, Waukegan Historical Society, John Wedge, Al Westerman, and Patty Yopp. The author is indebted to Charlie Groth, who spent hours scanning images for this endeavor.

Last but not least, a special thanks to Jill Martin, fellow historian and genealogist, and member of the Warren Township Historical Society. Martin encouraged me to take on the task of compiling this work and was my mentor throughout the process.

INTRODUCTION

It is often asked, "What is in a name?" There have been different theories about the origin of the name Avon given to township 45 north, range 10, east of the third principal meridian. One theory posed is that settlers came from a town called Avon in the state of New York. It is known that early residents either came from or were descendants of people from Sommersetshire, located along the Avon River in England. The name Avon was chosen at a meeting held in a school, later known as Avon Centre School, in 1850. Other suggested names were Haines and Eureka. The first supervisor of the township was John Gage.

The history of the area predates the formation of townships in 1849 and the naming in 1850. Before 1839, Lake County was part of McHenry County. When the county was organized, eight voting districts were created. At that time, most of what became Avon Township was in the Fort Hill precinct.

The Potawatomi Native Americans were in the area before they were told by the federal government to vacate the land in the early 1830s. Evidences of their existence were found for over 100 years. They left trail trees, which have been lost to development. Farmers found stone points, commonly called arrowheads, as they tilled the soil.

The mid- to late 1830s found nonnative settlers coming into the area. These early settlers were called squatters, as they could not purchase the land until it was surveyed in 1840. Land purchasers then traveled to the Chicago land office where they paid $1.25 an acre for a land patent.

Elijah Haines, in 1852, wrote that the early settlers of this township were Noer Potter and sons, Churchill Edwards, Delazan E. Haines, Harley H. Hendee, David Hendee, David Rich, Levi Marble, George Thomson, Thomas Renehan, Leonard Gage, Thomas Welsh, A. T. Miltimore, Lawrence Forvor, Freeman Bridge, Nathaniel King, and William Gray.

It appears that most of the firsts of Avon Township happened near the southwest corner. Levi Marble, whose landholdings were near present-day Belvidere Road and Fairfield Road, was the first justice of the peace. The first school was the Marble School. The first permanent minister, who was of the Congregational faith, preached at the Marble School and at Hainesville. The first post office was at Fort Hill.

Many of today's highways follow old Native American trails. One source notes that Hainesville Road was once such a trail. In 1848, realizing that a surfaced road would be more passable in wet weather and therefore increase commerce, a plank road from Waukegan to the McHenry County line was proposed. By 1851, the road was completed as far as Squaw Creek, west of Hainesville. It had three toll stations along its route with one being at Hainesville. The cost of upkeep caused the demise of the tollway before 1877. The road became a "hard road" in 1918. Route 120, also known as Belvidere Road, is the former plank road.

Early Avon Township had several settlements whose growth was lost to neighboring communities. Monaville was in Avon Township until Lake Villa Township was formed in 1912. It is at the junction of Fairfield and Monaville Roads. Like many early communities, it has undergone name changes: Caine's/Cany's Corners, Barne's Corners, Tweed's Corner. By the 1870s, it had become Monaville. The name is thought to have originated because many settlers came from the Isle of Man, which is also known as Mona. It had a post office from 1850 to 1902, but it was called Fox Lake. In 1886, when the Wisconsin Central Railroad built its tracks two miles east due to the encouragement of E. J. Lehmann, Monaville declined. East Fox Lake Cemetery is the final resting place for many of Monaville's early residents.

Another early post office was the Fort Hill post office that was originally in Fremont Township but moved to the Marble farm in the southwest part of Avon Township around 1840 and continued until 1904. Fort Hill Cemetery is near this location. A section of Fairfield Road was once called Fort Hill Road.

From 1874 to 1904, there was a post office at Rollins. It also had a milk depot located along the Wisconsin Central Railroad. The location today would be Hook Drive and Route 83. That section of Hook Drive was once part of Rollins Road.

Now located in Lake Villa Township but originally part of Avon Township, Sand Lake had a post office. It was first Angola in 1847, changed to Sand Lake in 1863, and discontinued in 1882. Again an early cemetery remembers this community. That cemetery is located on Grand Avenue between Lake Villa and Lindenhurst.

In 1912, a referendum was held to form a new township. The first supervisor of Lake Villa Township, John Stratton, was elected in 1913. Lake Villa Township was formed from Grant, Antioch, and Avon Townships. Avon lost the northern two rows of sections. This left the township 6 miles long and 4 miles wide, consisting of 24 square miles. The eastern boundary is basically Route 45 except where it goes around Druce Lake. The western boundary is a couple blocks west of Fairfield Road. On the north the boundary is approximately a block north of Rollins Road. Town Line and Sports Club Roads help delineate the southern border.

It is hoped that with the help of images, the reader will gain a broader understanding of the history and growth of Avon Township and its villages.

One

HAINESVILLE

In 1842, Charlotte Haines Bowen bought the east half of the southeast quarter of section 28, consisting of 80 acres, from the federal government. In 1844, her son Elijah Middlebrook Haines purchased the east half of the southwest quarter and the west half of the southeast quarter of the same section. In the same year, Elijah's brother John C. Haines purchased land in the adjoining section 27. Thus begins the story of Hainesville.

Elijah married Melinda Griswold, daughter of Amos Wright, in 1845. In his lifetime, Elijah was a land surveyor and writer of township law. He is best known for being the progenitor of the village of Hainesville. In 1846, Haines platted his namesake and almost immediately the new community had not only a post office but also a tavern, store, blacksmith shop, wagon maker, tailor shop, schoolhouse, and around 50 residents. When it incorporated in 1847, it became the first village to do so in Lake County.

Elijah studied law and was admitted to the bar in 1851. He moved to Waukegan and, in 1852, published *Historical and Statistical Sketches of Lake County, State of Illinois*. Elijah died on April 25, 1889, and was buried in Oakwood Cemetery in Waukegan.

Early Hainesville became known for its lyceum hall and for having a toll station for the plank road. When the village did not get a railroad station, it started to decline as businesses moved elsewhere, including Grayslake and Round Lake. Not only did businesses leave, but other entities did as well. A store building was moved from Hainesville to Grayslake's Park Avenue where it became a residence. The Rising Sun Masonic Lodge No. 115, which was chartered in 1852 in Hainesville, moved to Grayslake where it continues to be active. The post office closed in 1919. Hainesville once had a cemetery, but it too has disappeared.

As of 2007, the village is once more alive. Even though it is the oldest incorporated village in Lake County, the only signs of earlier times are the images found in this and other books.

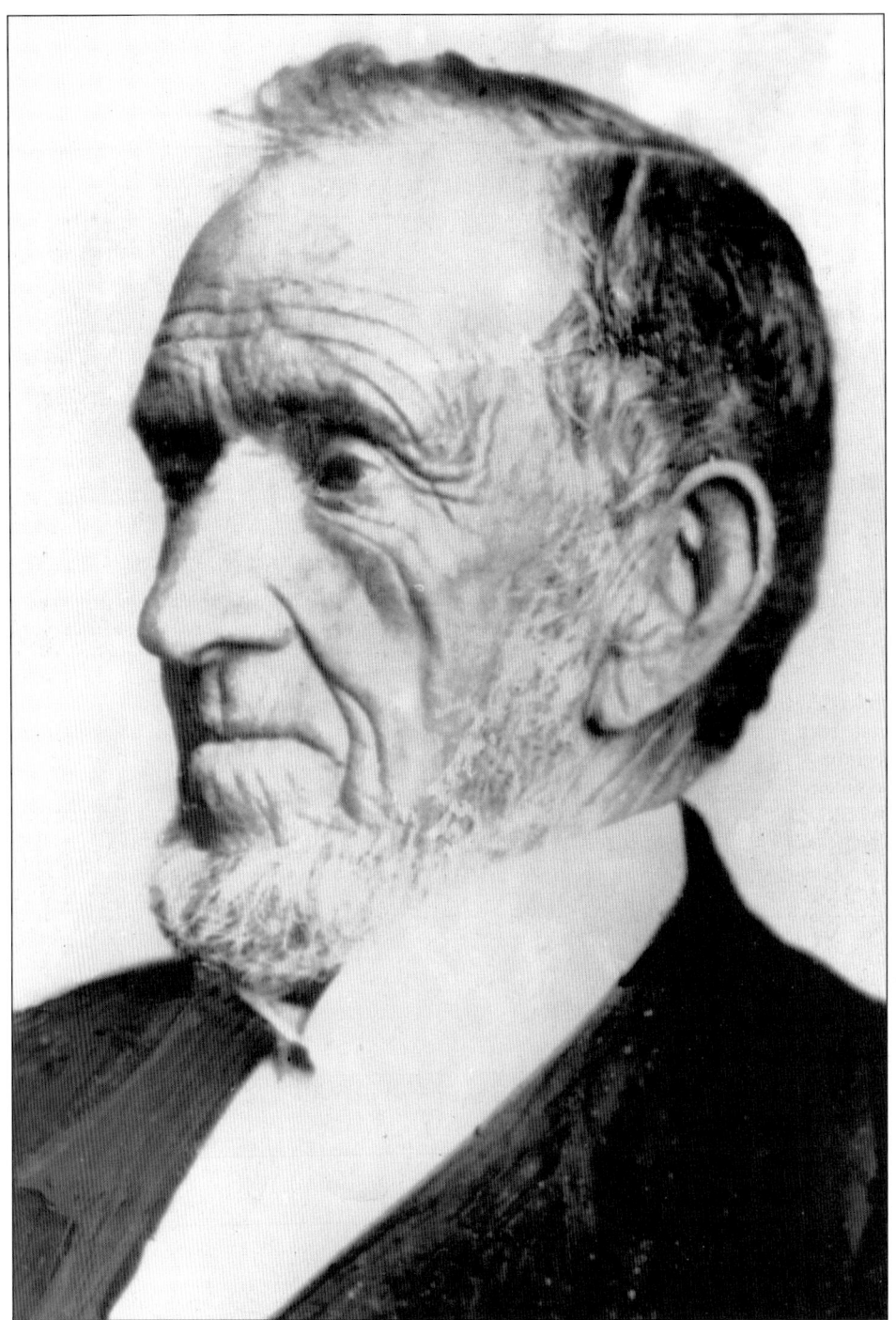

Elijah Middlebrook Haines was born in the state of New York in 1822. In 1838, he came to northern Illinois and settled in what became Hainesville. He married Melinda Griswold Wright and had two children. During his lifetime, he was a teacher, county school commissioner, justice of the peace, surveyor, postmaster, lawyer, state representative, and writer. He died in 1889 and is buried in Waukegan's Oakwood Cemetery. (Courtesy of Waukegan Historical Society.)

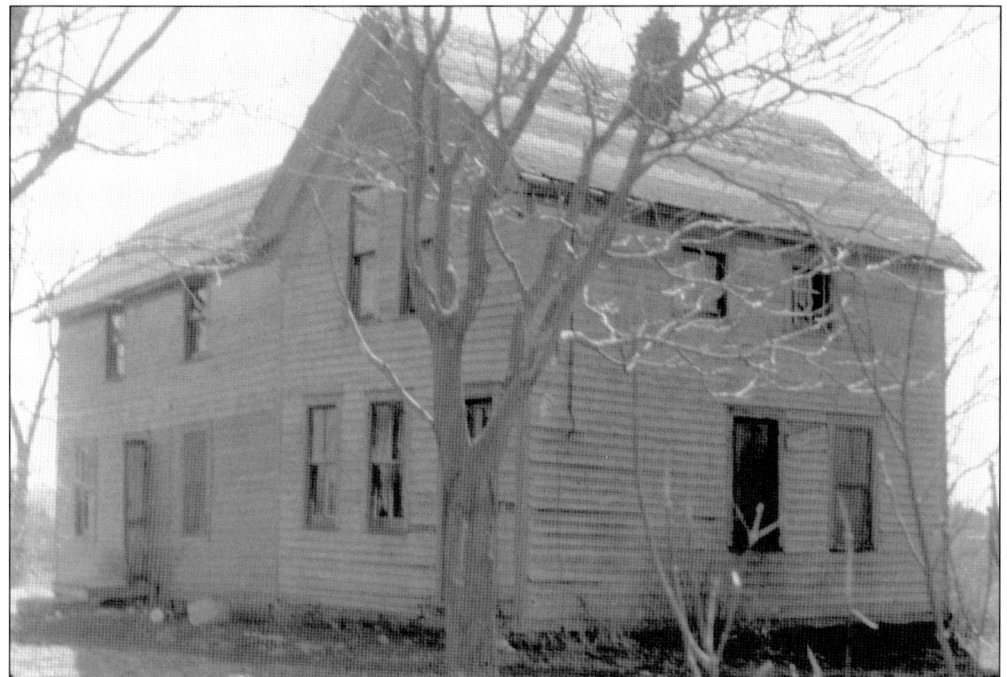

Construction for the Lake and McHenry Plank Road began in 1848. It was planned to extend from Waukegan to the McHenry County line. By 1851, it was completed to Squaw Creek, west of Hainesville. It had three toll stations along the way. The older part of the Charles Hall house was the former toll station in Hainesville, near the fork for Routes 120 and 137. (Courtesy of Grayslake Historical Society, Ruth Mogg Collection.)

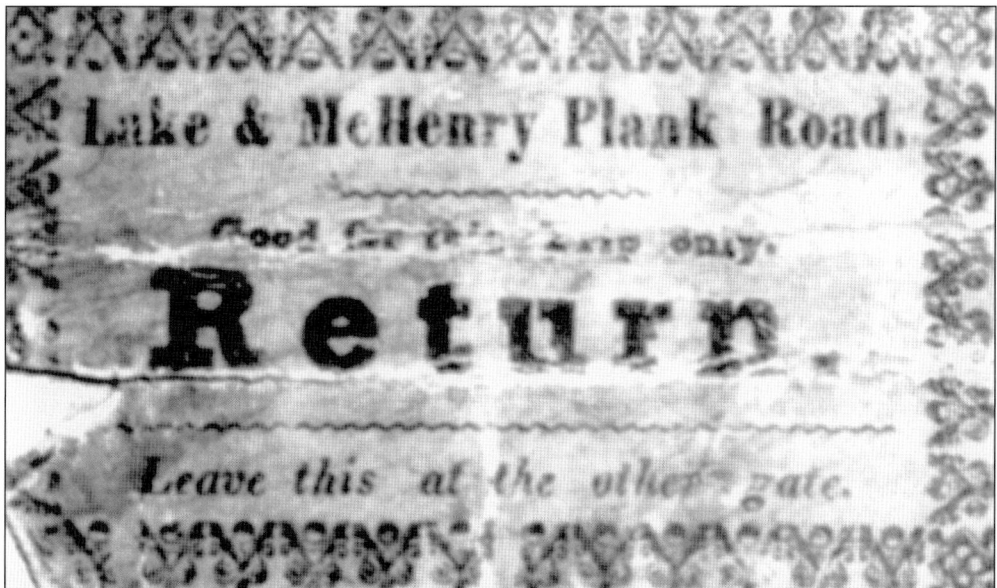

Travelers on the Lake and McHenry Plank Road paid a toll: each four horses and coach wagon or sleigh, 3.5¢ per mile; each two horses or oxen and wagon or sleigh, 2.5¢ per mile; each horse and buggy and wagon or sleigh, 2¢ per mile; each head of cattle, .5¢ per mile; each head of sheep or hogs, .25¢ per mile. (Courtesy of Grayslake Historical Society, Ruth Mogg Collection.)

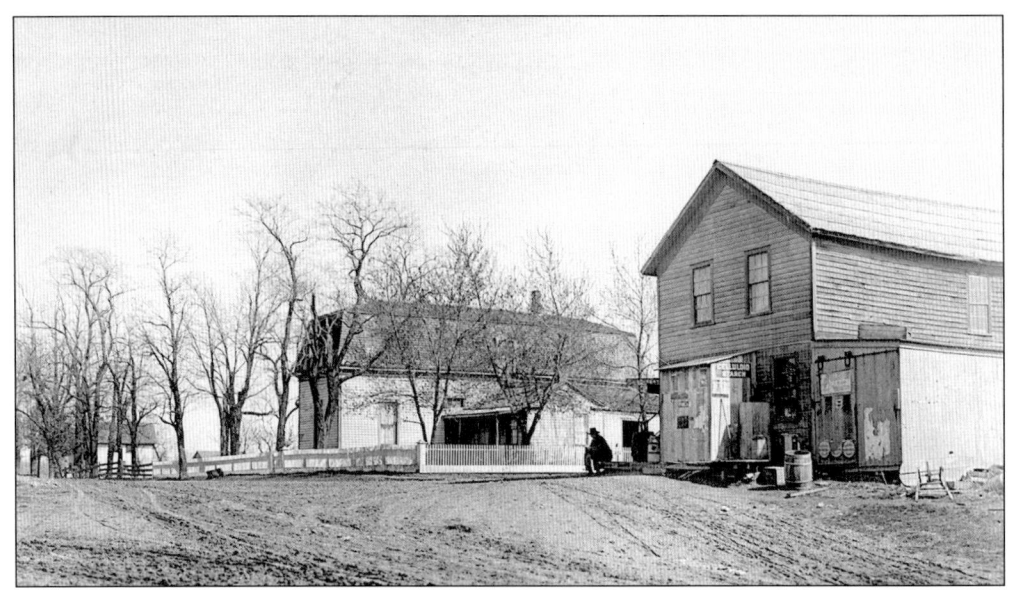

The notation on this postcard identifies the road pictured as Broad Street in Hainesville. Broad Street was the site of the Lake and McHenry Plank Road, today's Belvidere Road. (Courtesy of Grayslake Historical Society, Longabaugh Collection.)

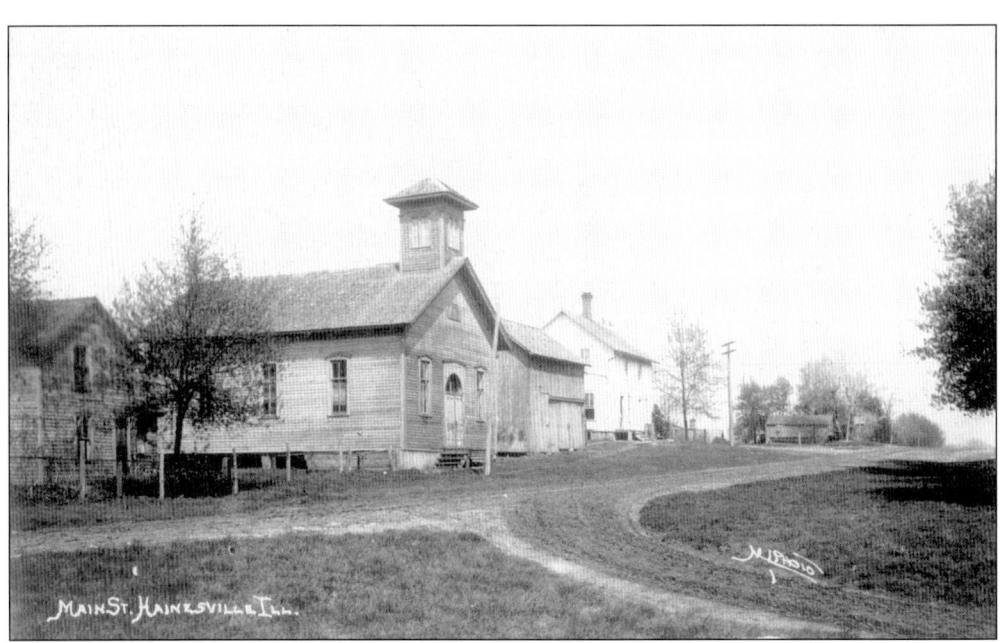

This postcard image calls the road Main Street. Again it is the former Lake and McHenry Plank Road or present Belvidere Road. In the foreground is Hainesville's lyceum hall.

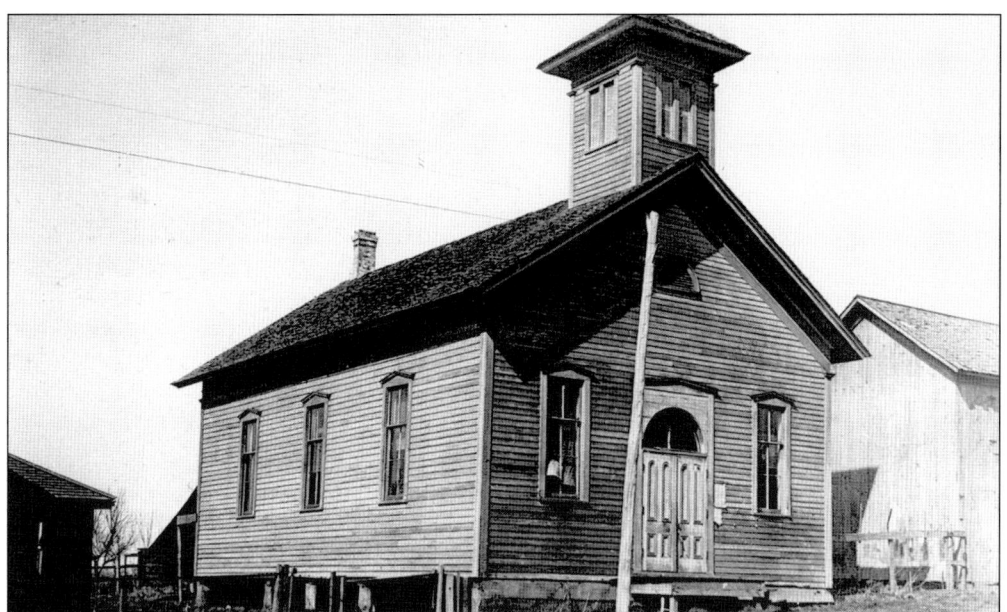
Many early communities had a lyceum hall. This was Hainesville's. It was a place of learning. Citizens spoke on various topics and debates were held. Catholic church services were held here from 1906 to 1908. (Courtesy of Grayslake Historical Society.)

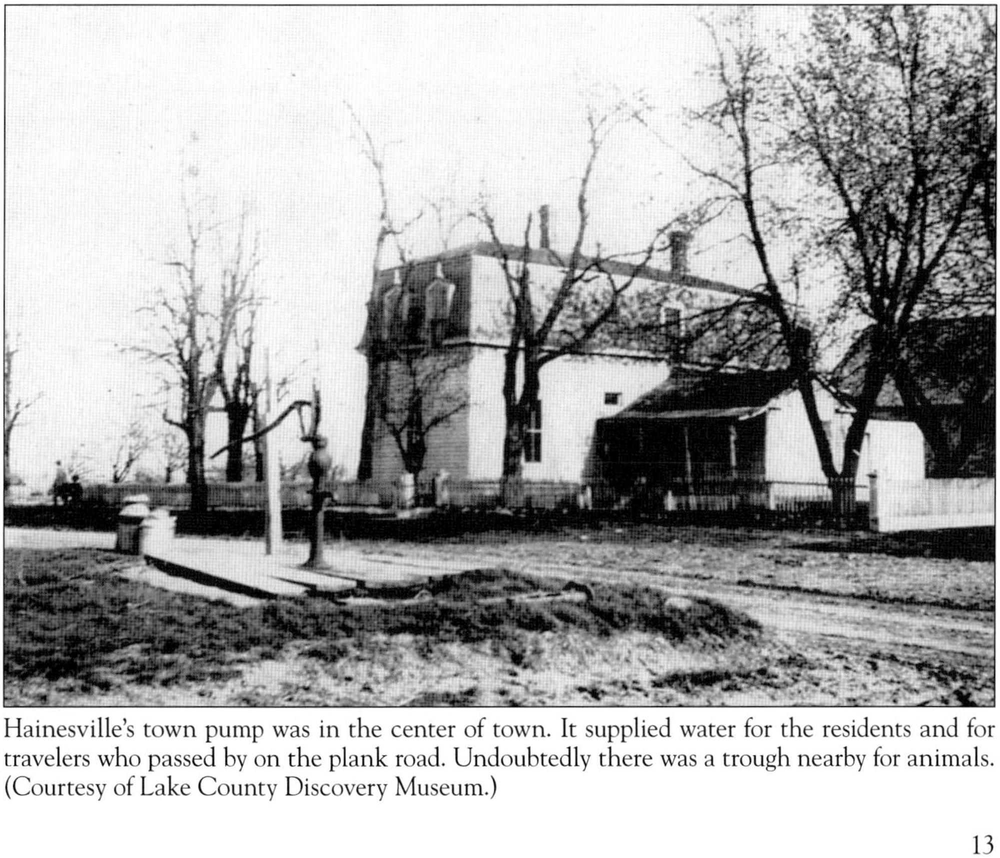

Hainesville's town pump was in the center of town. It supplied water for the residents and for travelers who passed by on the plank road. Undoubtedly there was a trough nearby for animals. (Courtesy of Lake County Discovery Museum.)

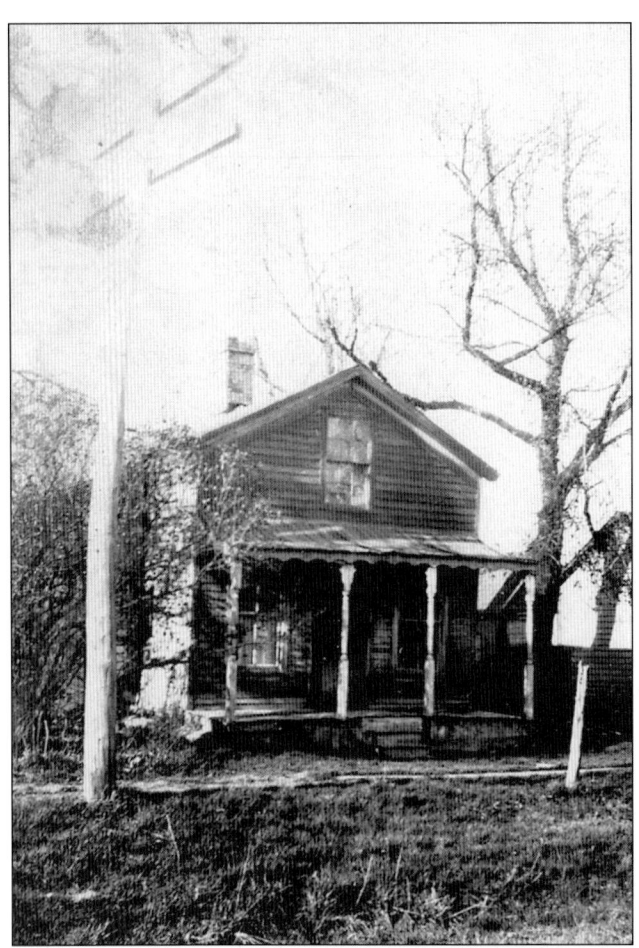

In 1918, the schoolchildren of Illinois were directed to write a history of their area in observance of Illinois's centennial year. The Fort Hill School children included pictures in their history. They wrote that the picture to the left was the first frame house in Hainesville and that the picture below was the Hendee house built in 1840. Locations were not noted. (Courtesy of Lake County Discovery Museum.)

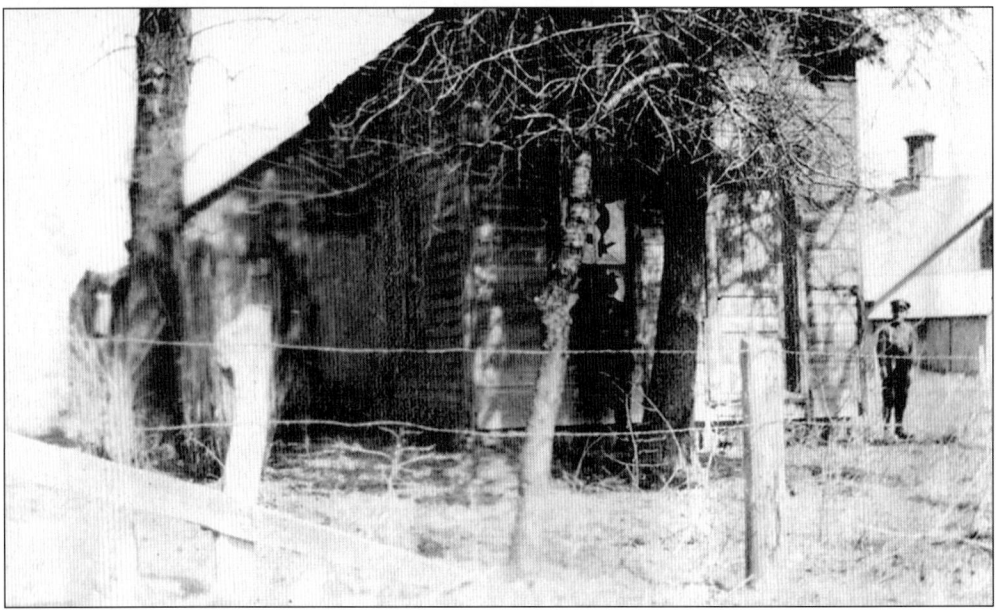

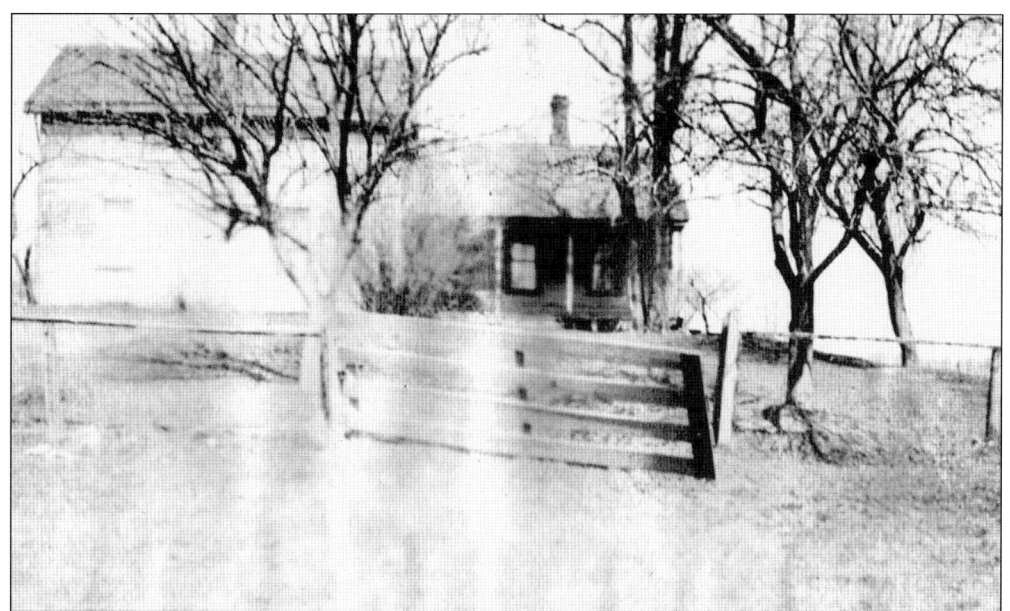

The Battershall family had a residence, store, and farm in Hainesville. The residence is shown here. George Battershall was Hainesville's postmaster twice. The Battershall General Merchandise business moved to Grayslake in the 1890s, where it built one of the older structures in that village. (Courtesy of Lake County Discovery Museum.)

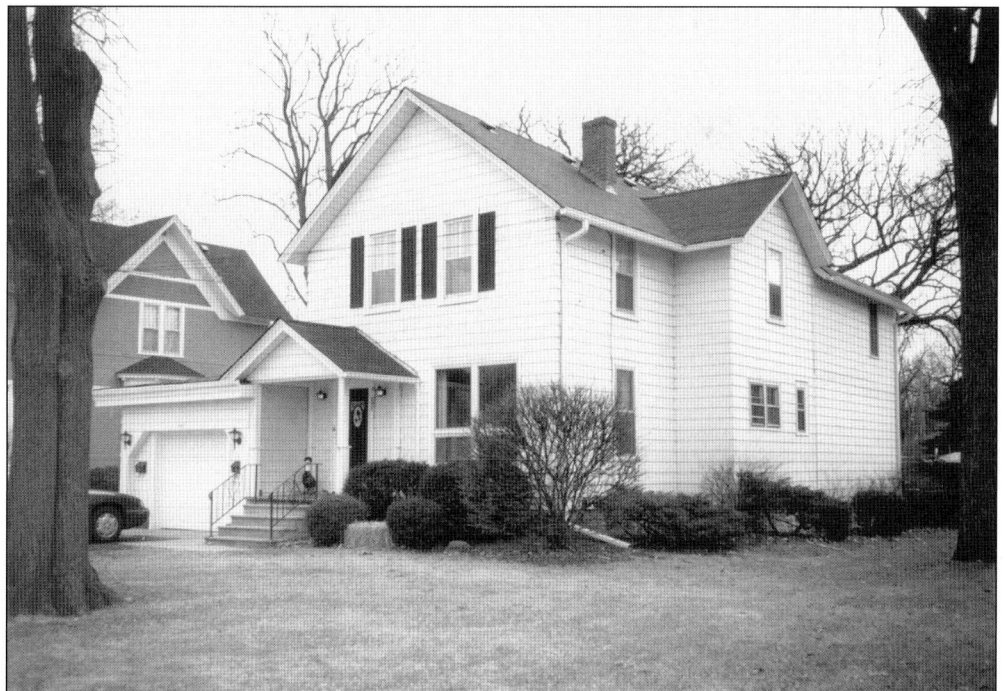

This house at 141 Park Avenue in Grayslake was formerly Merub Forvor's store building in Hainesville. It was moved from Hainesville to Grayslake around 1900 and has been enlarged. Forvor was the postmistress in Hainesville from 1891 to 1894.

New Year's Party,
AT
The Wightman House, Hainesville,
Friday Evening, December 31st, 1869.

Your Company, with Ladies, is Invited.

ROOM MANAGERS:

GEO. WRIGHT,   W. CONVERSE,   GEO. CLEVELAND,   WM TUPPER.

MUSIC---Morrell & Bryant's Band.

BILL, $2.00.   JAMES WIGHTMAN, Prop'r.

The 1870 Avon Township census says that James Wightman was the keeper of a public house. It is not known what happened to the Wightman hotel, as in 1880 Wightman was a stock dealer and single. Wightman family history relates that the family lived in Hainesville and then moved to a farm about a mile west on the old plank road. (Courtesy of Nancy Wightman Pease.)

CHICAGO, MILWAUKEE & ST. PAUL TIME TABLE

Saturday Special 149 Lv. Chicago 1:25 p m Ar. Hainesville 2:41 p m

Lv. Hainesville		Ar. Chicago.	Lv. Chicago.		Ar. Hainesville
136—7:07 a m	ex Sunday	8:25 a m	131—7:35 a m	ex. Sunday	8:43 a m
138 7:25 a m	Daily	9:55 a m	147—7:25 a m	Sunday only	8:59 a m
140—8:52 a m	Daily	10:05 a m	153—9:45 a m	Sunday only	11:14 a m
142—11:59 a m	ex Sunday	1:05 p m	135- 2:01 p m	Daily	3:58 p m
146 –7:05 p m	ex Sunday	8:20 p m	137—4:05 p m	Daily ex.Sun.	5:07 p m
150—7:24 p m	Sunday only	8:55 p m	139 5:10 p m	Daily ex.Sun.	6:17 p m
			143—6:03 p m	Daily	7:14 p m

Monthly ticket $12.00   25 rides $14.00   One way 86c

For further particulars call or write to the

AVON PARK HOTEL AND COTTAGES

GEO. P. RENEHAN, PROP.

Telephone Grayslake 101.   Postoffice—Grayslake, Ill.

When the Chicago, Milwaukee and St. Paul Railroad arrived in Avon Township in 1899, the train stopped in Hainesville. Hainesville lost its station to Round Lake when the local landowner George Battershall overpriced his land and the railroad bought elsewhere.

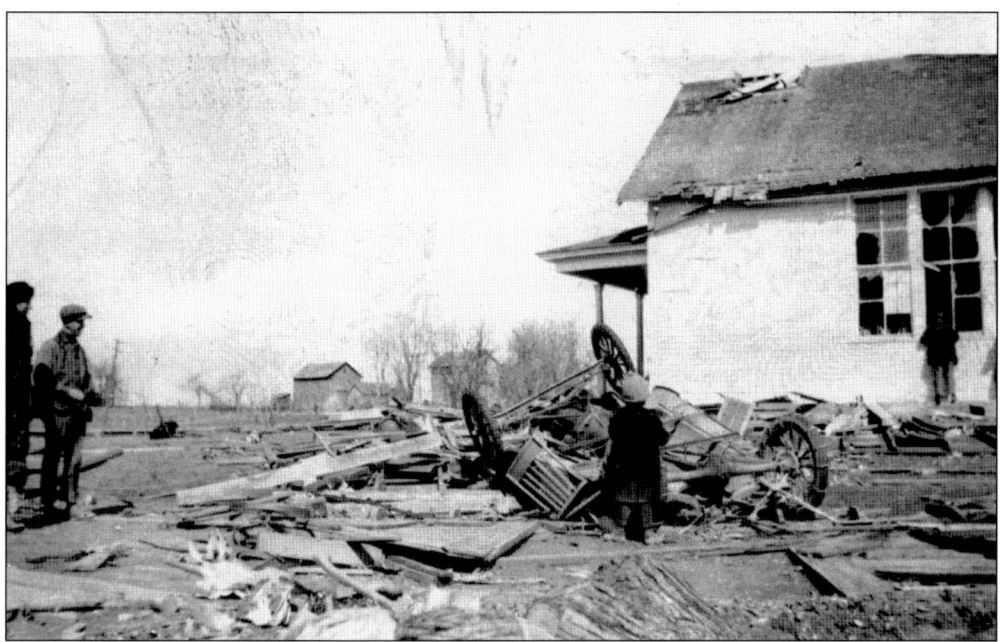

During the 1920s, a tornado hit Avon Township, and Hainesville received damage to several structures. The Shanks farm, later known as the Grayslake Gelatin Company farm, was hit. This image shows the destruction of the Hainesville schoolhouse. (Courtesy of Grayslake Historical Society.)

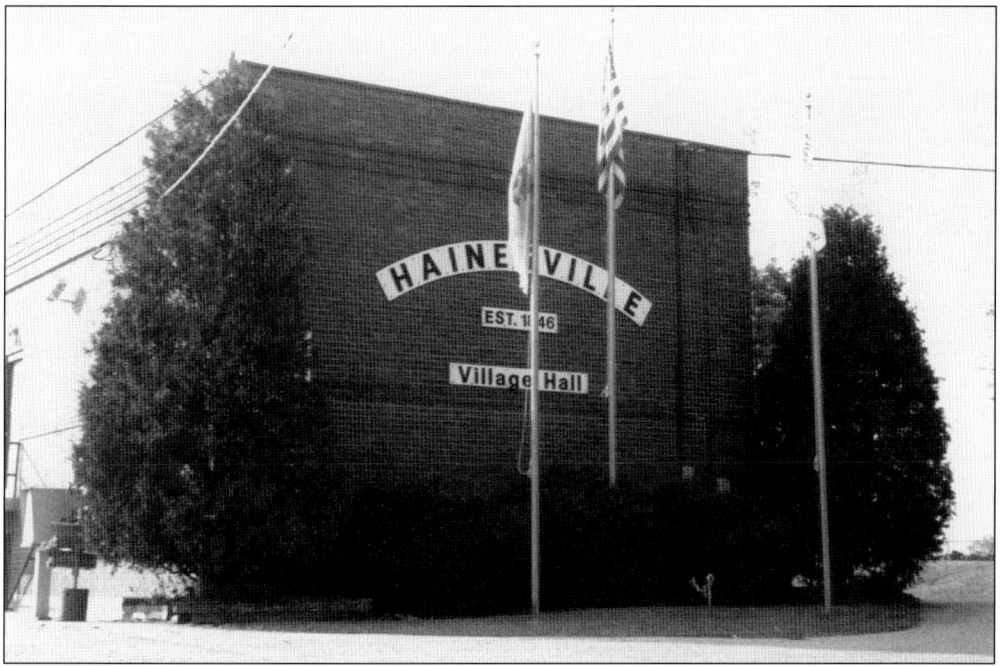

The brick structure at the northwest corner of Hainesville and Belvidere Roads was built in 1940 and became the fourth building to be used to educate students of the area. In 1945, the school became part of the Round Lake School system. In 1982, the building became Hainesville's village hall. The building was vacated in 2005 after a new village hall was built on Hainesville Road.

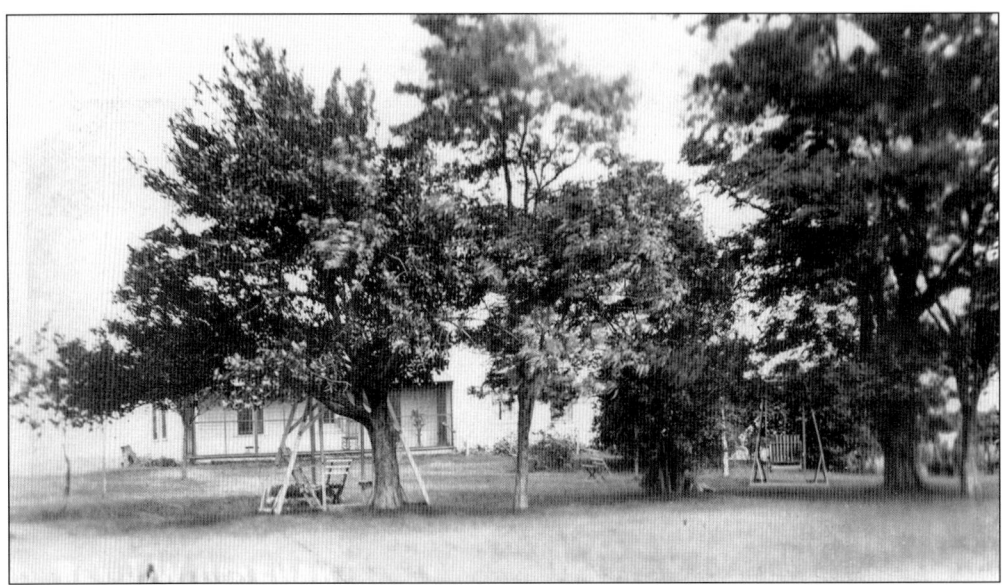

Jason Renehan, a descendant of the pioneer Renehan family, had a farm near the southeast corner of Hainesville Road and Renehan Road, now Washington Street. He and his wife rented rooms in their farmhouse to vacationers. The barn on the property was destroyed by fire in 1940. Part of the farm is now the location of the Avon Township Youth Baseball Fields, while the rest is subdivided.

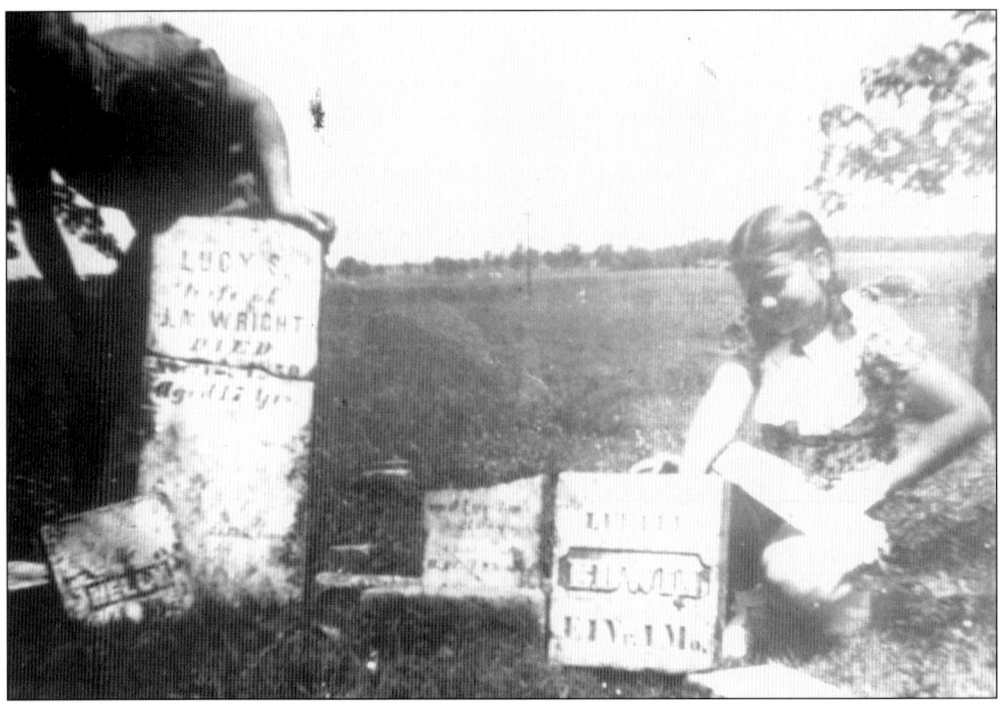

This 1938 picture is all that remains of the Cranberry Lake Cemetery. The tombstones record information about Cordelia Whitney and Lucy S. Wright, plus little Nelly and little Edwin. Cranberry Lake is still visible on the landscape. Years ago cranberries were harvested along the shore of the lake. (Courtesy of Grayslake Historical Society, Ruth Mogg Collection.)

Two

GRAYSLAKE

Settlers in the Grayslake area before 1840 include David Rich and William M. Gray from Allegany County, New York, and Lawrence Forvor from Lorain County, Ohio. Gray settled along the south shore of an unnamed lake, which became Grays Lake. The Gray family left the area before 1865. As the land became available for purchase, more settlers came, mostly farmers from the east.

In the mid-1880s the Wisconsin Central Railroad needed a right-of-way to complete its line between Wisconsin and Chicago. When Frank Beak was reluctant to grant a right-of-way through his farm, Henry E. Hawley, Charles Whitney, and Chase E. Webb purchased the farm. The railroad right-of-way was secured and the farm subdivided into 10 blocks. The subdivision of Grays Lake was officially recorded in 1886.

The area already had a school and a cemetery on land deeded by Forvor, and the railroad accelerated its growth. A lumber company came, houses were built, a fourth-class post office was established, a church was organized, and businesses soon followed. The community had low land and for a period of time was nicknamed "Parker's Landing" after Rhoderick Parker, the first postmaster.

By 1895, there were enough people to petition the government to incorporate. The petition was granted, and an election was held with George Thomson elected the first mayor. The village was incorporated as Grays Lake. It is said that it was changed to Grayslake for postal reasons.

Before 1900, a branch of the Chicago, Milwaukee and St. Paul Railroad passed near the southern edge of the village. The trains made it easier for people to come to the country to enjoy the area lakes. Summer cottages were built on the southwest and north shores of Grays Lake. Eventually these summer residences became year-round homes.

The growth continued with farmland converted to other uses. The village boundaries were expanded. In the 1980s, Grayslake started expanding into surrounding townships: Warren Township to the east, Fremont Township to the south, and Lake Villa Township to the north.

Grayslake is the home of the Lake County Fair, the College of Lake County, and the University Center of Lake County.

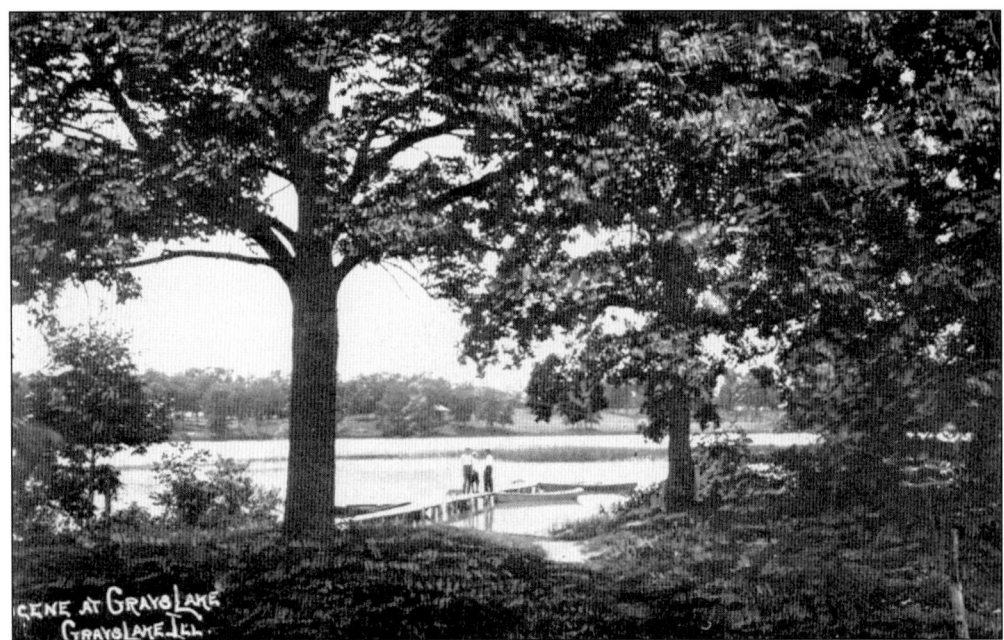

Sometime before 1840, William M. Gray came from Allegany County, New York, and purchased land along the south shore of an unnamed lake, now known as Grays Lake. The lake covers approximately 97 acres and is spring fed. This image of the lake is from around 1930.

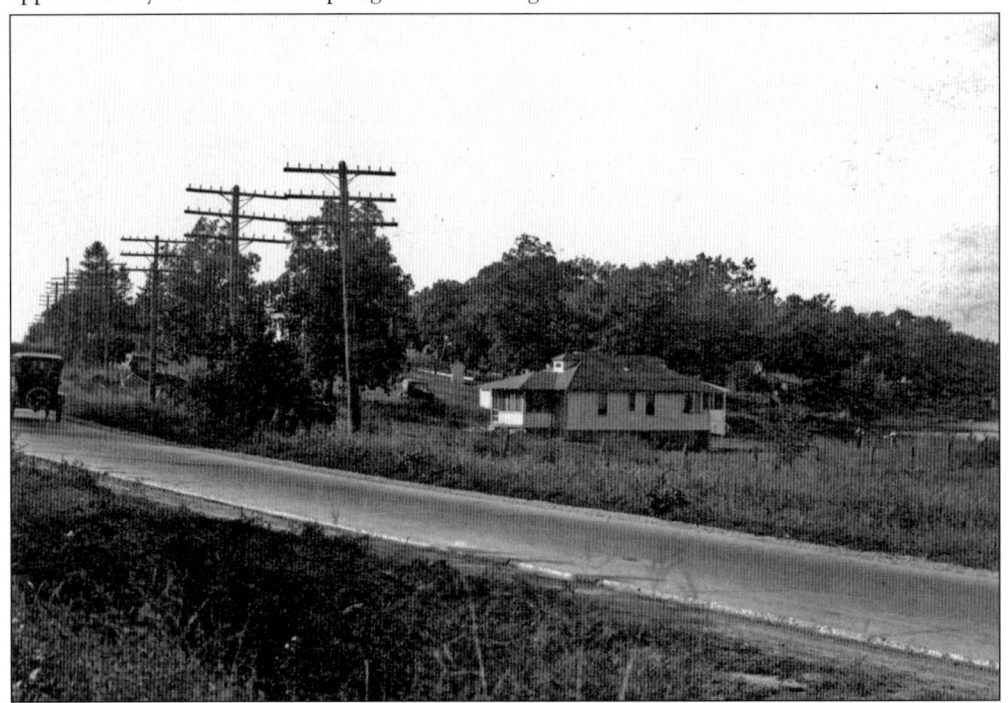

Belvidere Road follows the route of the former Lake and McHenry Plank Road. The early plank road had deteriorated and returned to dirt and gravel. In 1918, it was cemented and became a hard road. This section of the road is along the south shore of Grays Lake, looking west toward Hainesville.

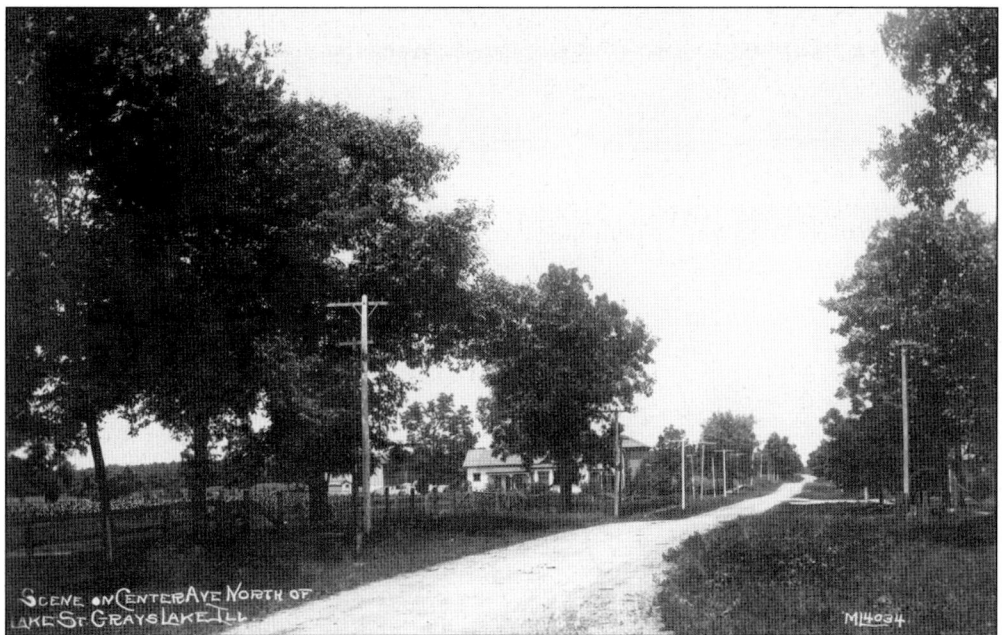

This picture was taken around 1910 at the corner of Lake and Center Streets looking north. At the time, the dirt road was known as Center Avenue. Today it is called Lake Street. Grayslake's first downtown streetlights are at this intersection.

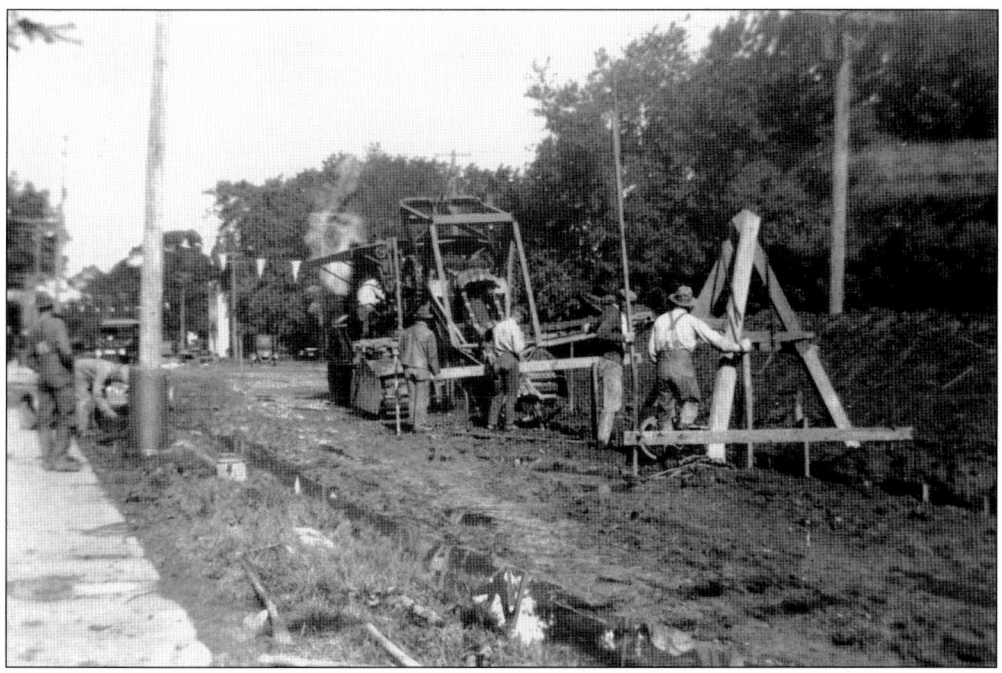

The main street of Grayslake became a hard road in 1926. It was about this time that Lake and Center Streets exchanged names. (Courtesy of Grayslake Historical Society.)

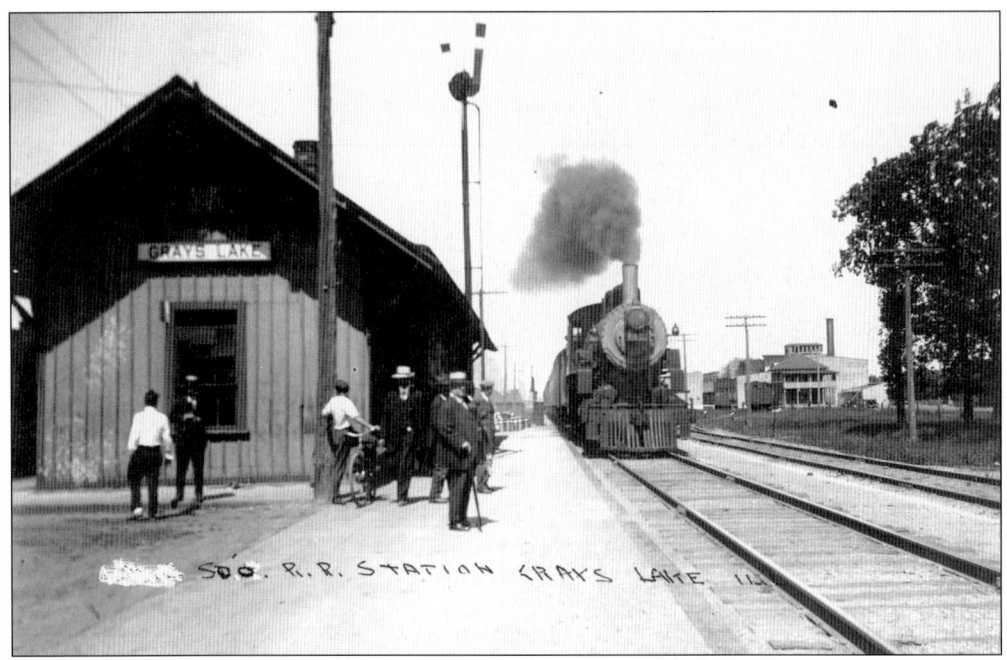

The Wisconsin Central train depot in Grayslake was completed in 1886. The Wisconsin Central was later known as the Soo Line Railroad. This postcard, dated 1916, shows the Wisconsin Condensed Milk Company at the far right.

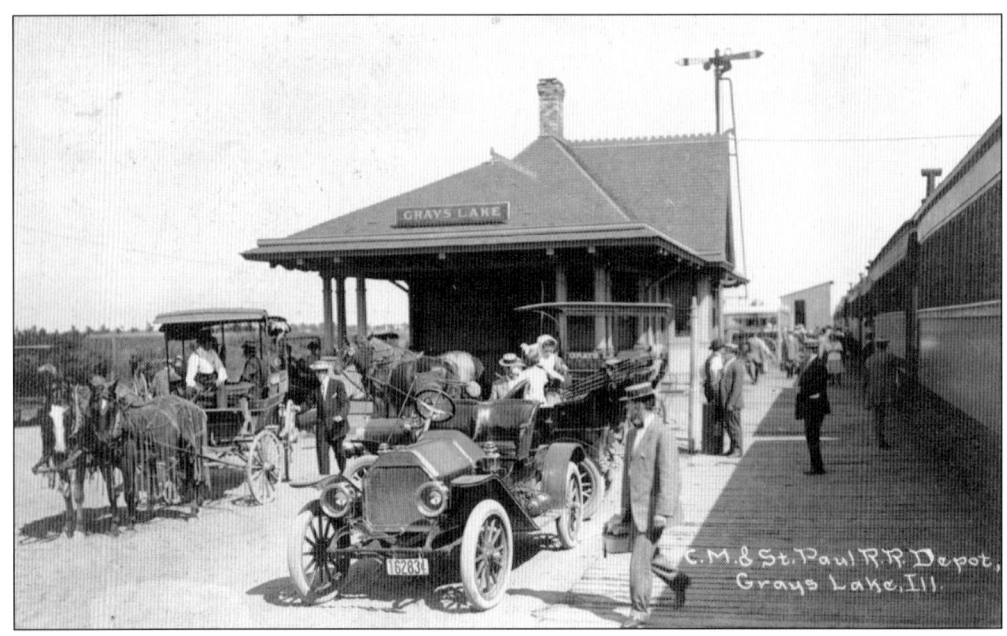

Tracks of the Chicago, Milwaukee and St. Paul Railroad, the second in Grayslake, passed the south end of the village in 1899. This c. 1920 image shows the various means of travel during that time frame. Trains would carry ice from the lakes and milk from the farms to the city.

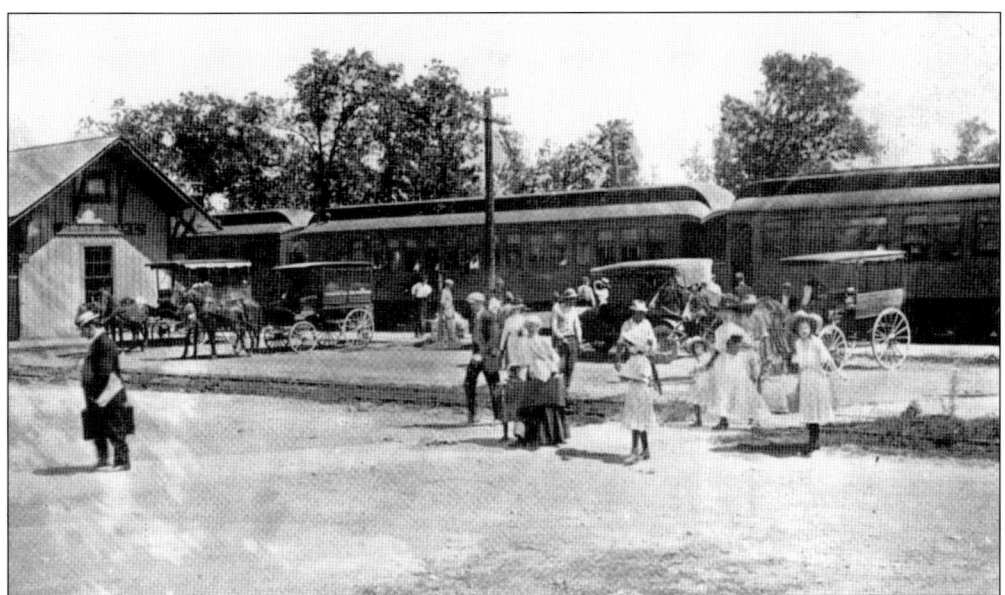

Before the popularity of motorized vehicles, people from the city came by train to vacation in the country. Horse-drawn buses would meet the trains and transport vacationers to the various summer hotels and resorts located on the shores of the nearby lakes. This scene is at the Soo Line station in Grayslake.

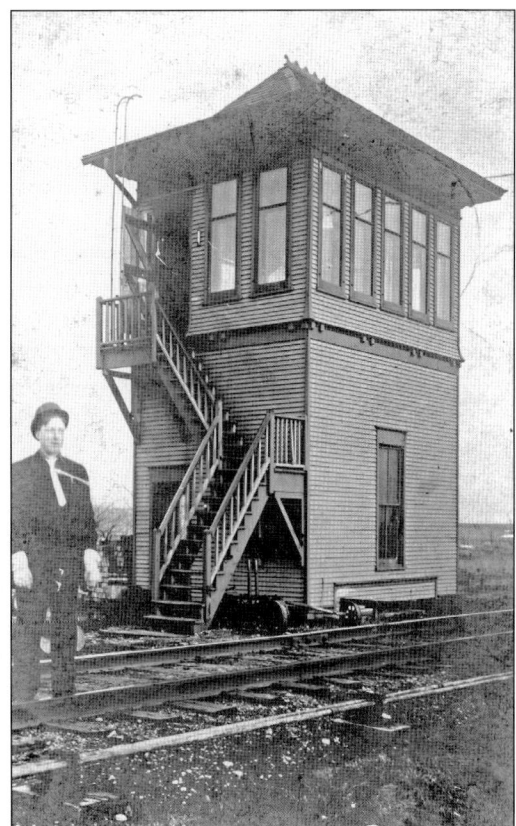

Grayslake's two train lines, the Wisconsin Central and the Chicago, Milwaukee and St. Paul Railroads, cross south of the village. The early switching tower is shown here. (Courtesy of Grayslake Historical Society.)

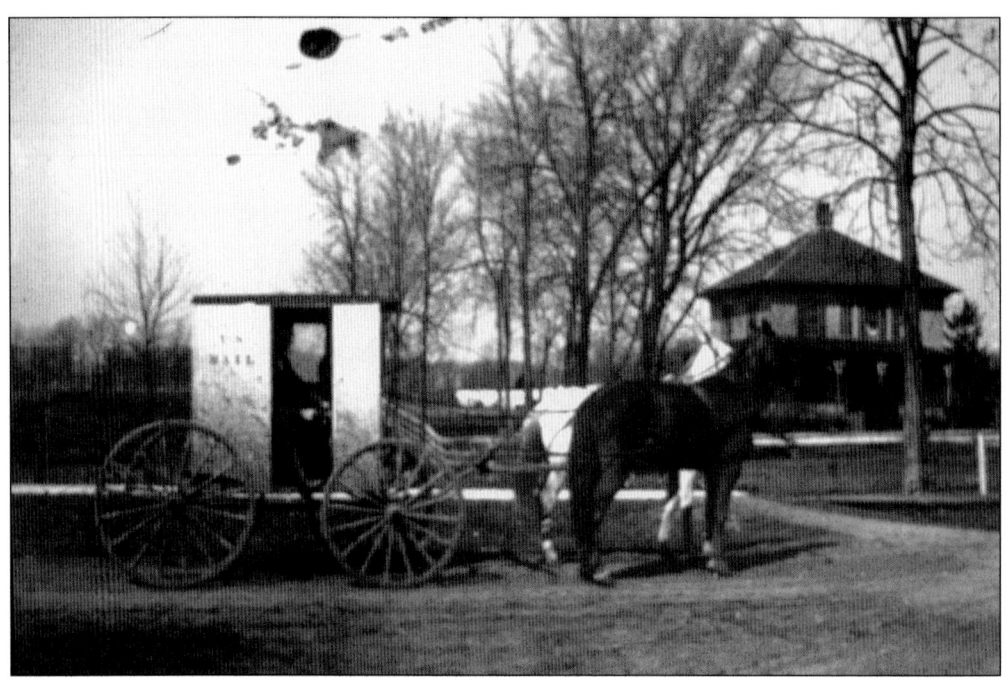

The property at the west end of present-day Center Street was once the farm of John Hook. His farmhouse is shown in the photograph above. The farmland was purchased by Pete Newhouse in 1924. He developed Grays Lake Park as shown in the picture below. The property, which extended from the corner of Lake and Center Streets to the lake, was sold and developed around 1951. Part of the land was used for a grocery store with a parking lot and the rest became a small subdivision. The house was moved to Hickory Street. Today a business/condominium building is at this location.

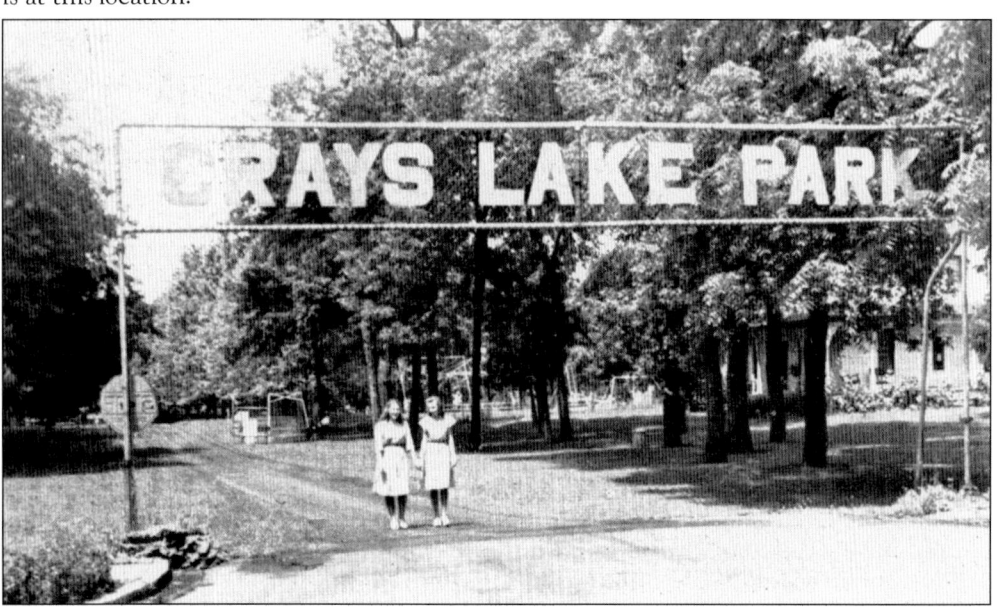

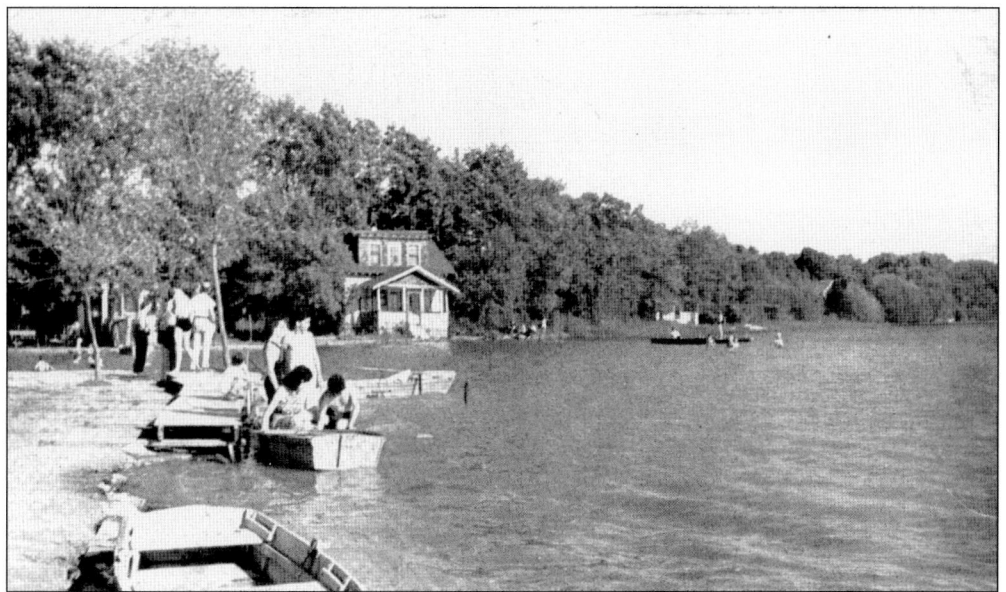

People came from the city to spend a day at Grays Lake Park. They enjoyed picnicking, using playground equipment, and playing baseball. They swam in the lake or waded in a small adjoining area. Owner Newhouse rented boats, and patrons leisurely rowed across the lake or tried their luck at fishing.

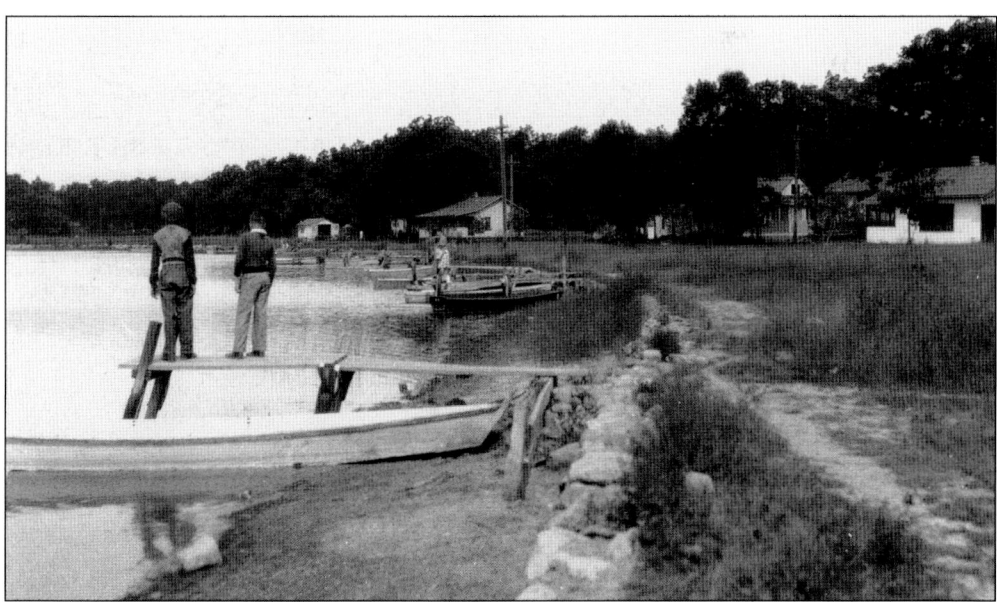

Harvey's Subdivision along the northern shore of Grays Lake was developed by dentist Earl Harvey in 1921. The summer cottages, seen here in the 1930s, have given way to year-round homes. (Courtesy of Grayslake Historical Society.)

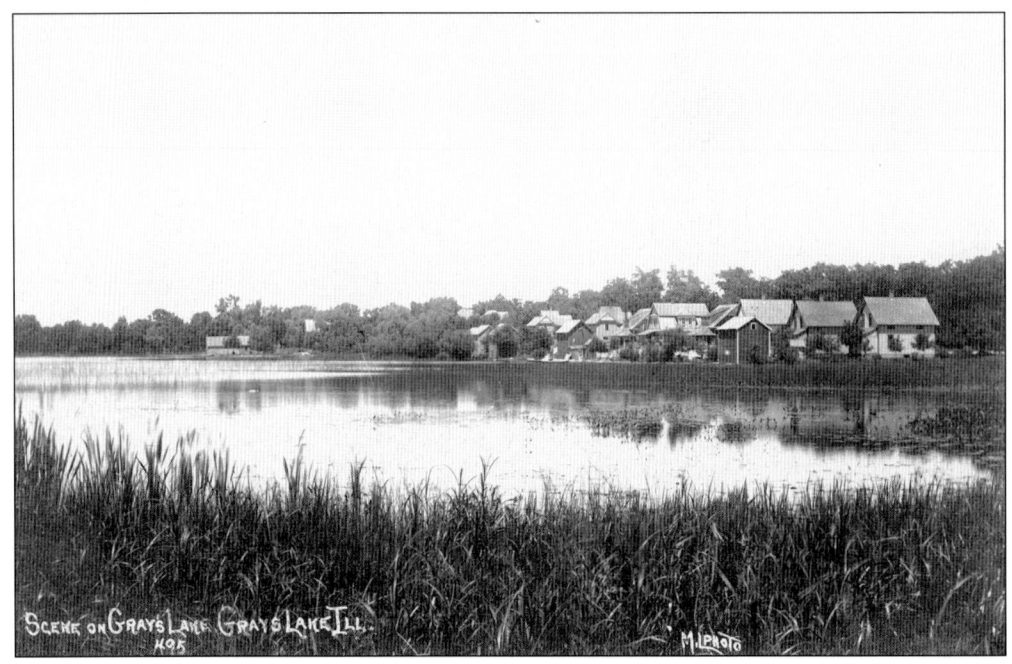

Banker P. A. Robinson platted a subdivision along the eastern shore of Grays Lake in 1901. The lake has been dredged in this area to make a more defined shoreline. These lakefront homes face present-day Lake Street and are visible form Belvidere Road in this c. 1913 image.

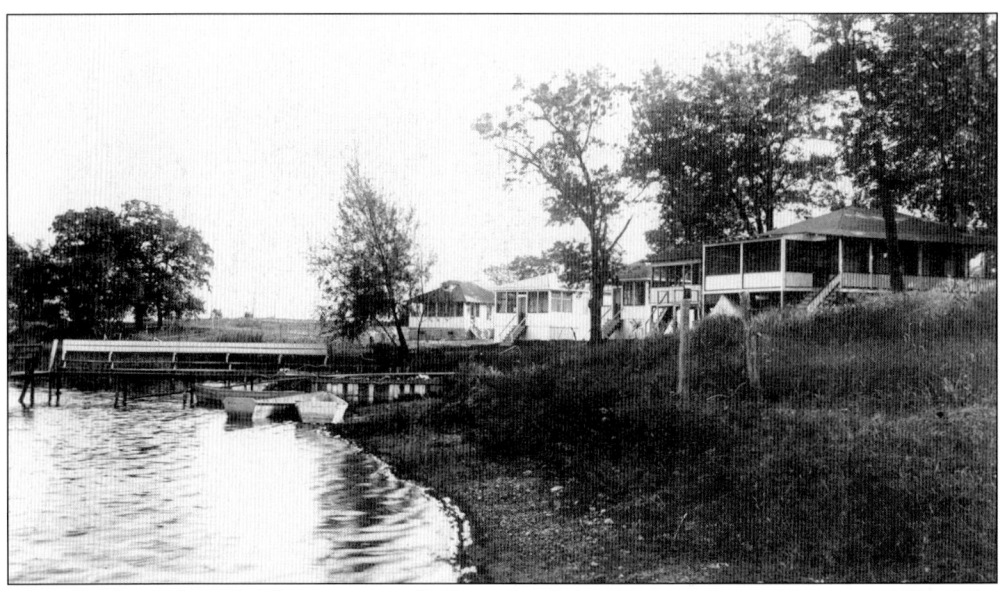

The plat for Tobias Subdivision was filed in the Lake County Court House in 1921. The subdivision, located north of Belvidere Road and east of Bluff Avenue along the shore of Grays Lake, was initially composed of summer cottages. (Courtesy of Grayslake Historical Society.)

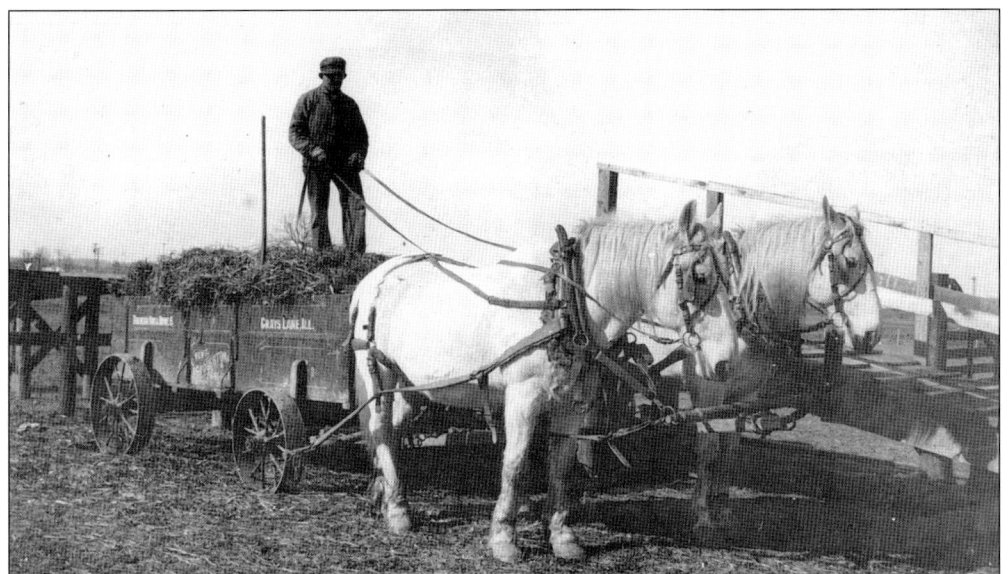

Grayslake had three canning factories. The Fisk Kyle Company started canning sweet corn in 1904. In 1910, it sold its buildings to the Hohenadel Company, which also canned peas. The final factory belonged to the Inderrieden Canning Company, which is believed to have closed in 1926. Farmers would bring their produce to the factories at the end of Railroad Avenue by horse and wagon. (Courtesy of Grayslake Historical Society.)

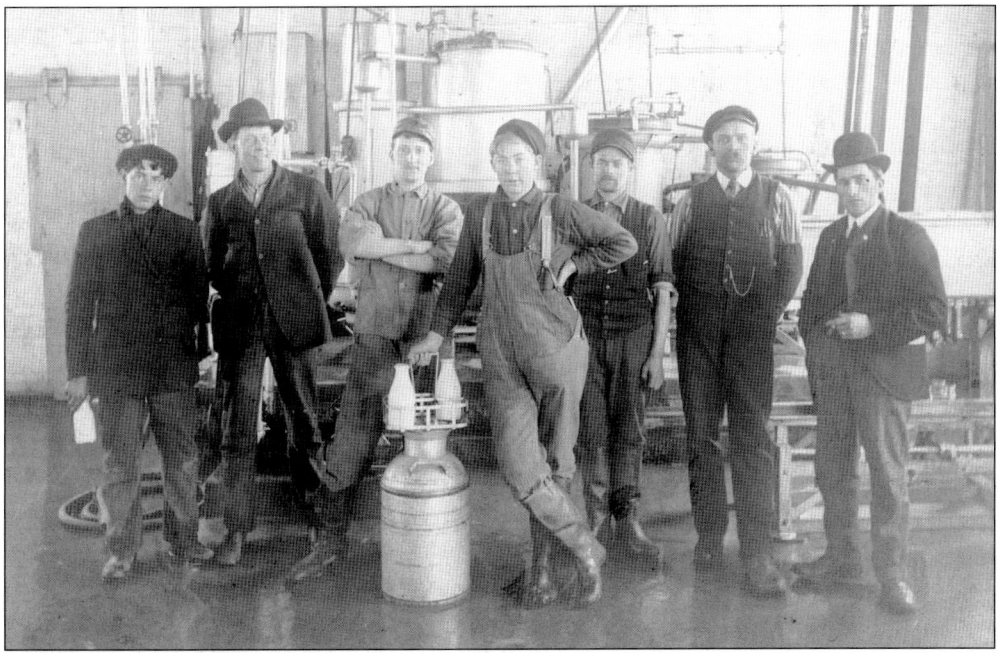

The Wisconsin Condensed Milk Company followed the railroad and came from Burlington, Wisconsin, in 1912. Later the condensery was sold to Nestle's. The workers seen here were local residents. (Courtesy of Grayslake Historical Society.)

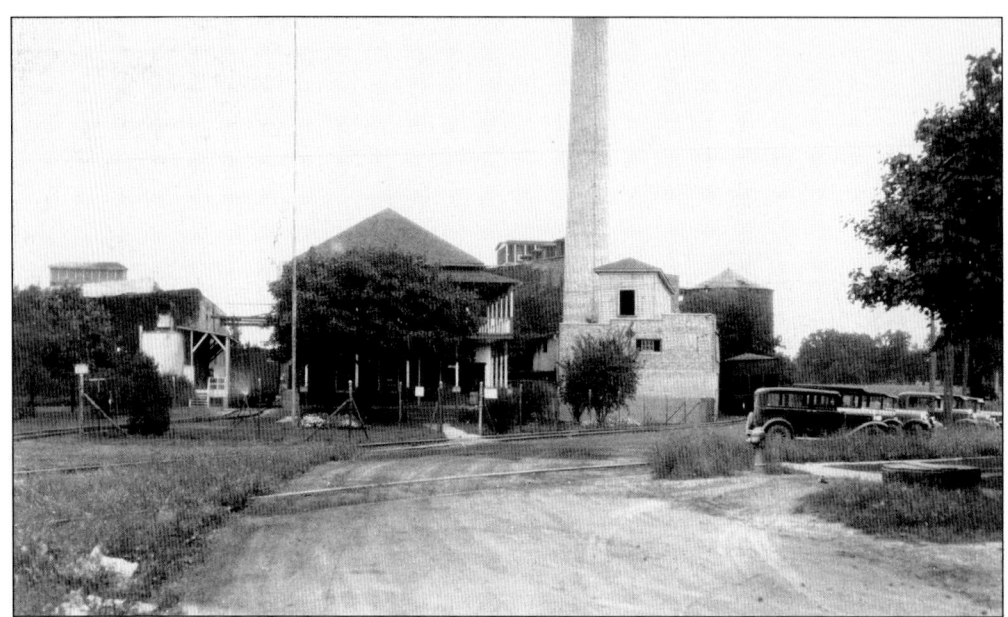

The Grayslake Gelatin Company started operations at the end of Railroad Avenue in 1922, in buildings formerly occupied by the condensery. The company, which was owned by the Epstein family, ceased the manufacturing of gelatin in 1982 but continued for a time to package the product. (Courtesy of Grayslake Historical Society.)

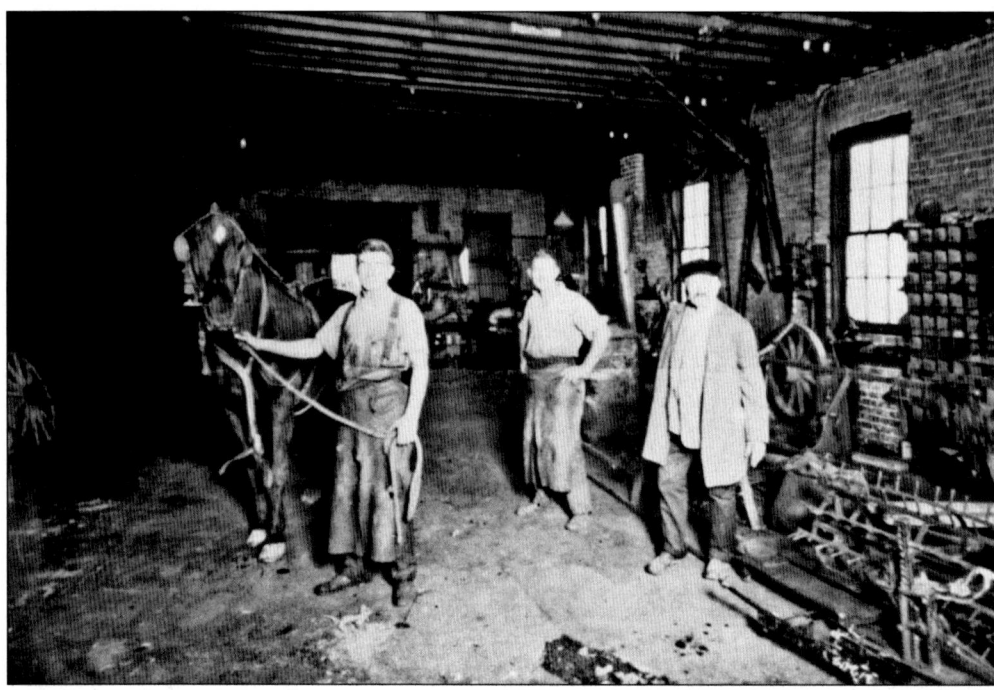

Grayslake has had several blacksmiths. This is the interior of the Joe Pester Blacksmith Shop, which was located at the northwest corner of Slusser and Center Streets. Pictured here are, from left to right, owner Joe Pester, employee Joe Davis, and an unidentified man. (Courtesy of Grayslake Historical Society.)

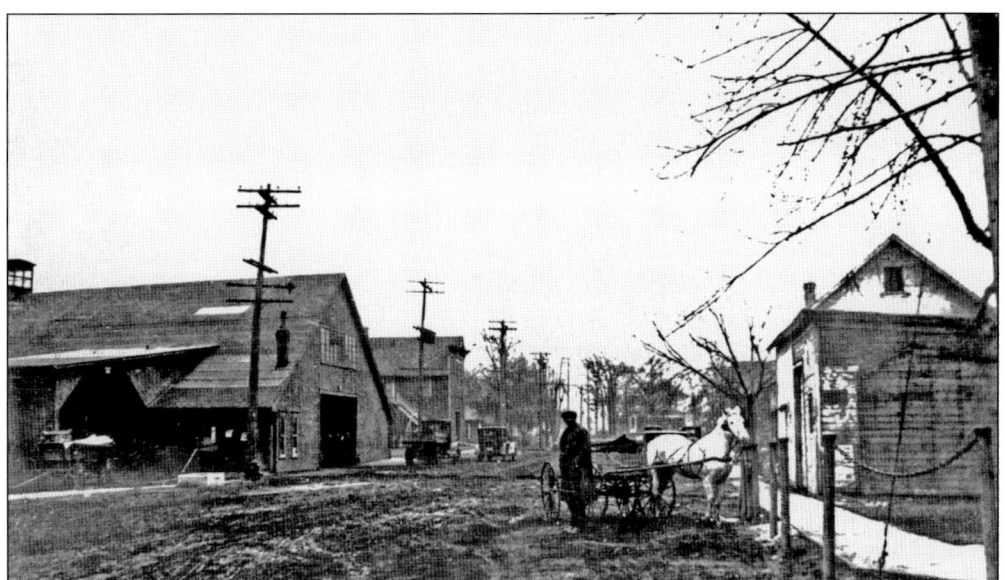

F. C. Wilbur brought his lumberyard from Burlington to the new subdivision of Grays Lake in 1886 and located it between the railroad tracks and Seymour Avenue. In 1970, the Everette Hook family purchased the company after being employed there many years. The lumberyard survived three fires, including one with a fatality, but succumbed to the challenge of the big box stores in 1994. (Courtesy of Grayslake Historical Society.)

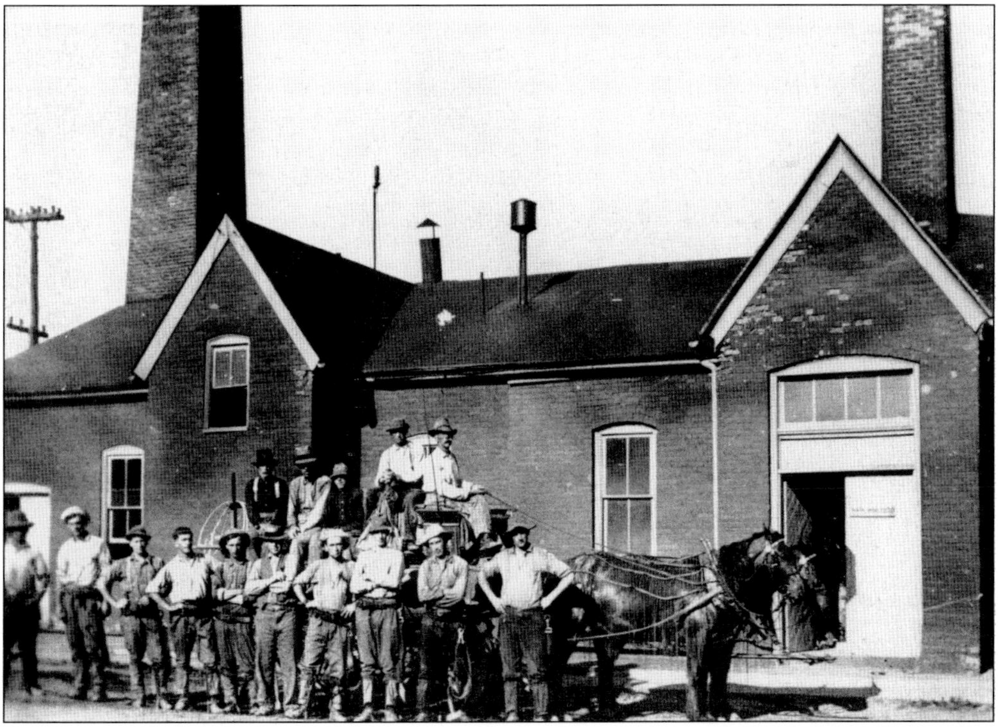

Grayslake's electric generating plant was across the street from Wilbur Lumber Company on Seymour Avenue. Charlie Kreuser is pictured here with other members of the first line gang. A gristmill was also at this location.

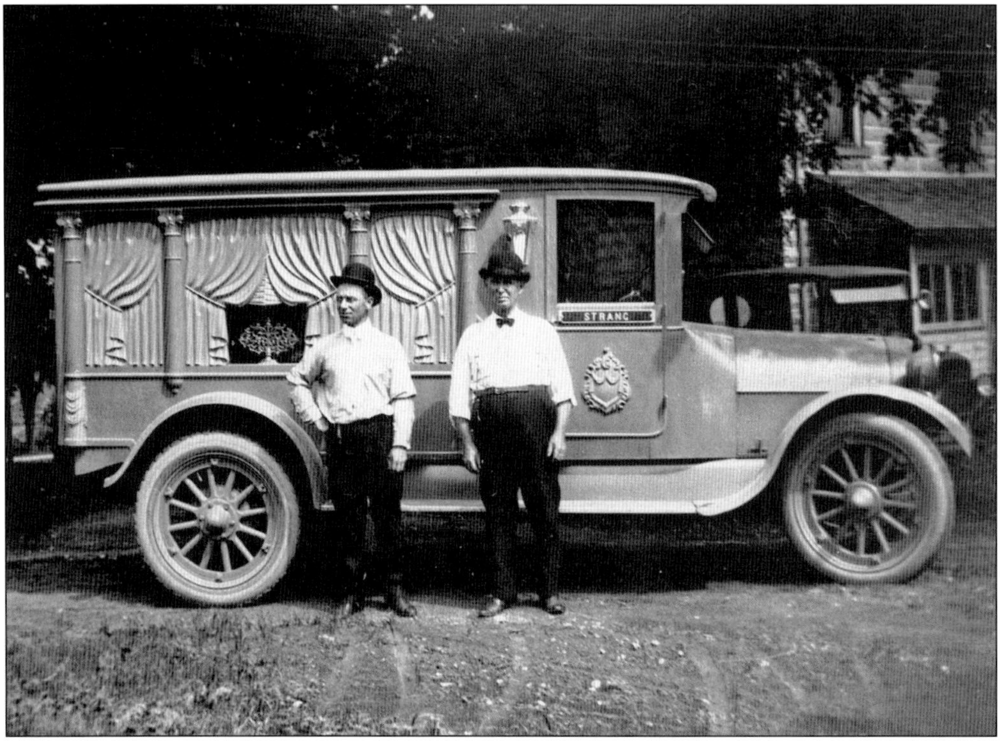

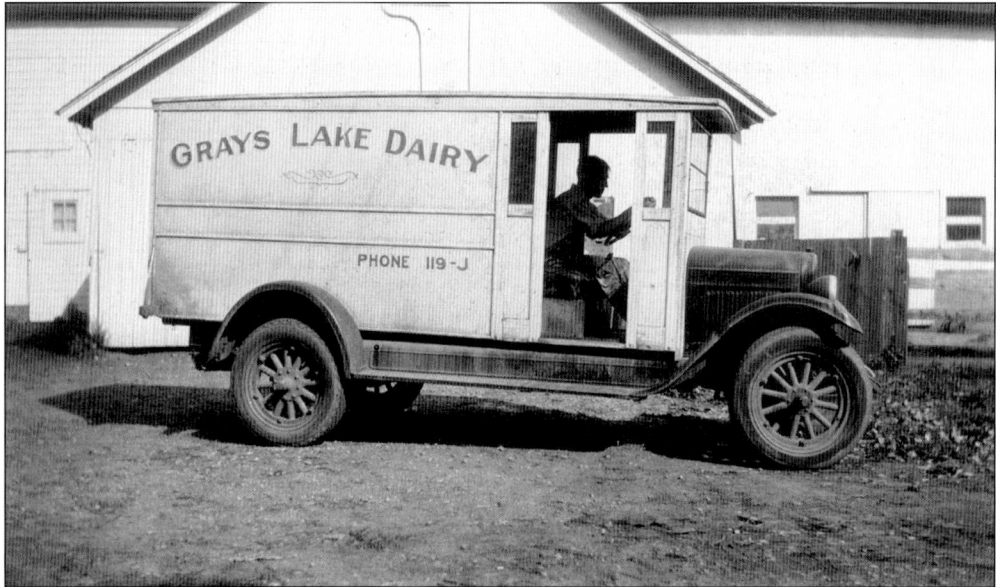

Lee Strang (left) and George Strang acquired their REO hearse in 1920. George started the undertaking business on present-day Center Street in 1898. Son Harold and grandson David moved it to Belvidere Road in 1958. (Courtesy of Grayslake Historical Society.)

Harley Darby sold his milk route to Charles W. Kuebker in 1925. Kuebker processed the milk produced by his cows and raw milk bought from other farmers. Milk, cream, and eggs were delivered door to door by truck to local housewives. Kuebker ceased operating the dairy about 1936 but continued to farm.

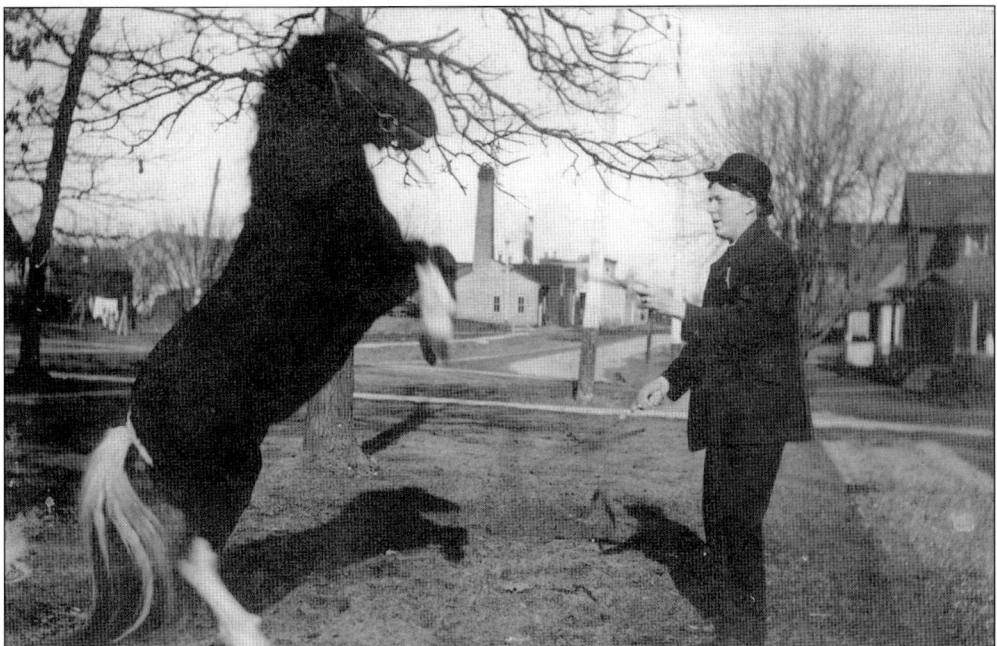

Photographer Lee Williams was responsible for this postcard imagine postmarked 1909. His lens was looking north down Seymour Avenue from Park Avenue. To the right is Buck Shute's house, and the smoke stack is on Grayslake's electric generating plant.

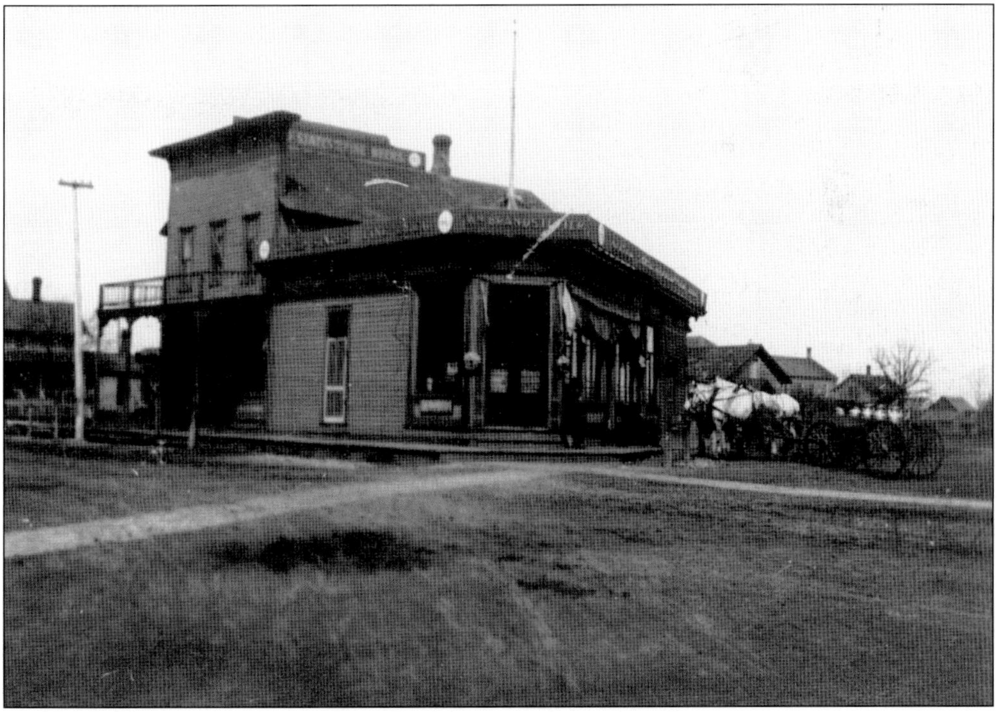

William Brandstetter came to Grayslake in the 1890s and opened a saloon at the corner of present-day Center Street and Seymour Avenue. Prohibition caused him to go into the general merchandise business. (Courtesy of Grayslake Historical Society.)

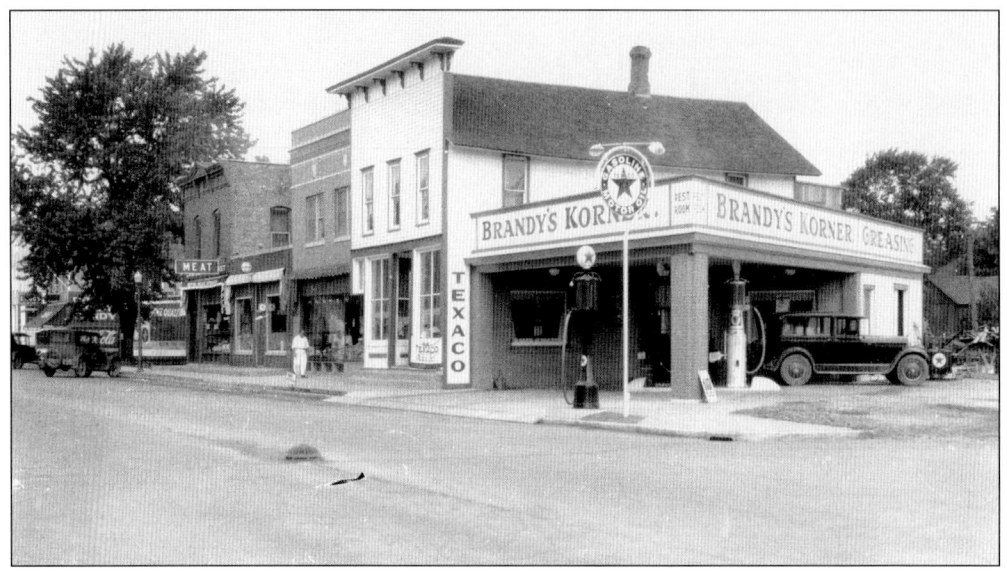

Saloon keeper William Brandstetter had three sons. Son Irvin's gas station was at the location of his father's former saloon as seen in this photograph from the late 1920s. Grandson John took over the operation before the business passed out of the family's hands in the 1950s. (Courtesy of Grayslake Historical Society.)

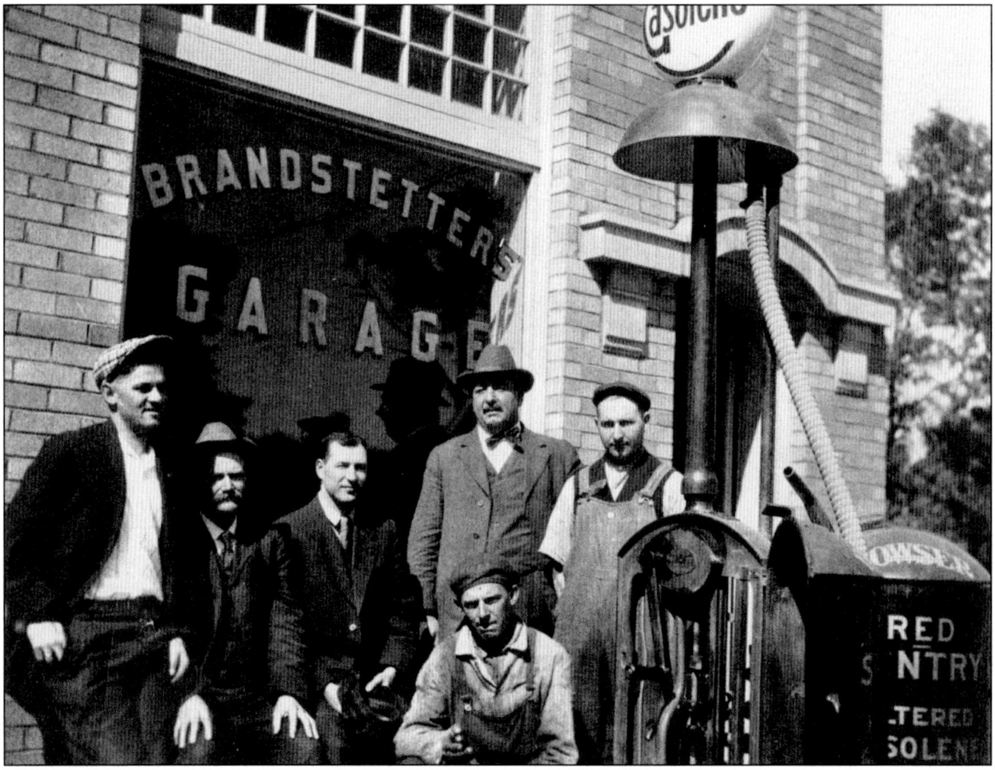

Standing in front of Brandstetter's Garage at 2 South Lake Street are, from left to right, Frank Winkle, William Rehbein, George Brandstetter, Joe Schlosser, and owner Fay Brandstetter. Cliff Frazier is kneeling in this c. 1918 photograph. (Courtesy of Grayslake Historical Society.)

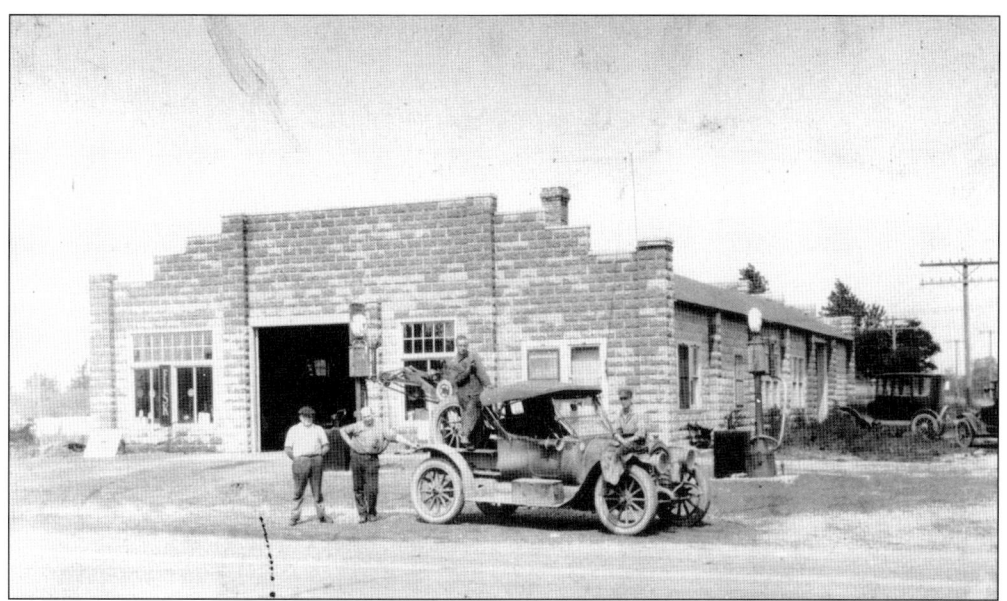

In 1924, Fay Brandstetter opened the garage pictured here, a cement block building located at the northeast corner of Barron Boulevard and Center Street. This location has had many uses, including manufacturing. The building has been replaced, and the site is currently a restaurant. (Courtesy of Grayslake Historical Society.)

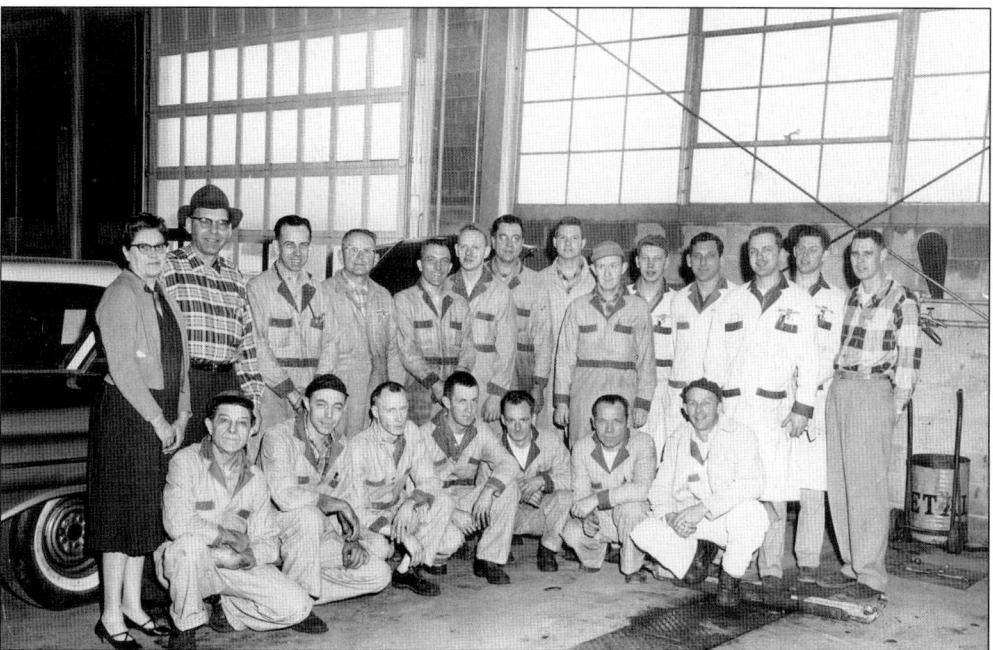

Robert Rockenbach started his garage business in 1926. In a new location, Rockenbach Chevrolet continues. This 1958 photograph recognizes employees. They are, from left to right, (first row) Harold Druce, Eugene Amann, Linc Gould, Dick Renehan, Bob Glick, Owen Litwiler, and Wes Druce; (second row) Jean (Mrs. Robert) Rockenbach, Rodney Rockenbach, Leonard Burge, George Flary, Bob Grodotz, Gene Herman, Ed Amann, George Schlung, Gene Lenzen, Bob Rockenbach, Jack Richardson, Don Toomey, Milt Stickels, and Doug Rockenbach.

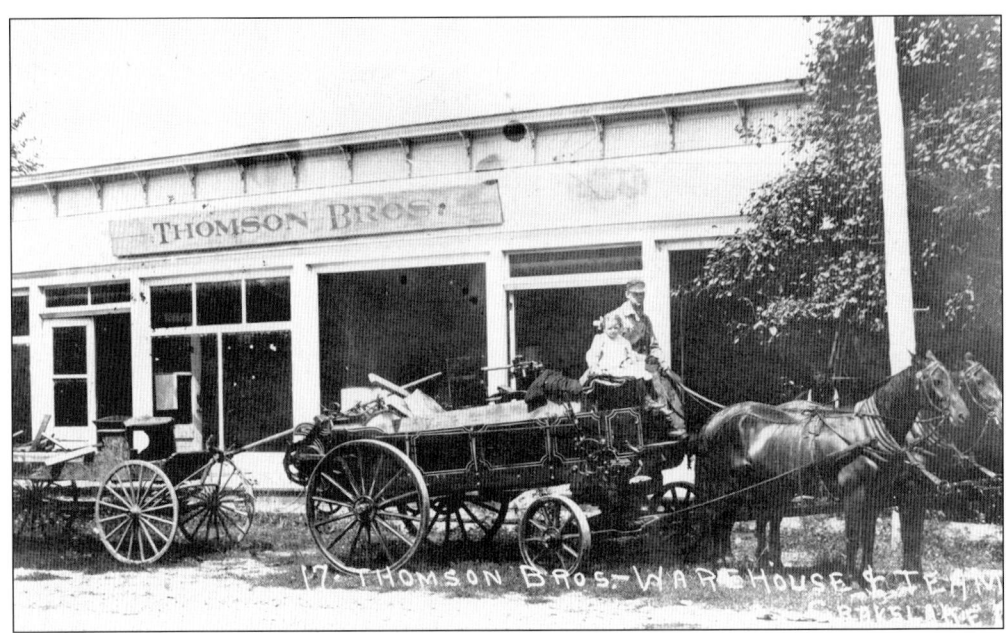

Ed Wagner was the delivery driver for Thomson Brothers Hardware Store. Seated with him is his daughter Bessie. Bessie became Mrs. Harkness and taught in the local grade school. The location today is approximately 164 Center Street.

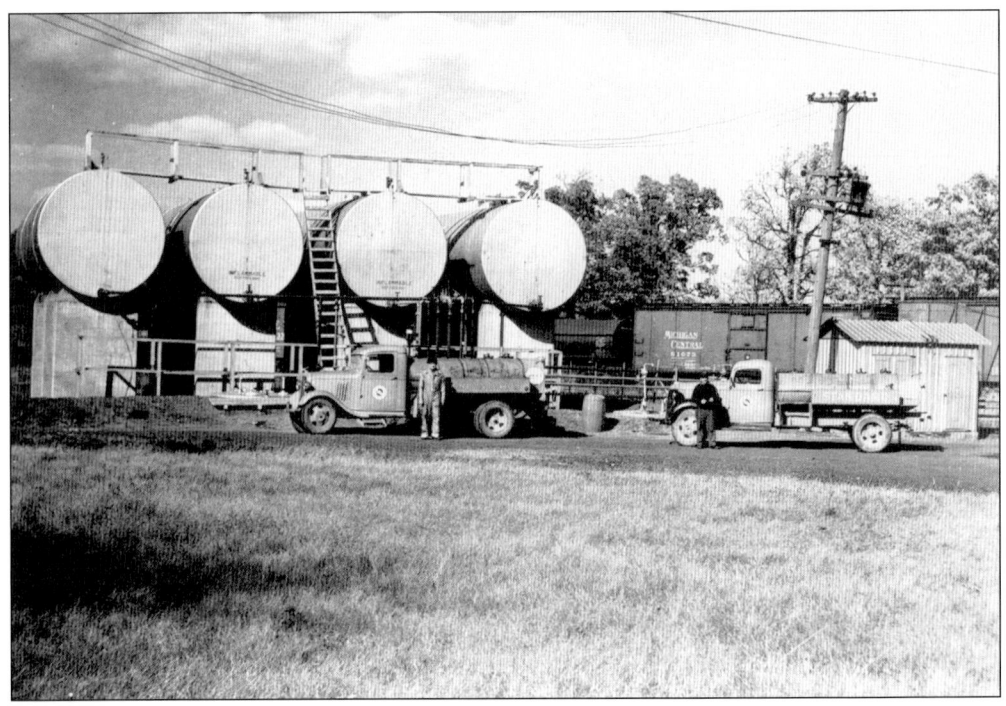

The Grayslake Park District maintenance building on North Lake Street now occupies the property formerly used by the Standard Oil Company for its bulk oil-distributing center. Fuel oil trucks delivered heating oil to homes and gasoline to filling stations and farms. (Courtesy of Grayslake Historical Society.)

The first Grays Lake election was held in 1895 in the Carmi Read building pictured here. Thomson Brothers Hardware Store was in the building, and George Thomson was elected the first mayor of the village. The building was moved and is now a residence at the corner of Lake Street and Harvey Avenue. After the building was moved, Henry Kuebker had a brick building built in its place in 1912. The c. 1918 picture below shows, from left to right, Sid Carfield; Sid's wife, Maude; a little girl, Irene Gelden; two clerks, Russell Meade and Cash Pester (who later became a partner); and an unidentified man. Carfield served twice as village mayor. The building is no longer visible as its facade is now part of the building to the east. (Below, courtesy of Grayslake Historical Society.)

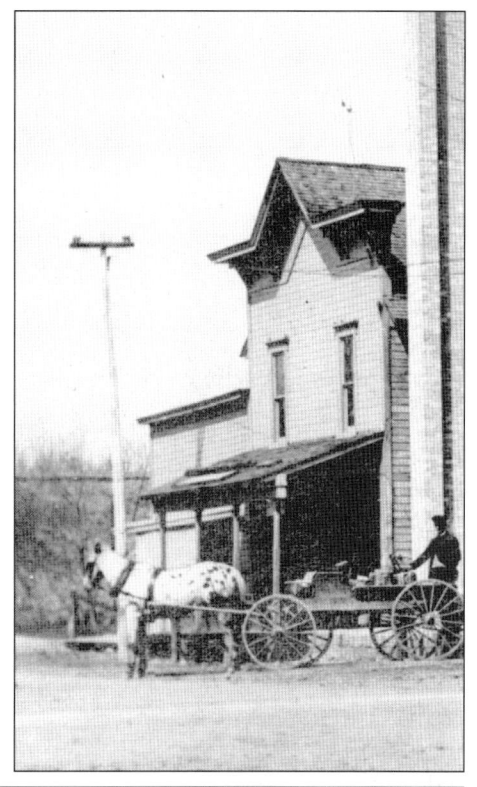

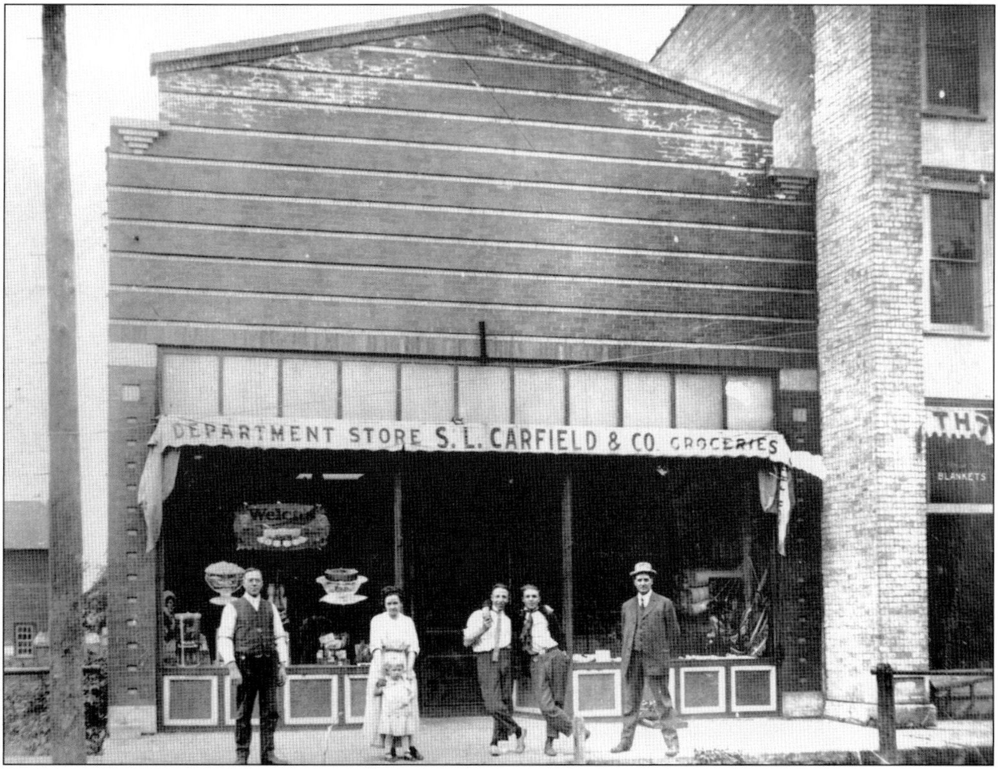

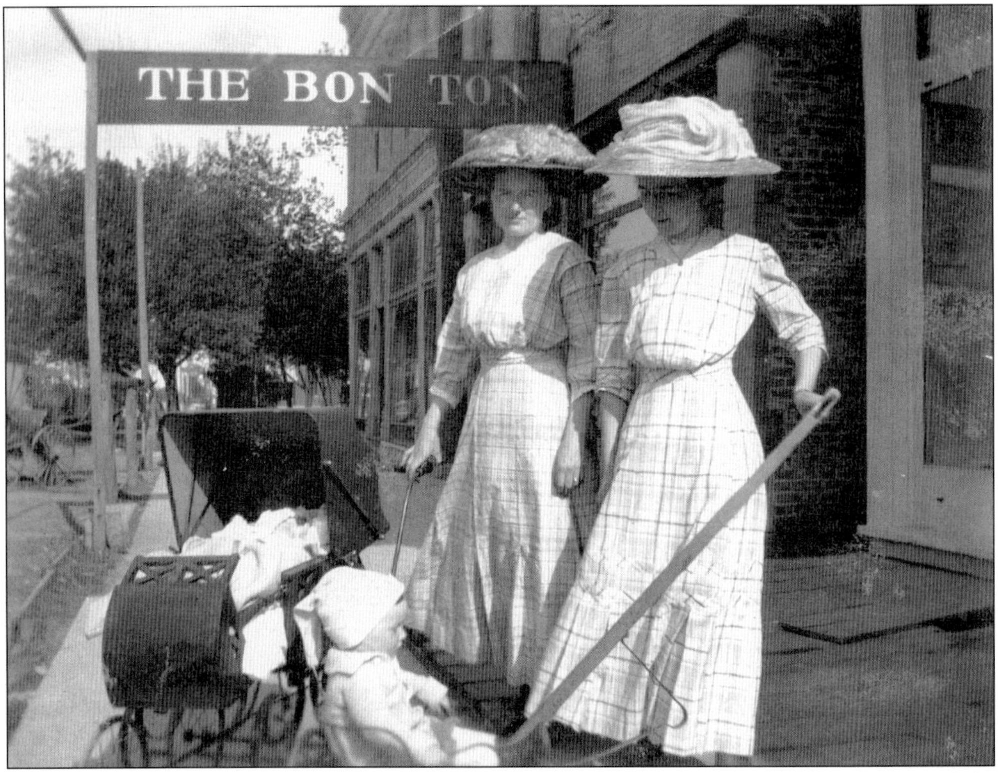

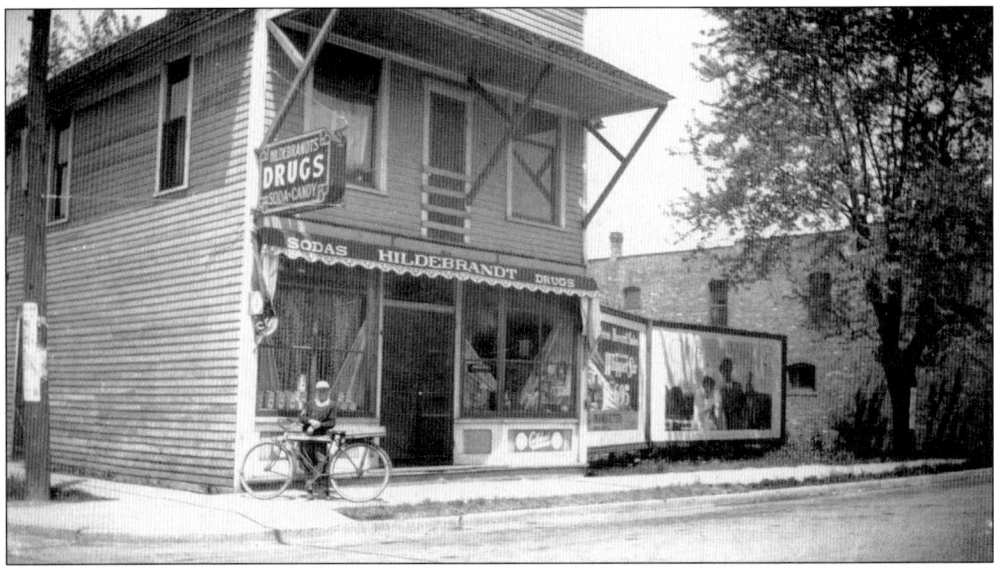

This photograph of two young women out for a stroll with their babies, typical of Grayslake scenes, was taken in front of Viola Burge's Bon Ton store between 1907 and 1910. (Courtesy of Grayslake Historical Society.)

In 1929, Phil "Doc" Hildebrandt opened a drugstore in the Bixler Building located at the northeast corner of Center and Whitney Streets and remained there for two years. The building was demolished in the late 1930s, and the vacant lot was then used for outdoor movies, carnivals, and an ice-skating rink. A bank is presently at this site. (Courtesy of Grayslake Historical Society.)

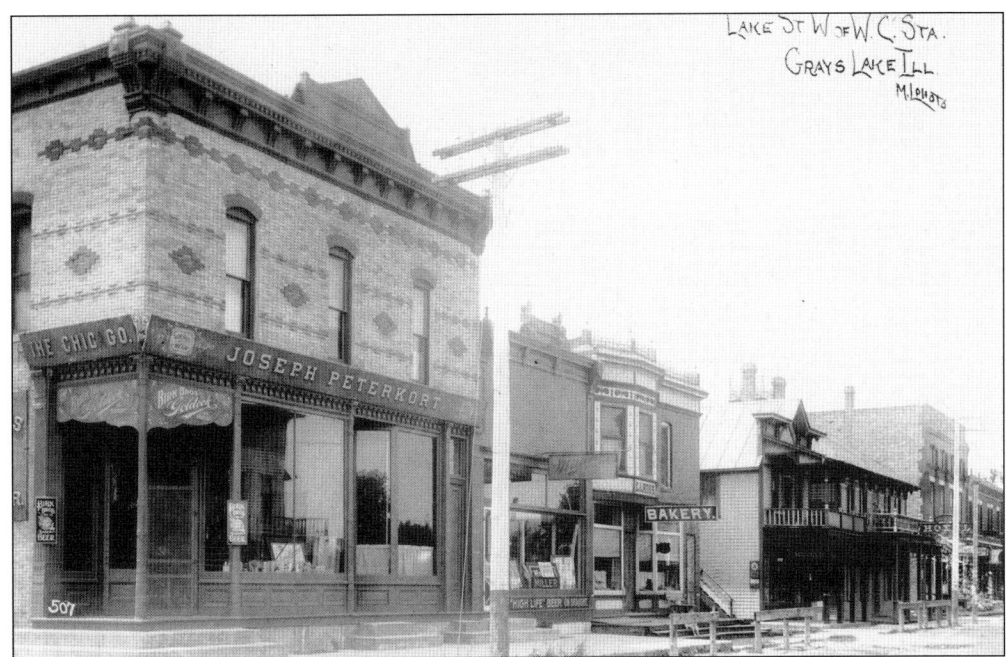

The corner building in this view burned in 1970 when it was a bowling alley. The structure had been built in 1894 for John J. Longabaugh. The first occupants were A. J. Leonard and Fred H. Kuebker, who operated it as a general merchandise store. In 1898, Joe Peterkort moved in with his saloon and hotel. The Peterkort family left the business in 1919.

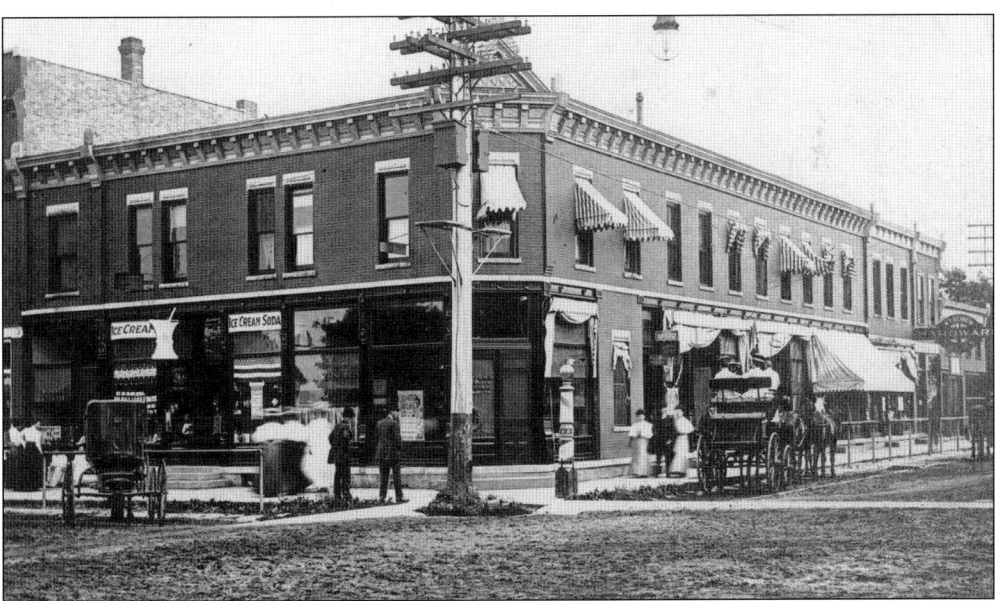

Banker P. A. Robinson came to Grayslake in 1899, and the following year, the Merchants and Farmers Bank was in operation at the southeast corner of Whitney Street and present-day Center Street. In 1903, R. W. Churchill opened his law office on the second floor. The bank was sold in 1906 to L. Y. Sikes. The building was demolished in 2007. (Courtesy of Grayslake Historical Society.)

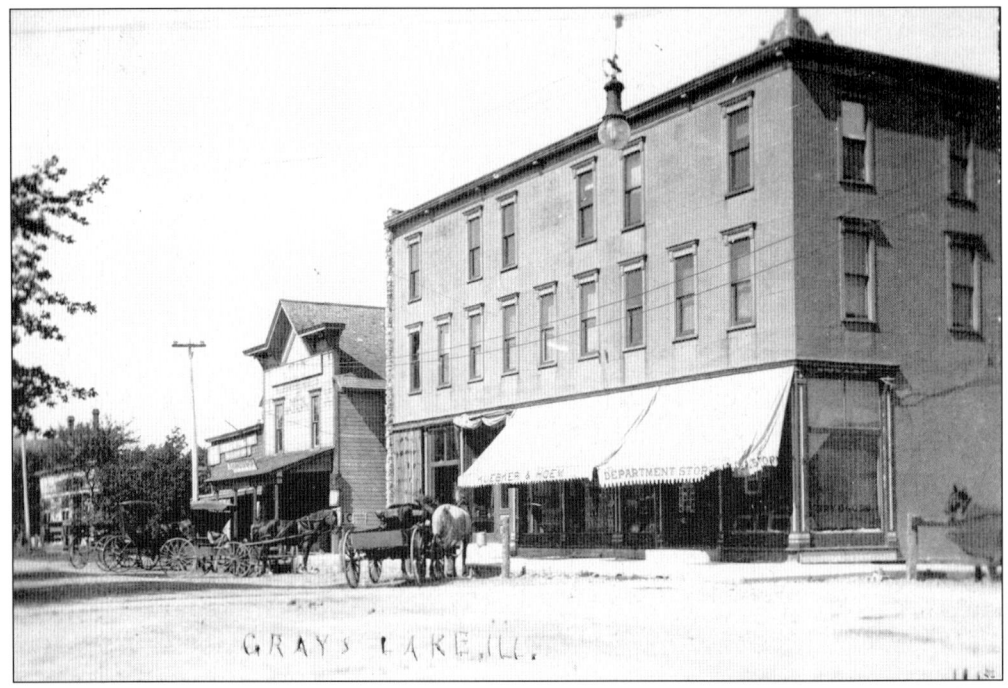

Fred H. Kuebker had his three-story building completed in 1897. The Kuebker building has been lowered from three stories to two stories but still stands at the northwest corner of Center and Whitney Streets. The building presently houses several businesses. In this view from a postcard dated 1908, the Carmi Read building is to the left.

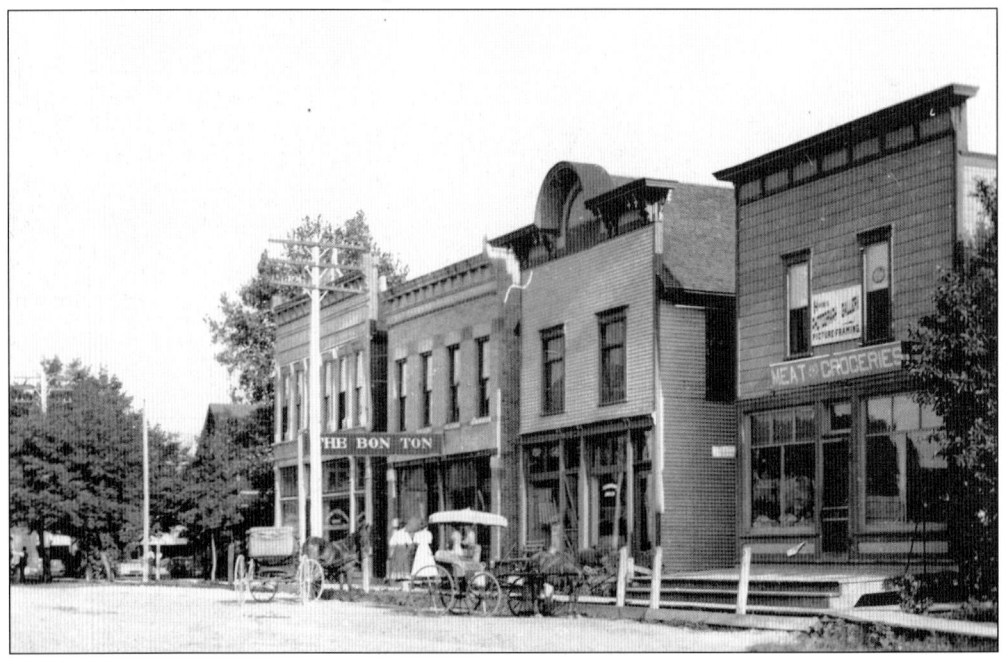

This view of the south side of present-day Center Street between Whitney and Slusser Streets was taken between 1907 and 1910. The shoppers purchased dry goods at Viola Burge's Bon Ton or meat at Ed Hook's market. (Courtesy of Grayslake Historical Society.)

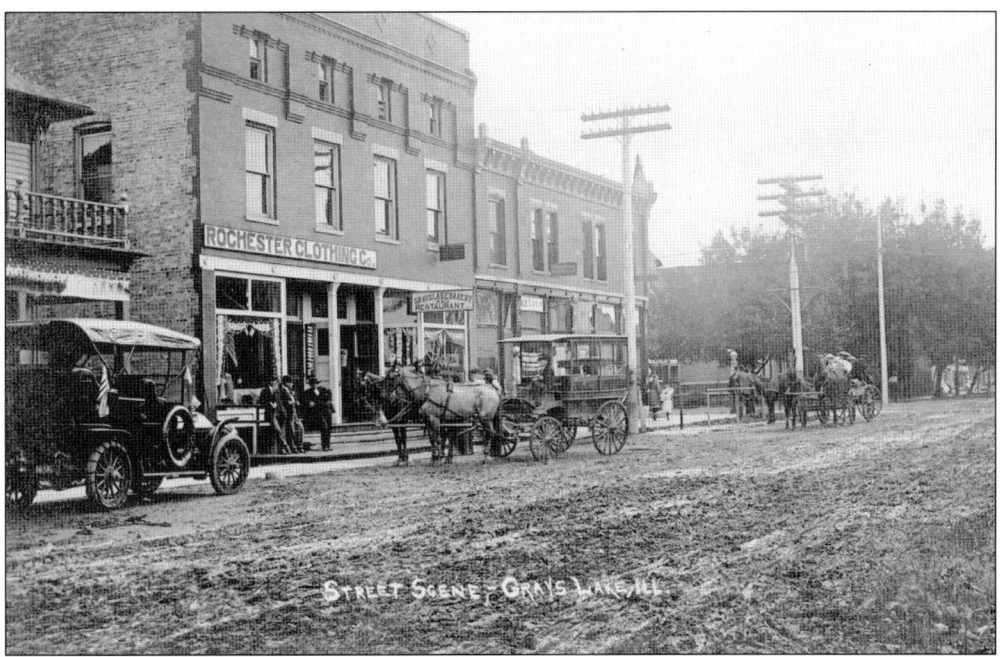

A corner of the Grayslake Hotel is showing in this *c.* 1910 view of Grayslake's main street. The opera house is to the right, followed by the bank building. After crossing Whitney Street, what looks like a wooded lot is the front yard of the first house built in the subdivision of Grays Lake.

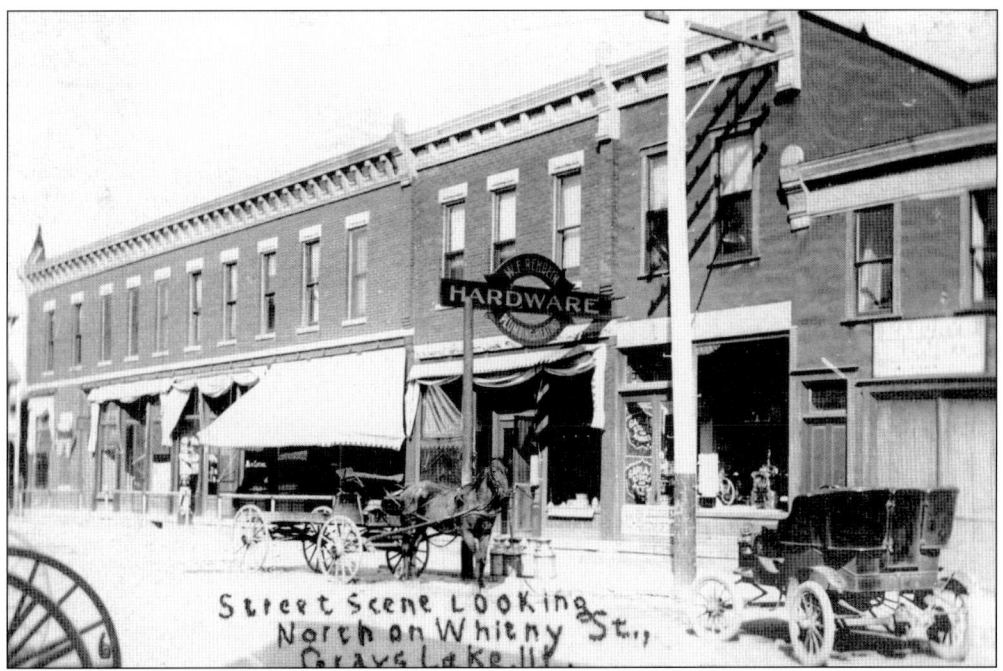

The east side of South Whitney Street is seen here. At the left corner is the former Merchants and Farmers Bank. W. F. Rehbein's store is shown in the center. Rehbein, a plumber by trade, did business at this location from 1903 to 1911. The buildings were demolished in 2007.

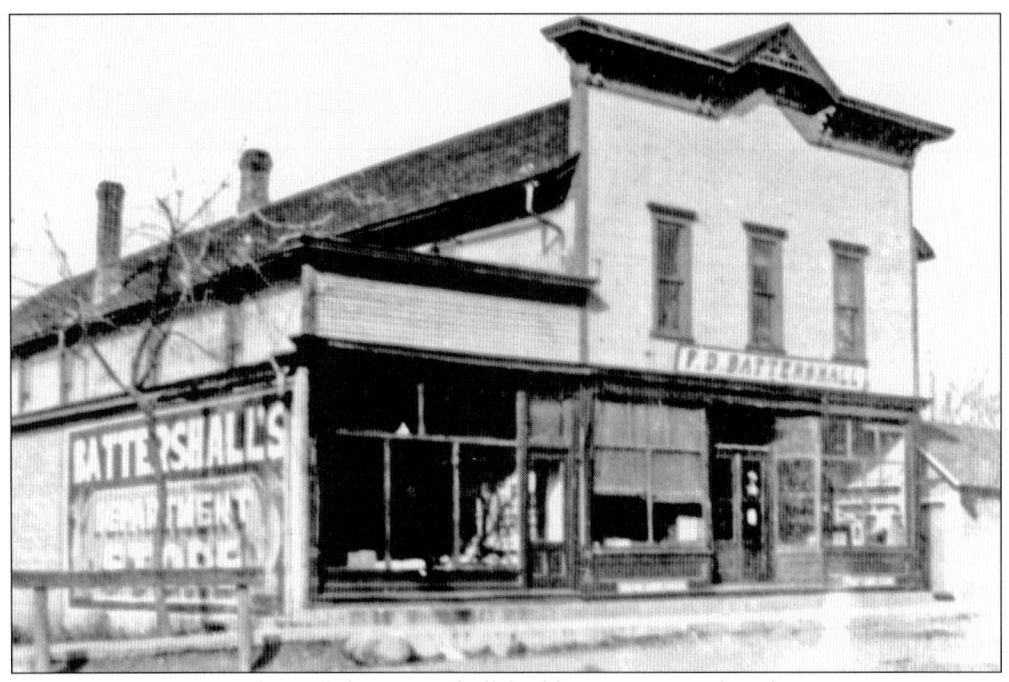

This c. 1910 photograph is of the Battershall building at 34 South Whitney Street. George Battershall and son Fred built this 1890s structure and moved their general merchandise business here from Hainesville. For more than 50 years, the *Grayslake Times* was published here. (Courtesy of Grayslake Historical Society.)

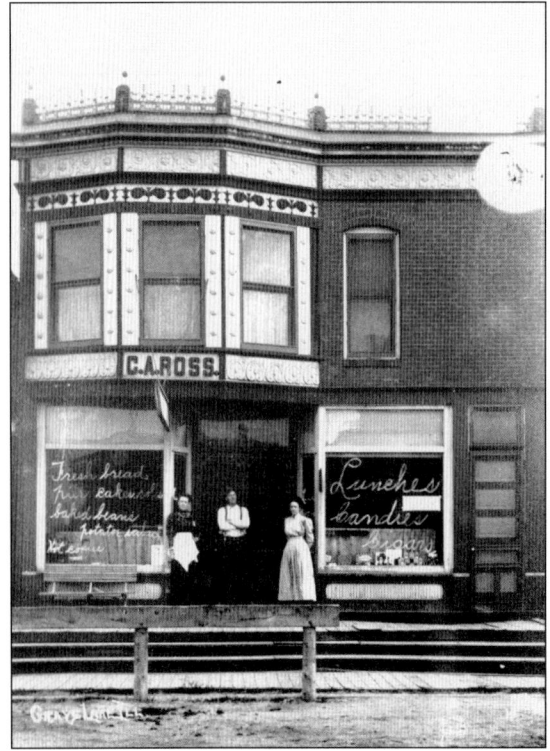

The building at 265 Center Street currently houses an accounting service. It was built in 1895 for Charles Ross as the Austin Hotel. Pete Newhouse published the *Grayslake Times* at this location from 1913 to 1928. It was the location of several bakeries through the years.

In early years, many communities had an opera house. School functions, dances, and sports events were held in Grayslake's opera house. At the time of this picture, it had a barbershop and bowling alley in the basement with businesses on the ground floor. T. A. Reynolds managed the Rochester Clothing Company from 1903 to 1913. A delicatessen was in the right-hand side of the building for numerous years.

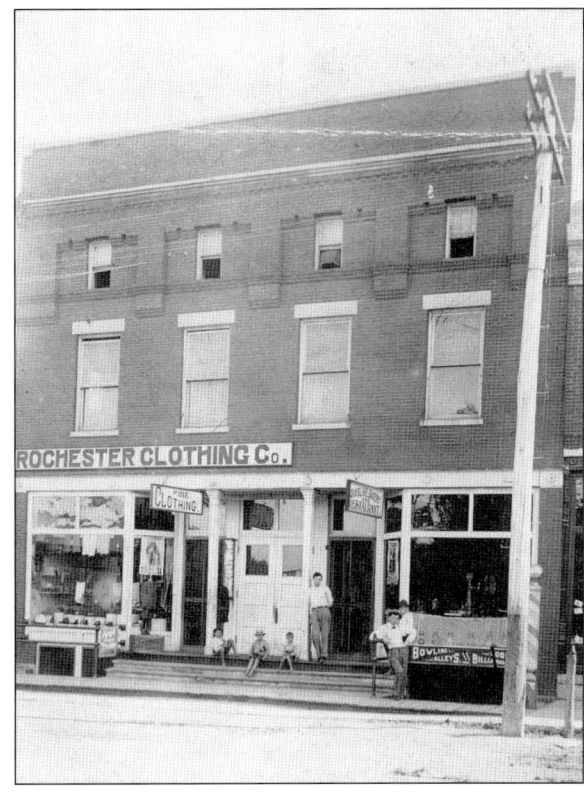

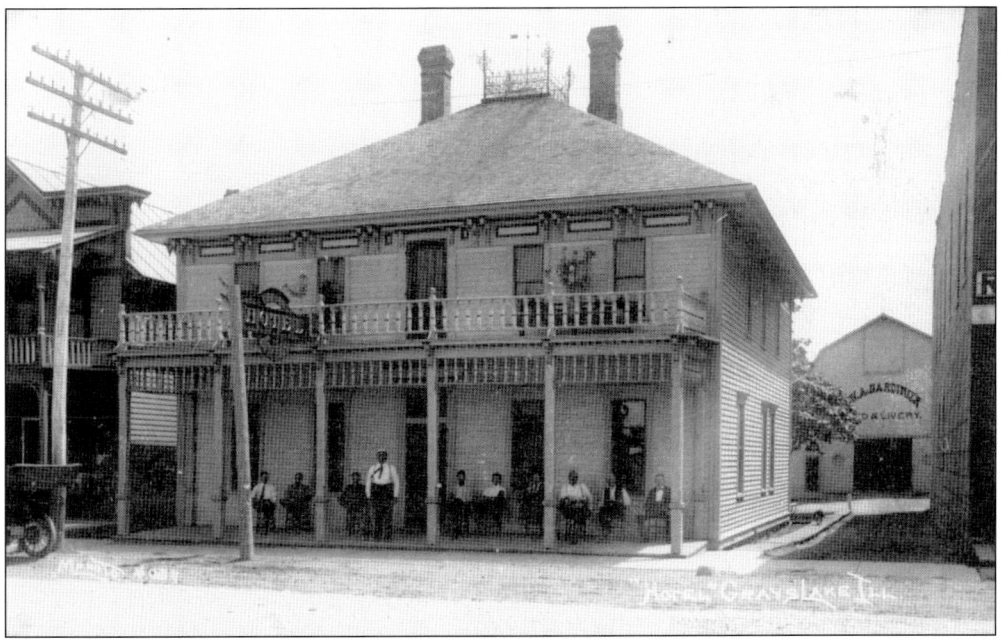

The frame structure at 229–241 Center Street was built as the Grayslake Hotel in the 1890s for Mary Ann Hook. Hook and her husband, Willis Gardinier, ran the establishment. The former hotel is now an investment office, while the alley leading to the livery stable is occupied by a restaurant. This image is from around 1910.

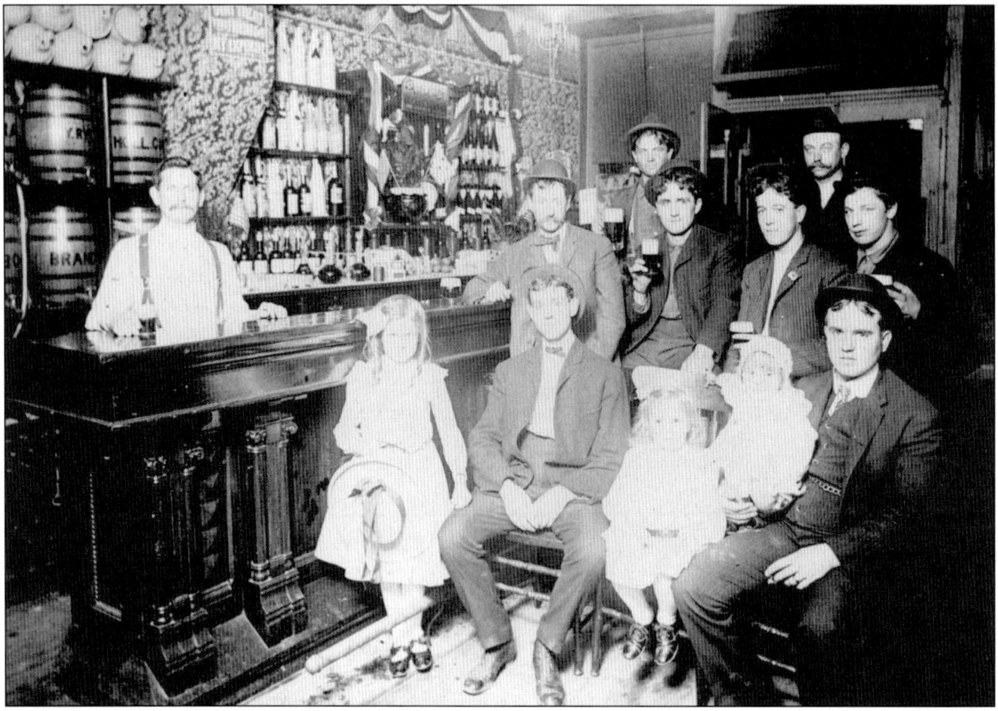

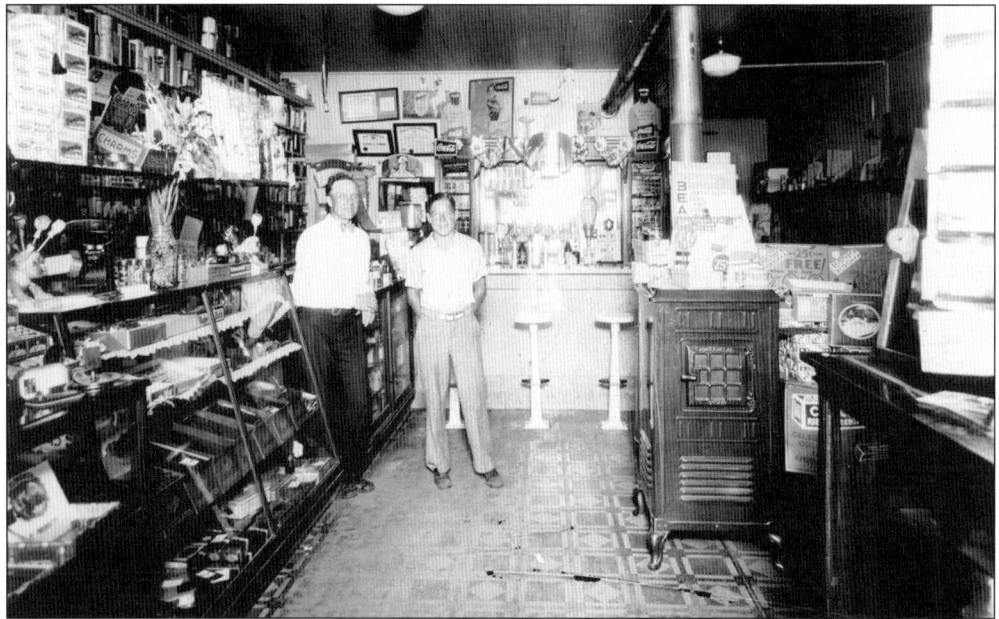

The interior of a Grayslake saloon shown here from around 1900 is believed to be the William Brandstetter establishment on what appears to be a special occasion. (Courtesy of Grayslake Historical Society.)

This interior view of the Bixler Building, between 1929 and 1931, shows Phil "Doc" Hildebrandt's drugstore. Hildebrandt had his drugstore in several Grayslake locations between 1917 and 1943. Standing in this image are Doc on the left and his son Phil Jr. (Courtesy of Grayslake Historical Society.)

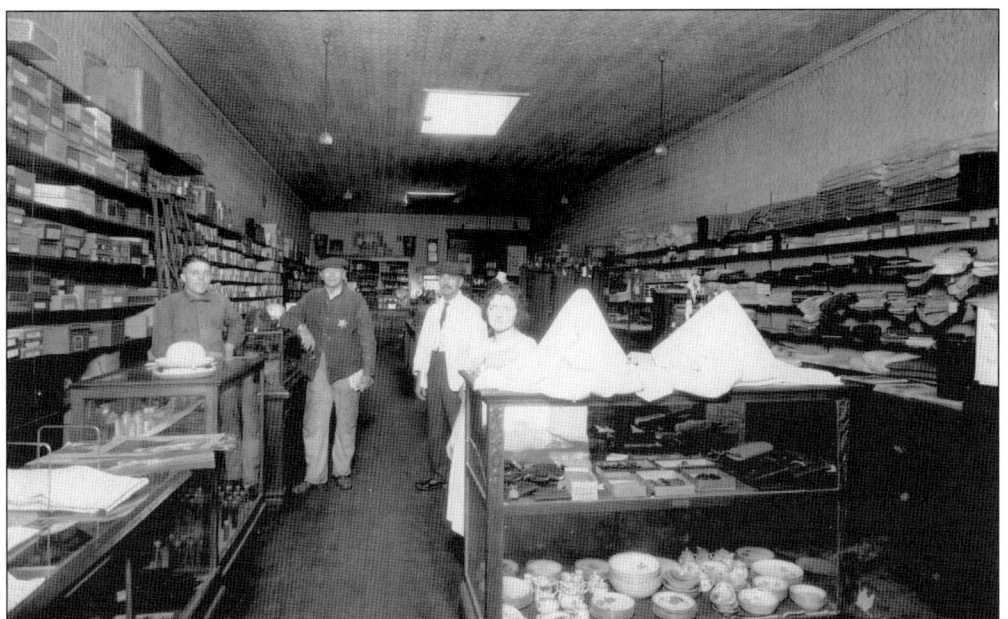

Cash Pester purchased the Sid Carfield general merchandise store in 1927. He phased out dry goods, and the business became a grocery store. Pester ran the store until he retired in 1948. (Courtesy of Grayslake Historical Society.)

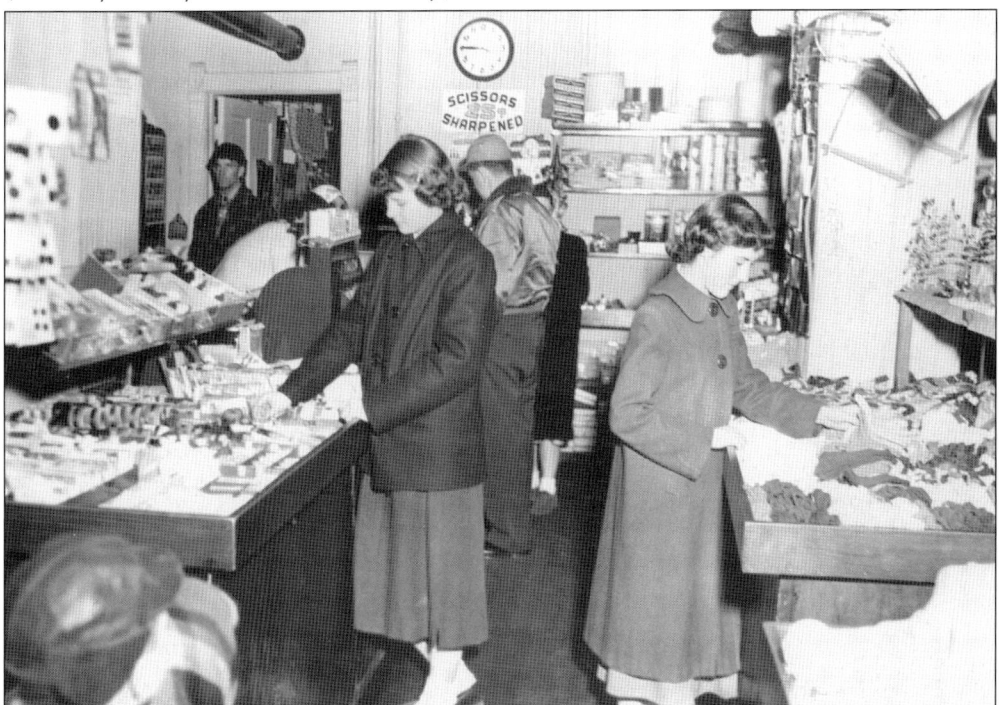

At the time of this photograph, about 1950, Sharon Wightman (left) and Maureen Walsh are shopping in the Old Dime Store. The Old Dime Store was known for its penny candy. Today the building is a part of a saloon and eating establishment. (Courtesy of Grayslake Historical Society.)

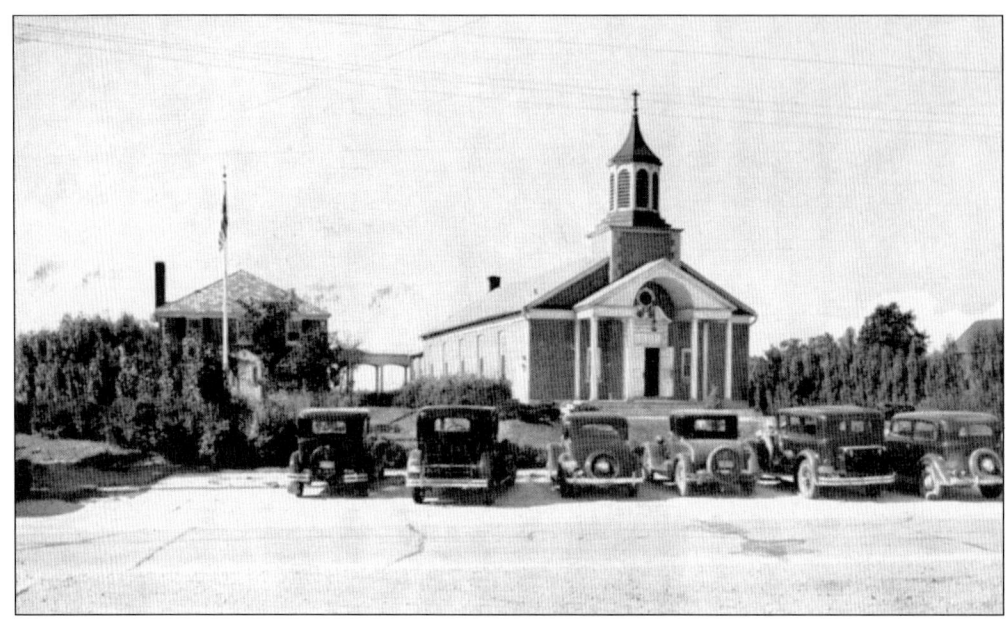

George William Cardinal Mundelein dedicated St. Gilbert Catholic Church in 1932. Although a new larger edifice has been constructed, the church pictured above, around 1938, on Belvidere Road, continues to serve the parish. In the 1930s, the inside of the original St. Gilbert Catholic Church looked as pictured below. For a period of time, it was a recreational facility for the parish school but is once more a place of worship.

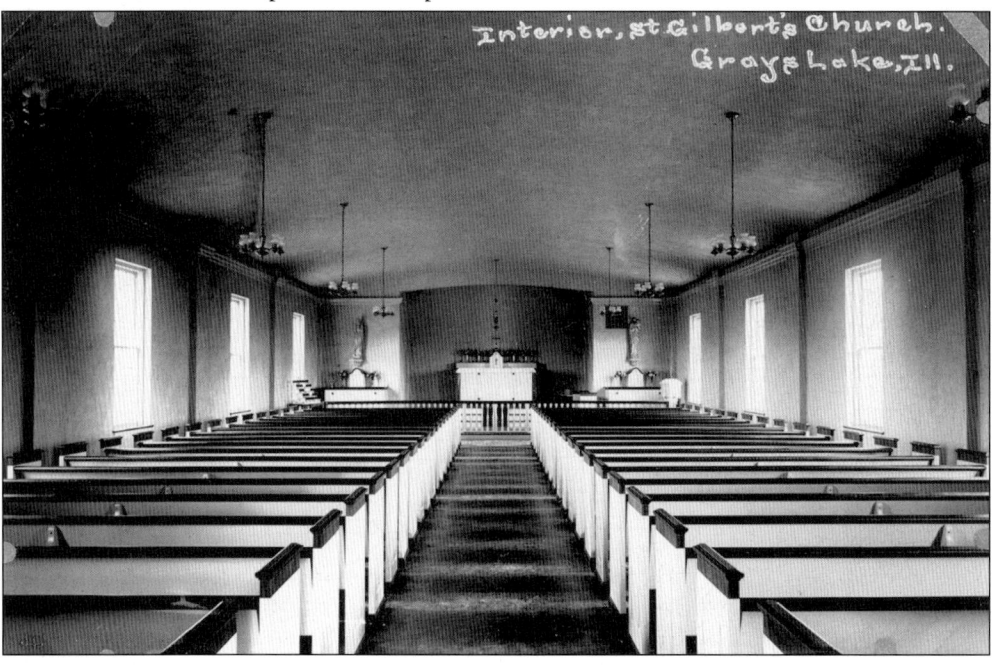

The first church building in Grayslake, pictured on the right, was dedicated in 1892 as a Congregational church. Previously the parishioners met in a store as a Sunday school class. The building exists today at the corner of Lake and Center Streets as the home of the Rising Sun Masonic Lodge. A postcard dated 1910 documents the interior, seen below, of the Congregational church at that time. The building was sold to the Masonic Lodge in the 1950s. (Courtesy of Grayslake Historical Society.)

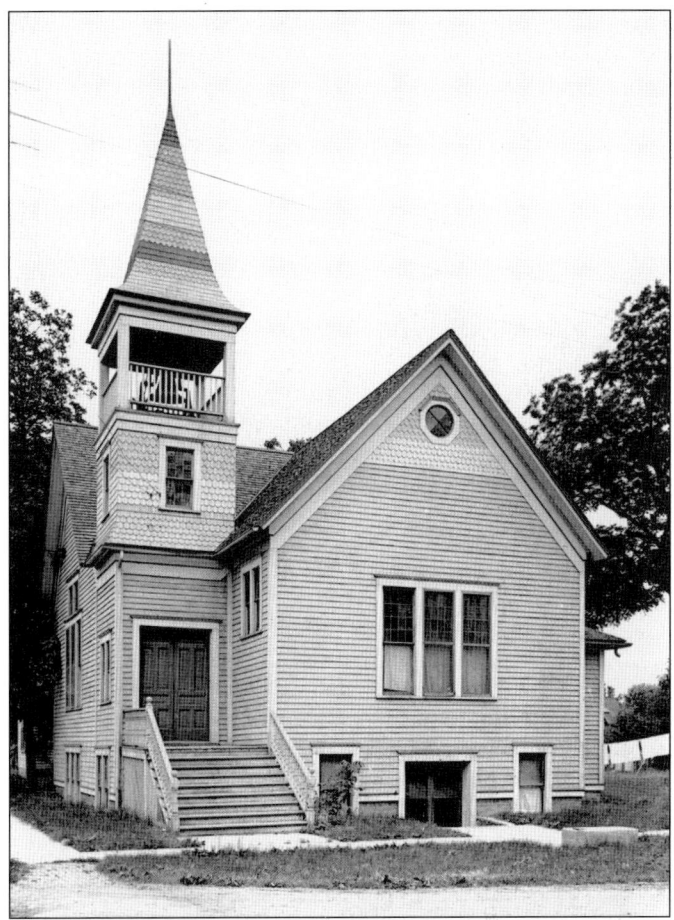

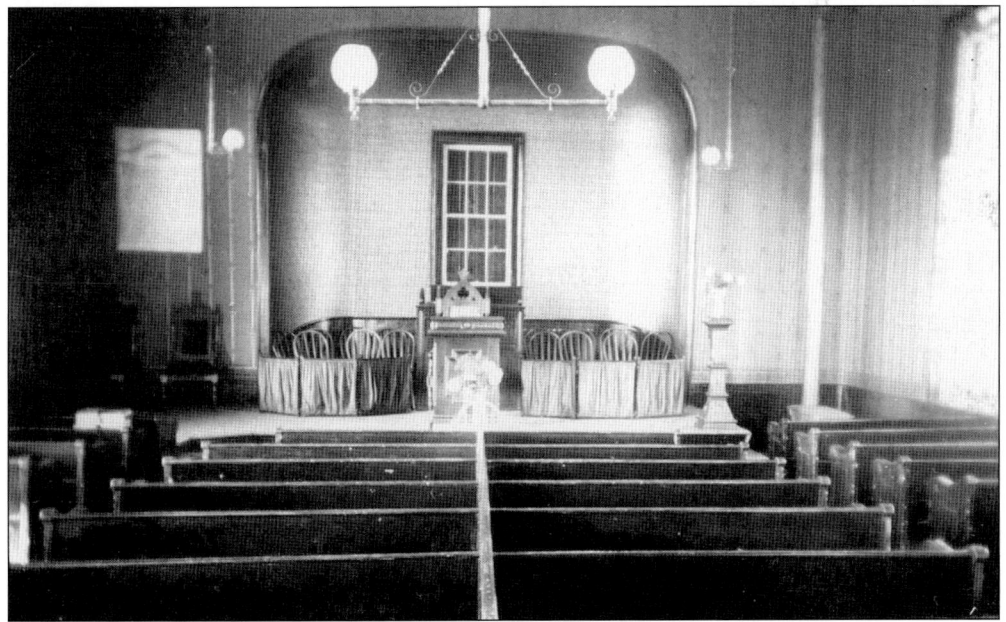

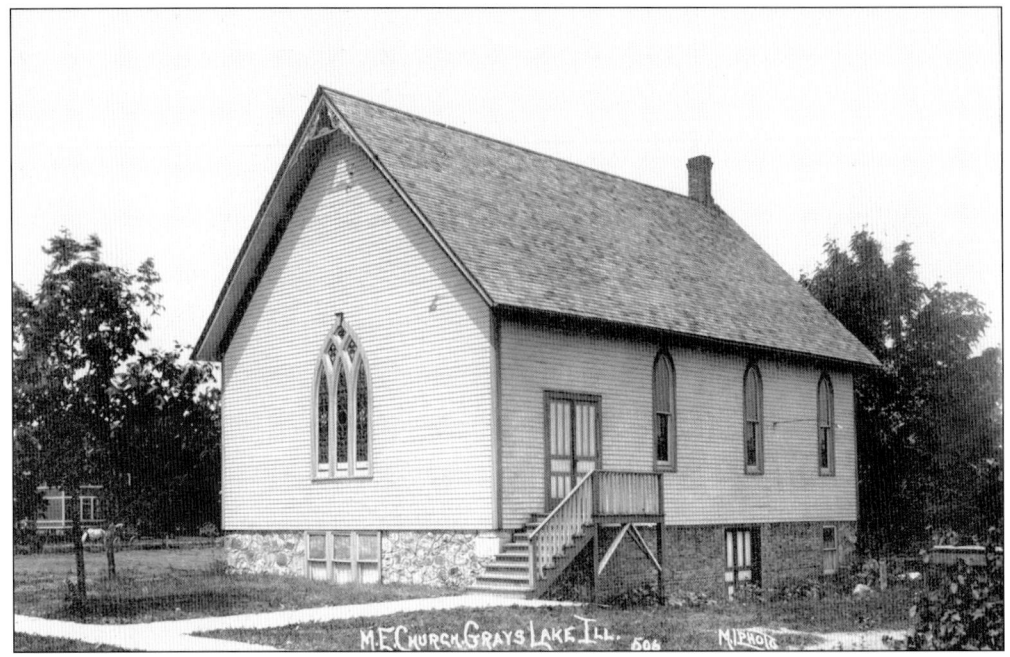

The Methodists of Grayslake built their building on Park Avenue between Whitney and Slusser Streets. The first service in the building was in 1903. In 1924, they moved the building closer to Whitney Street, turned it around 180 degrees, and added a vestibule. It was demolished in the early 1950s to make room for the United Protestant Church.

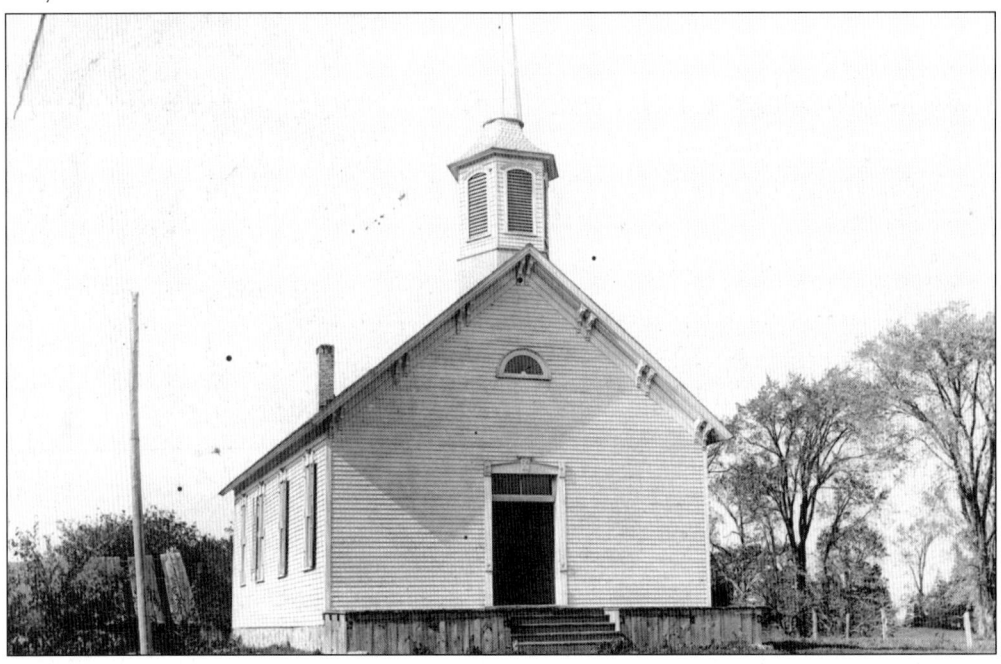

The Gages Lake Methodist Church, built in the 1880s, stood at the southwest corner of Routes 45 and 120. In 1922, the building was moved adjacent to the Grayslake Methodist Church on Park Avenue where it became a community hall. The former church was demolished in the 1930s. This postcard image is postmarked 1908. (Courtesy of Grayslake Historical Society.)

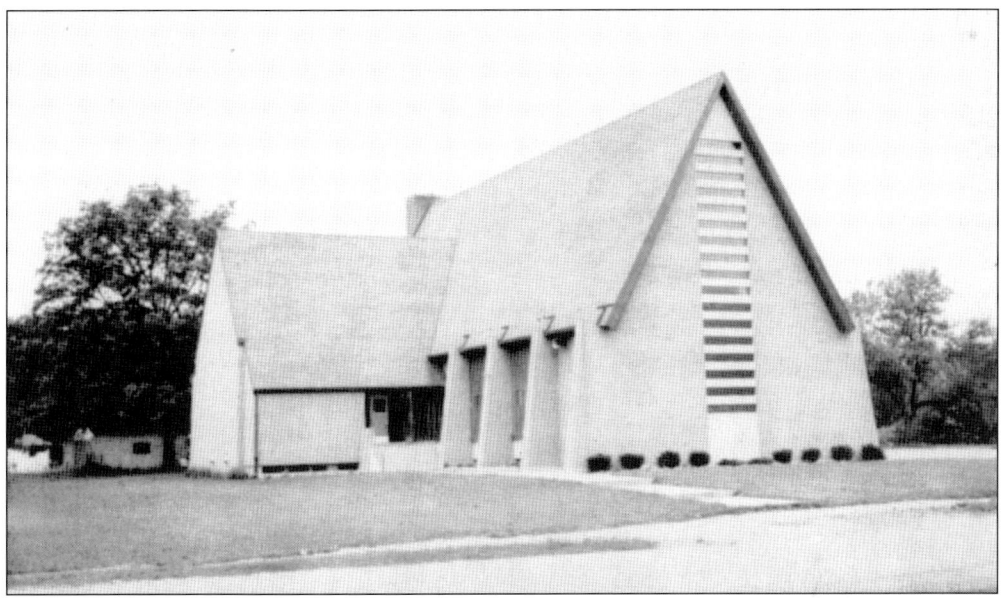

The United Protestant Church building was consecrated in 1956. The congregation was formed in 1950 when the Methodist and Congregational churches merged. Its building is on the site of the former Methodist church at the corner of Whitney Street and Park Avenue.

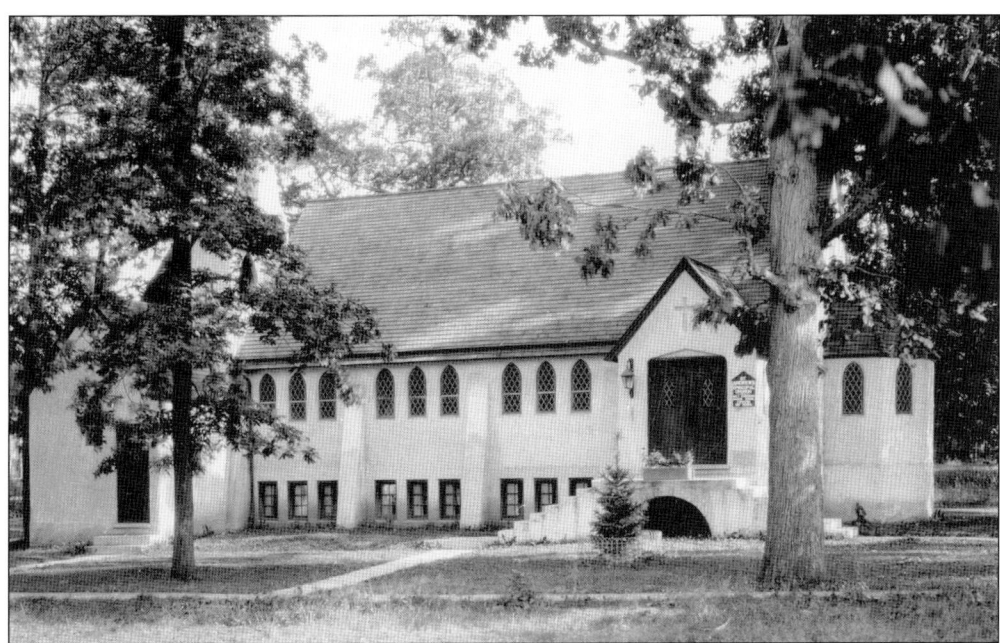

The original entrance to St. Andrew Episcopal Church faced Park Avenue when the first worship service took place in 1928. The entrance was changed to Lake Street when the educational wing was added in the 1960s. (Courtesy of Grayslake Historical Society.)

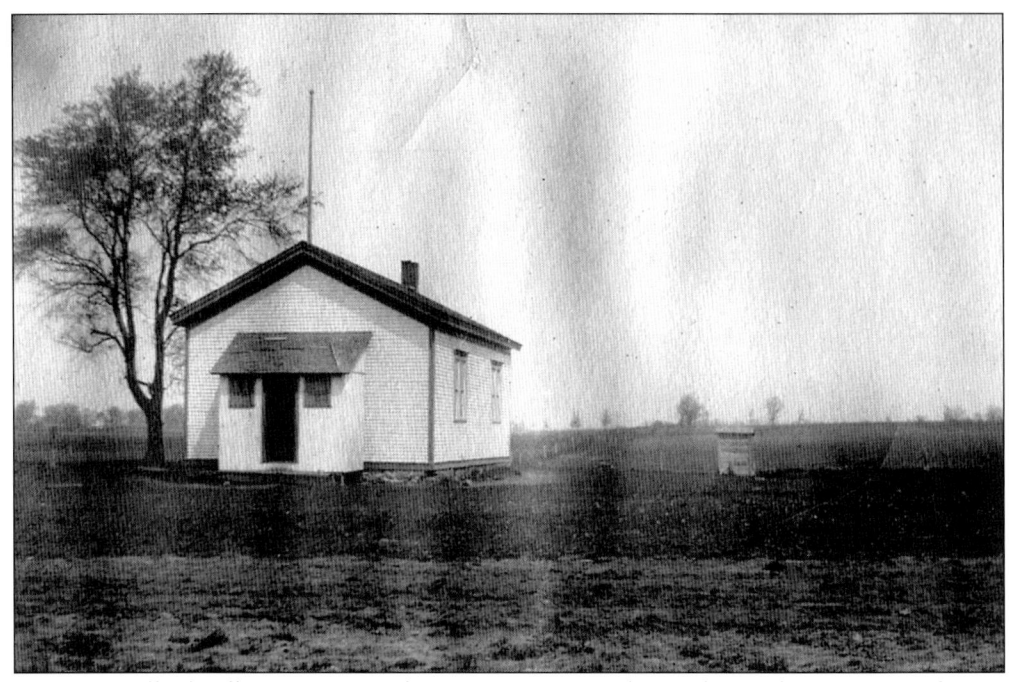

This Fort Hill schoolhouse was torn down in 1916. It stood near the southwest corner of Avon Township. (Courtesy of Lake County Discovery Museum.)

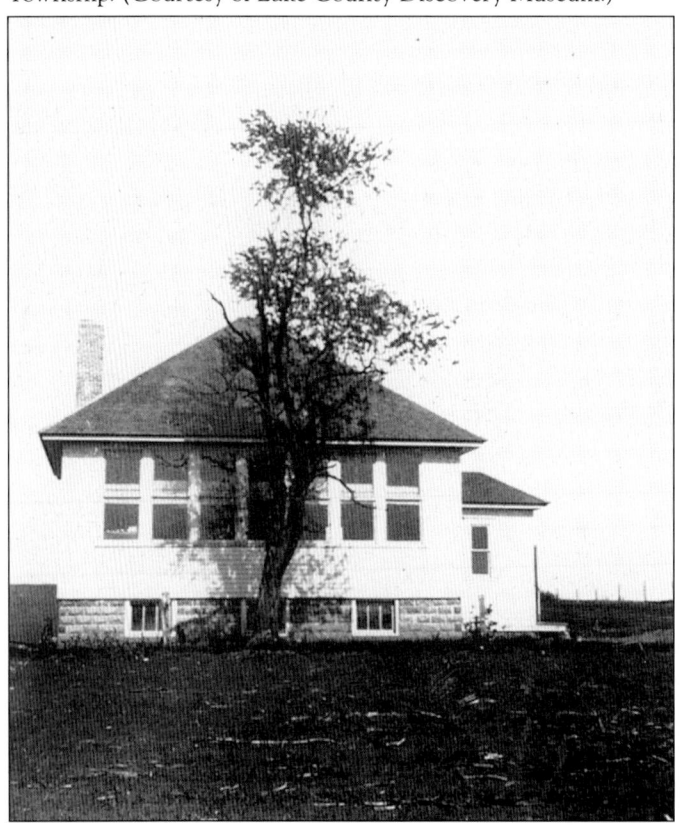

The Fort Hill school, located on Town Line Road in 1918, became a part of the Grayslake Community Consolidated School District 46 in 1949, and the former schoolhouse became a residence. (Courtesy of Lake County Discovery Museum.)

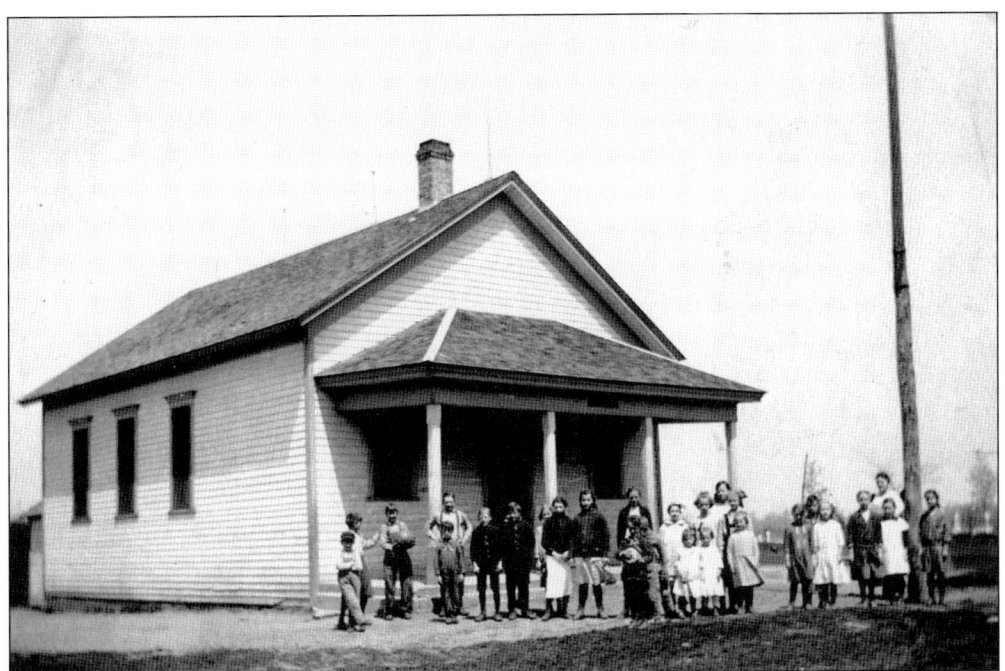

In 1916, as pictured here, the Avon Center School was located in the triangle bordered by Shorewood Road and Route 83. A brick two-room building was constructed in 1950 at 35373 North Highway 83 in the village limits of Round Lake Beach. In 1988, the school merged with Grayslake District 46. (Courtesy of Lake County Discovery Museum.)

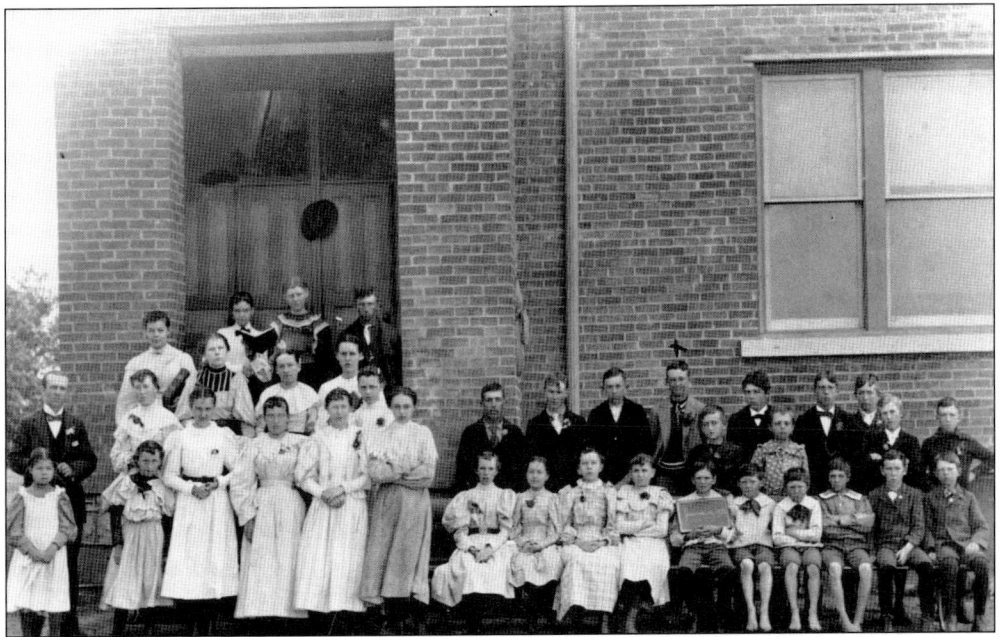

A two-room brick school was built at the northeast corner of present-day Lake Street and Belvidere Road in 1895. It replaced the one-room frame school, which had been moved to downtown Grayslake to become the Grayslake Village Hall. This picture of Grayslake School was taken around 1897. (Courtesy of Grayslake Historical Society.)

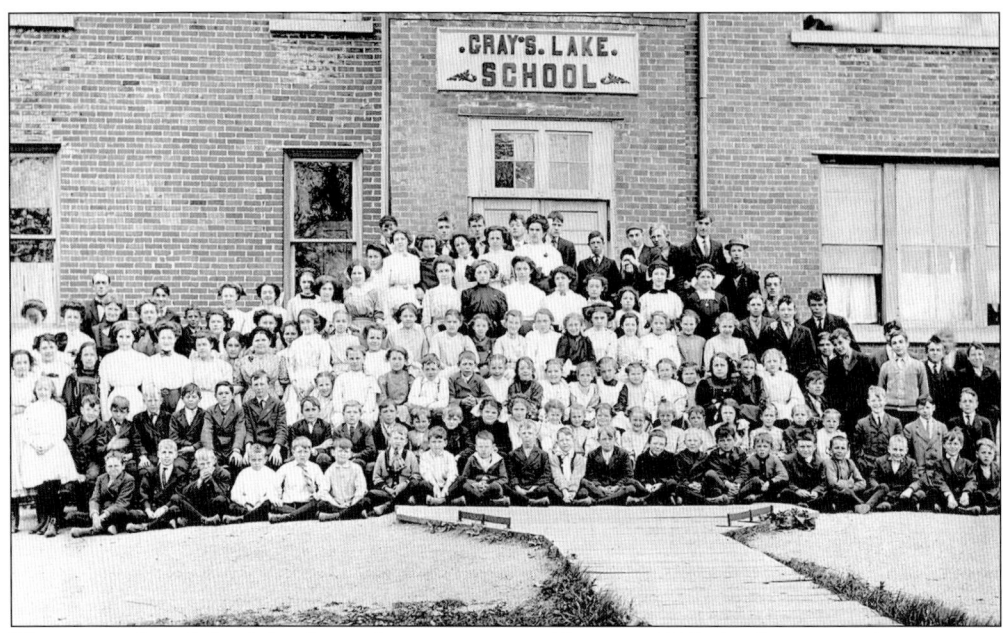

The entire Grayslake School population is pictured here in 1907. At that time, there was no kindergarten, but there were two or three years of high school.

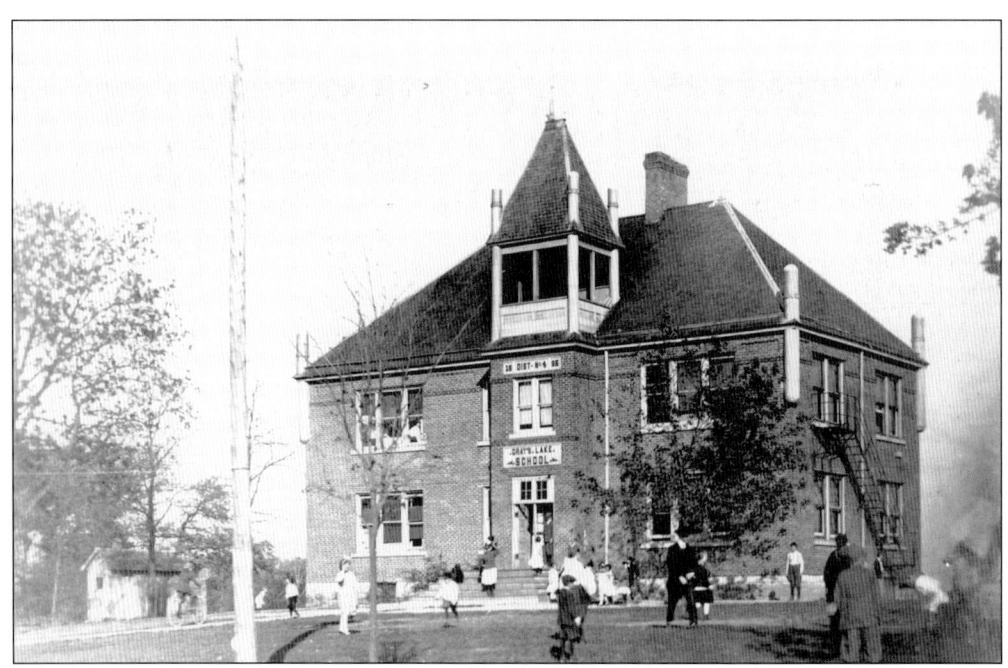

In 1901, two rooms were added to the Grayslake School. In this photograph, from around 1910, the sign over the doors states that it was District No. 4, which meant that it was the fourth school in Avon Township. (Courtesy of Grayslake Historical Society.)

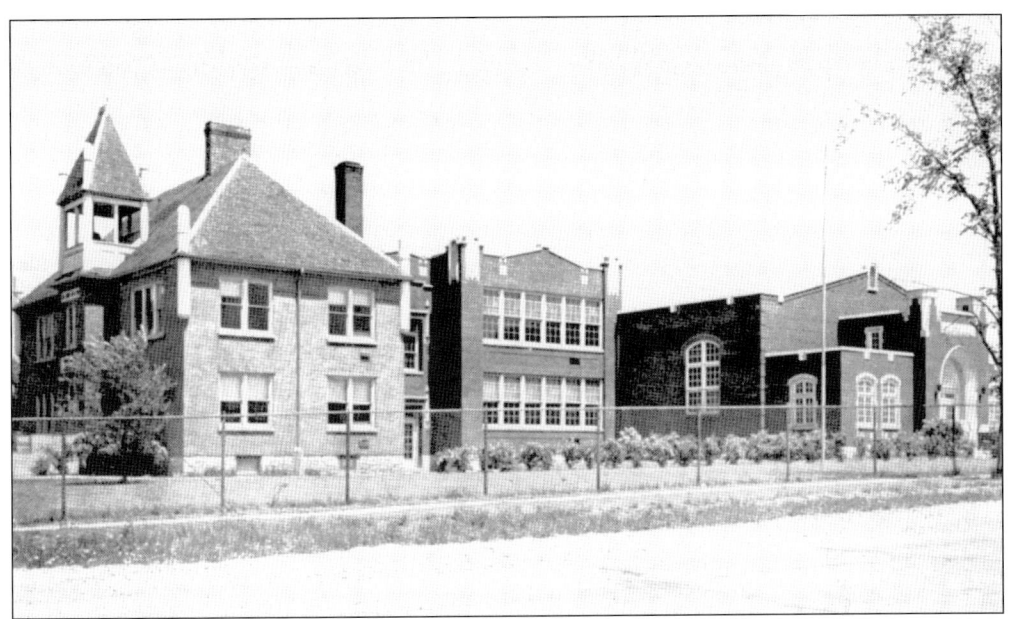

In the late 1920s, four classrooms were added to the Grayslake Grade School with the gymnasium being dedicated in 1933. The gymnasium included a stage, boys' and girls' locker rooms, washrooms, a coat check room, a kitchen, and a lobby. There was a projection room above the lobby. In 1951, the original building was replaced. When Woodview School opened, the building became known as Lakeview School. Lakeview School closed in 2002.

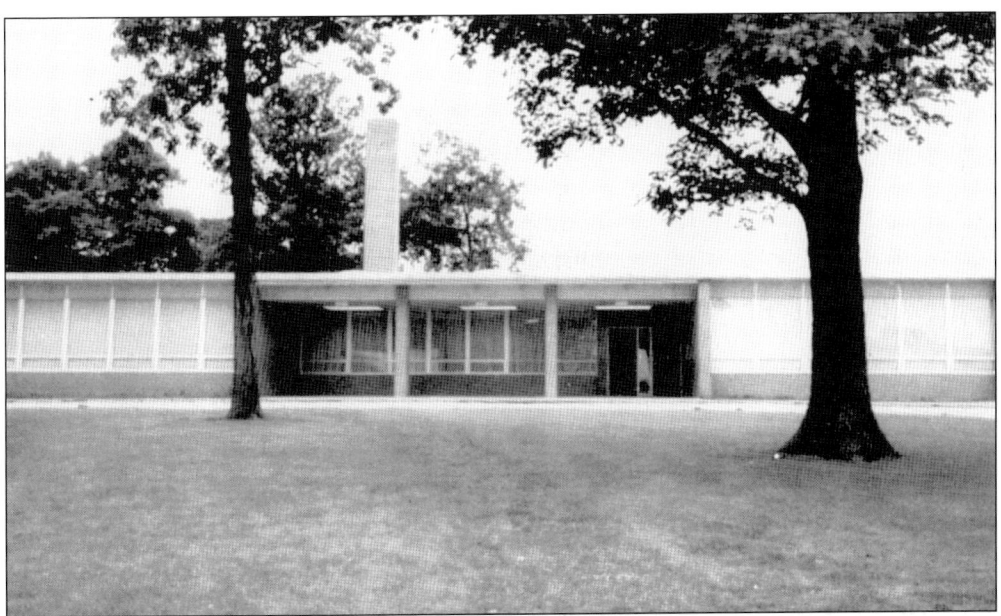

Woodview School, located at 340 Alleghany Road, opened its doors in 1956. It housed kindergarten through fourth-grade students, while older students went to Lakeview School. The building has had many classrooms added plus a gymnasium.

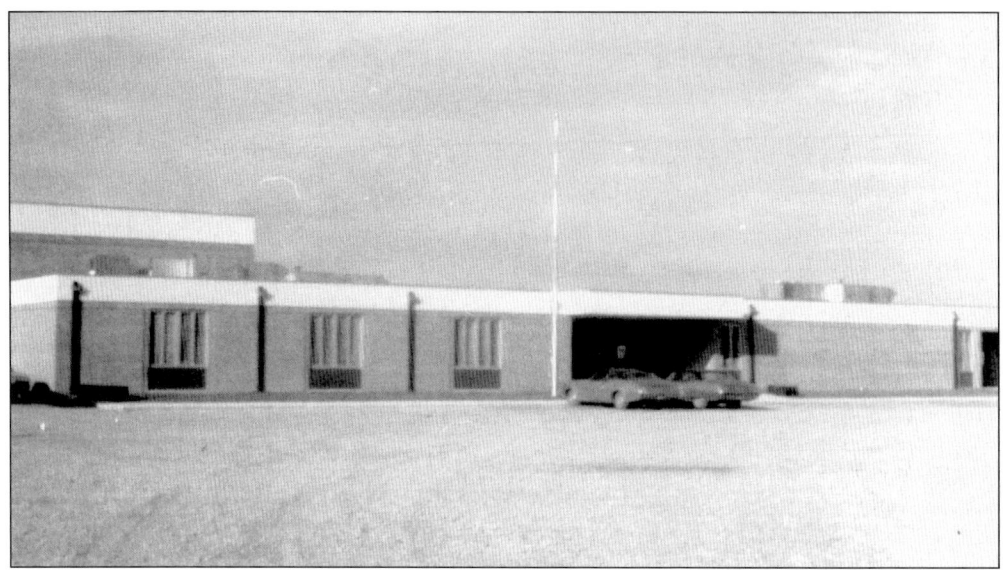

The Grayslake Junior High School was completed in 1969 on the former Kuebker farm. The school has a Barron Boulevard address and is now known as the Grayslake Middle School. This view shows the school when it opened.

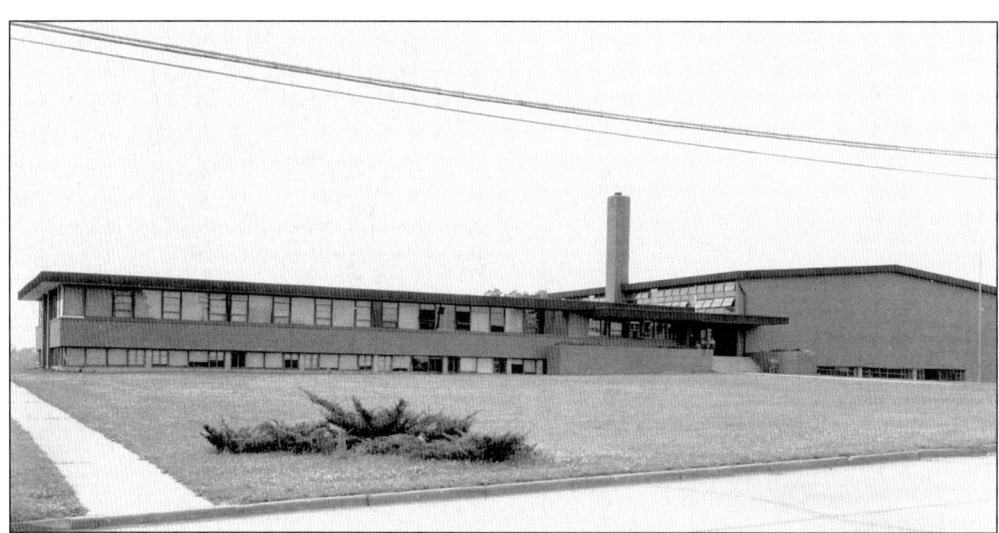

In 1946, Grayslake Community High School opened at 400 North Lake Street, on the former Harvey farm. Previously students attended area high schools, such as Warren Township in Gurnee, Grant Township in Fox Lake, Libertyville High School, or Antioch High School. With the recent opening of a second high school, the Lake Street campus became Grayslake Central High School. This 1948 view shows the school with a large front lawn.

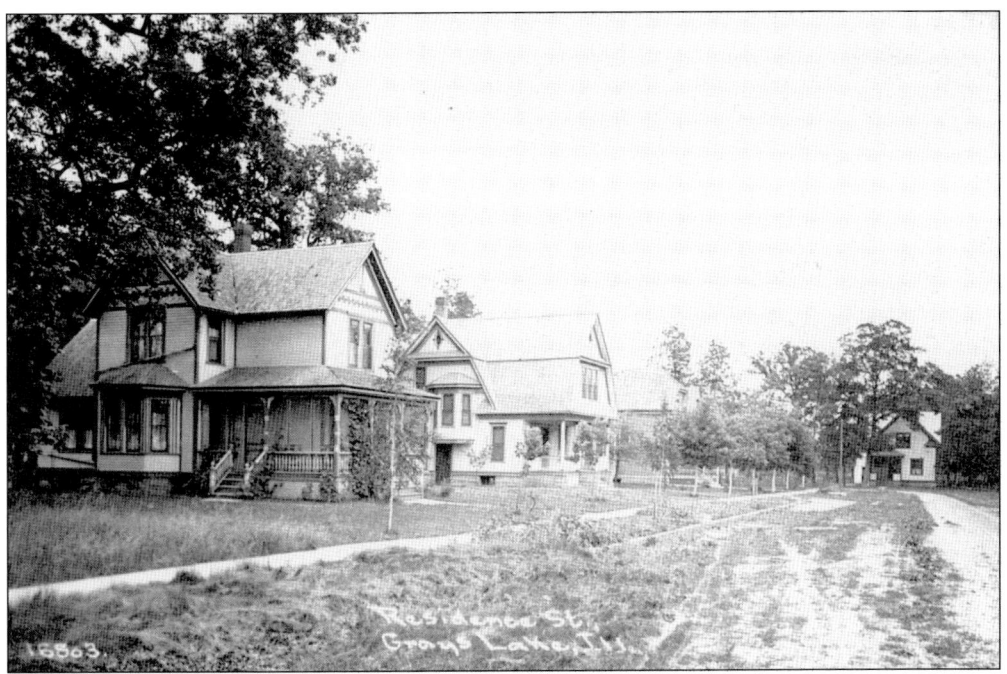

Oak Street is a one-block long street, between Slusser Street and present-day Lake Street. The photograph above shows the north side of the street. The house on the left was known as the Harvey house for many years. Also visible is the former Brandstetter house, while the Barron residence is hidden by trees. At the end of the street is the former Murrie house. The view below shows, from right to left, the catalog house built for lawyer R. W. Churchill in 1904 and the foursquare house built for banker L. Y. Sikes in 1907. Houses on both sides of street have undergone major renovations. (Below, courtesy of Grayslake Historical Society.)

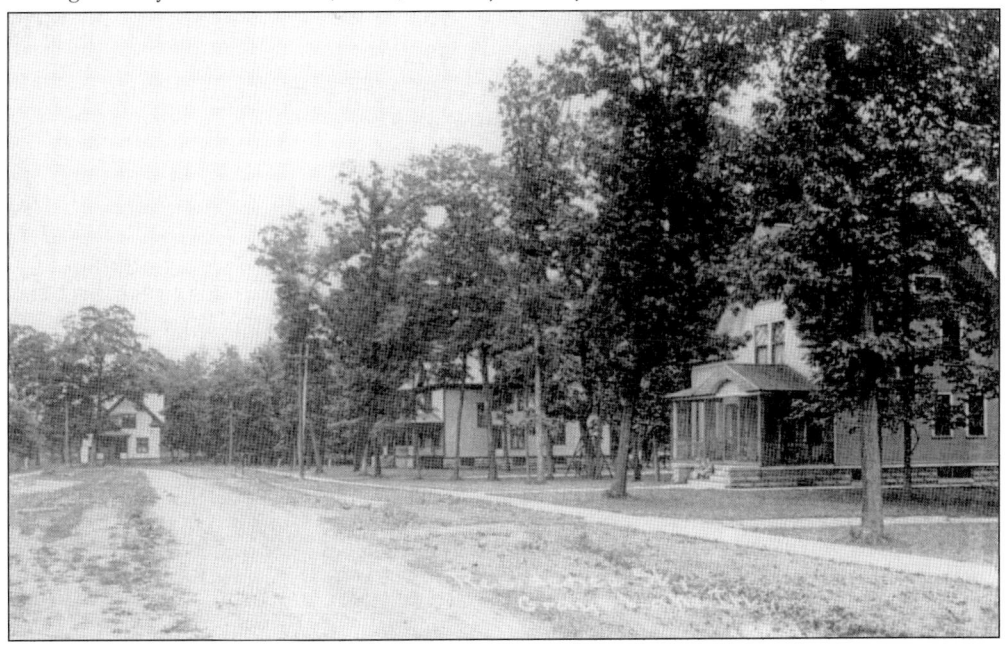

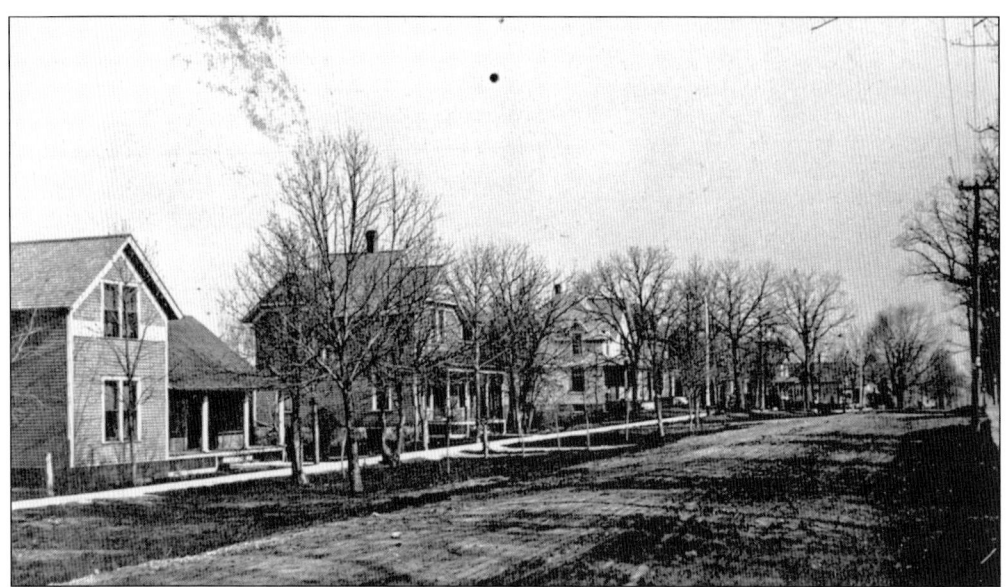

This view from a postcard from around 1926 was titled "Lake Shore Drive." The street was originally named Center Street and today is called Lake Street. The house at the left is at 150 South Lake Street. (Courtesy of Grayslake Historical Society.)

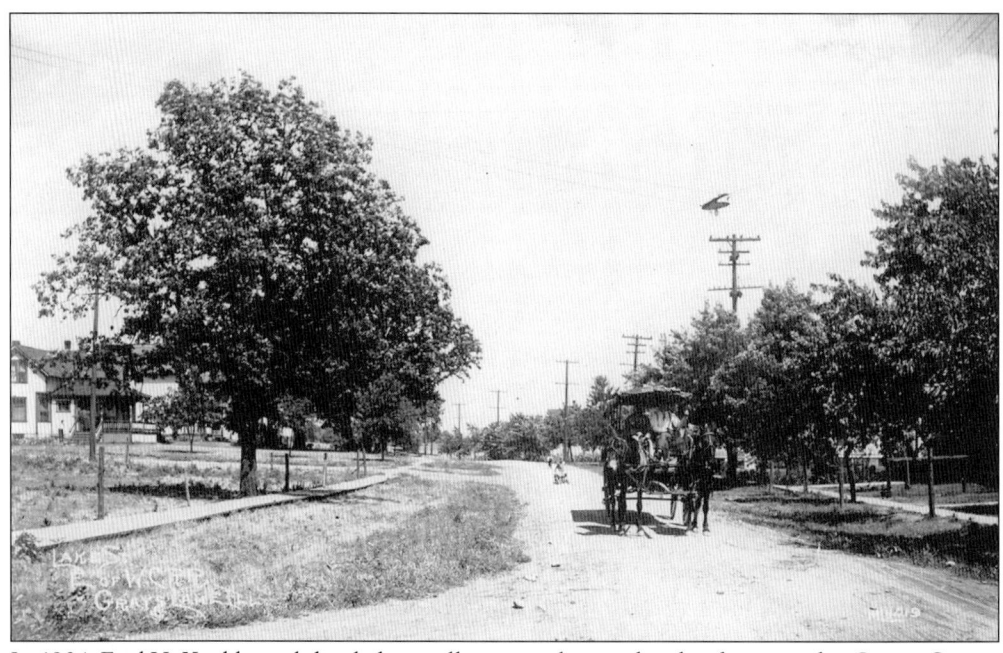

In 1904, Fred H. Kuebker subdivided a small area on the north side of present-day Center Street. The following year, he had the house at the corner of Webb and Center Streets built as an investment. During 1988 and 1989, the one-and-a-half-story house was remodeled to become a two-story house. A music school currently occupies the structure. This image is from around 1915. (Courtesy of Lake County Discovery Museum.)

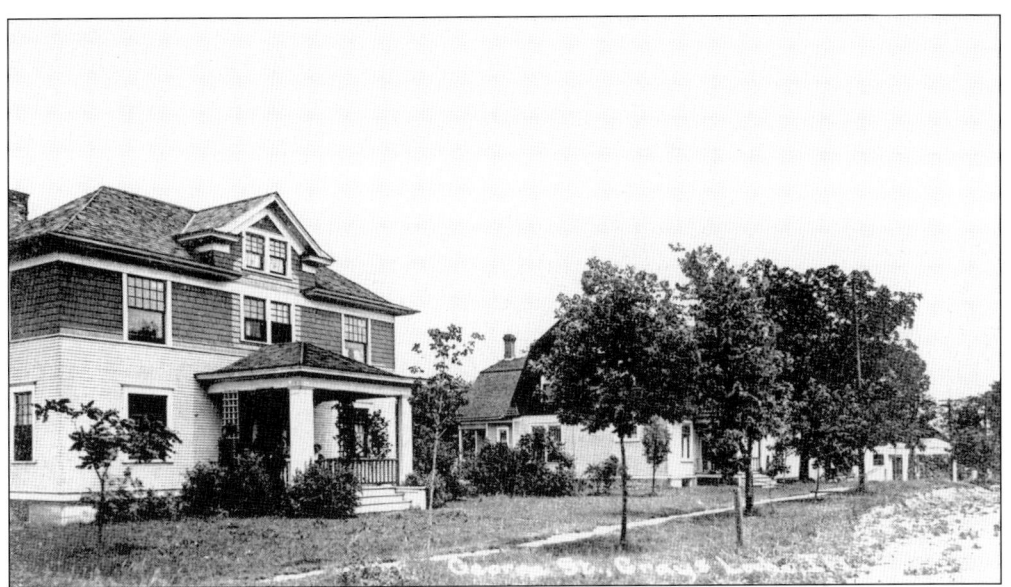

John Washburn built the house in the foreground on George Street in Palmer subdivision. It was probably built about 1908. Washburn and his brothers were well-known carpenters and built many fine houses in the Grayslake area.

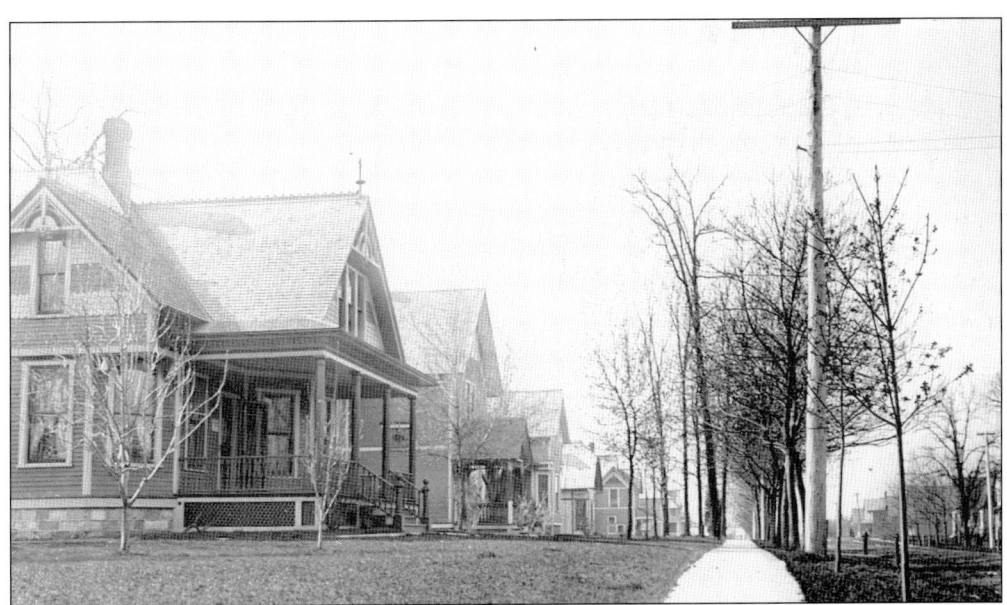

Albert W. Thomson lived on Westerfield Place. He, with his brother George, owned the Thomson Brothers Hardware Store and other businesses in early Grayslake. Westerfield Place is named for a railroad surveyor. This section of Westerfield Place was subdivided in 1891.

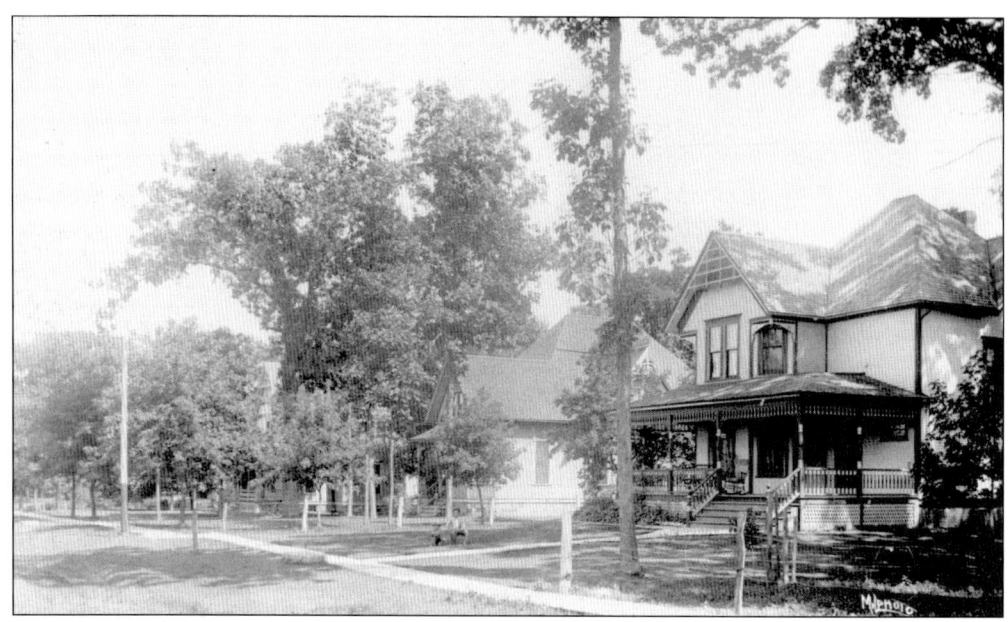

Dr. Robert Rickey, a Civil War veteran who came to Grayslake in the 1890s, paid for construction of the two houses on Park Avenue shown in the photograph. Rickey left the area around 1905. Mayor Ed Schroeder lived in the house to the right in the 1990s. In the 1940s, Mayor Ed Hook lived in the second house from the right. In its earlier years, Park Avenue was nicknamed "Miser Avenue." (Courtesy of Grayslake Historical Society.)

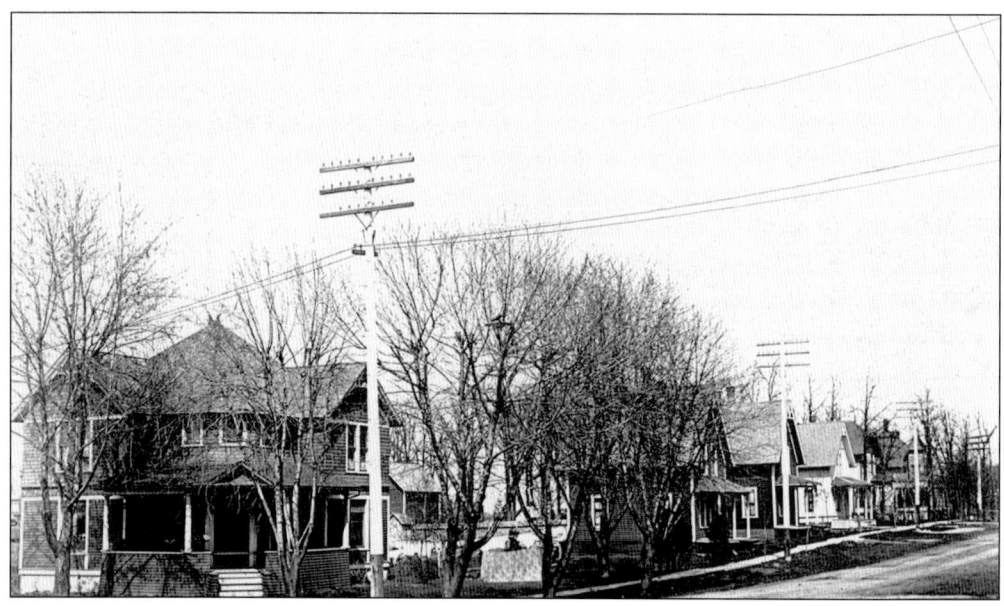

The residence of Buck Shute can be seen at the northeast corner of Seymour and Park Avenues. He was the carriage driver for Dr. Edward F. Shaffer, Grayslake's first doctor. Although enclosed for several years, the house once again has an open porch. The next three houses were identical houses built by Leonard Burge. (Courtesy of Grayslake Historical Society.)

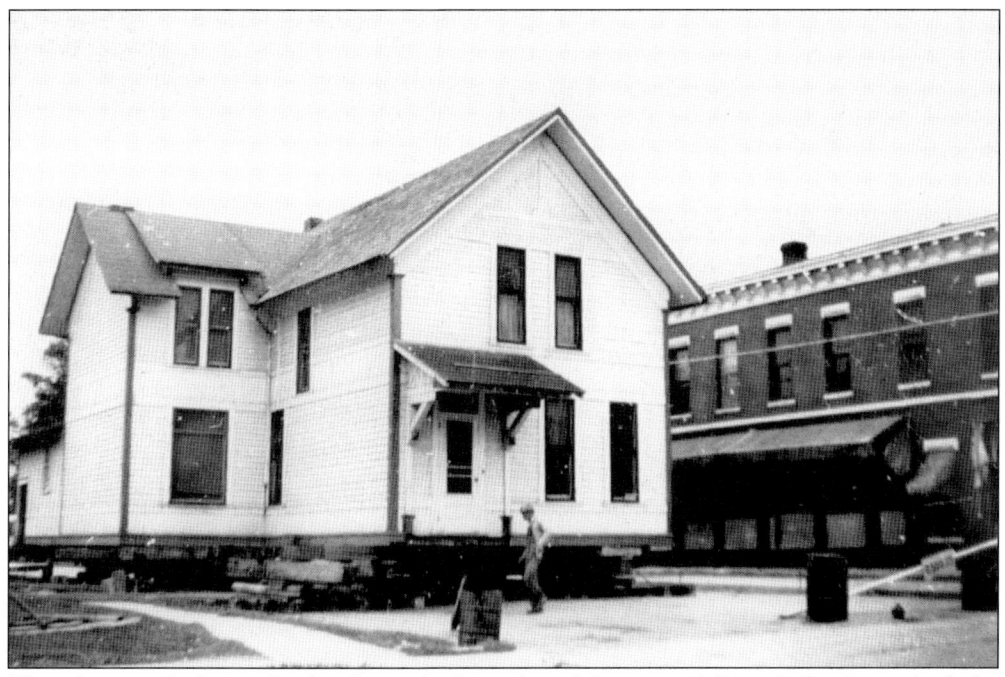

This photograph shows the first house built in the subdivision of Grays Lake. It was built for postmaster Rhoderick Parker in 1886 and stood at the southwest corner of Whitney Street and present-day Center Street. In 1941, it was moved to 49 South Whitney Street. From 1960 to 1969, it housed the Grayslake Public Library. (Courtesy of Grayslake Historical Society.)

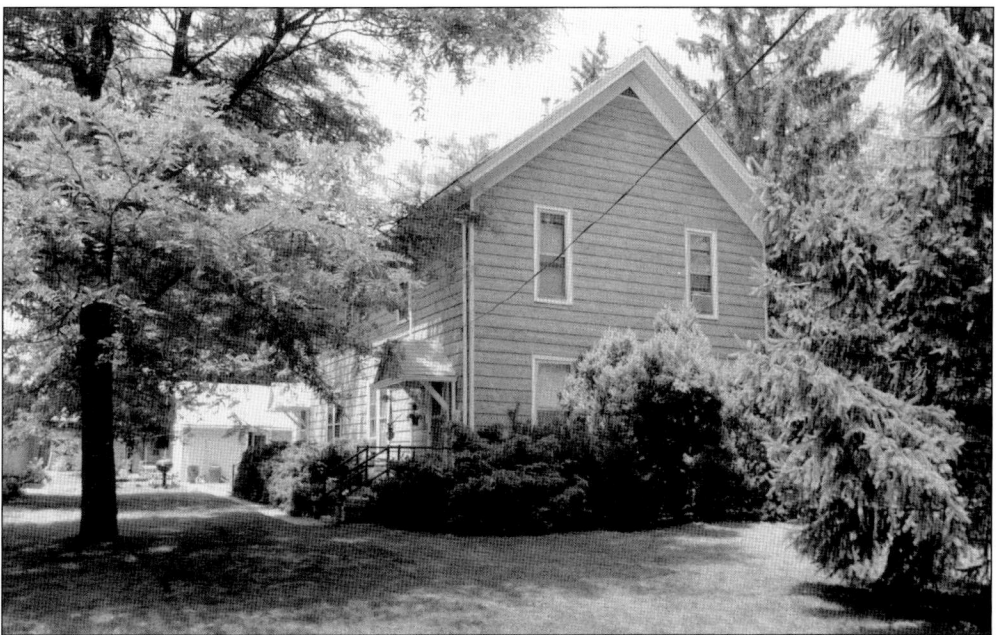

The residence at the corner of Harvey Avenue and Lake Street played an important part in Grayslake's history. It is the former Carmi Read building, which stood on the former Lake Street in downtown Grayslake before being moved. It was in the Read building that the first village election was held in 1895.

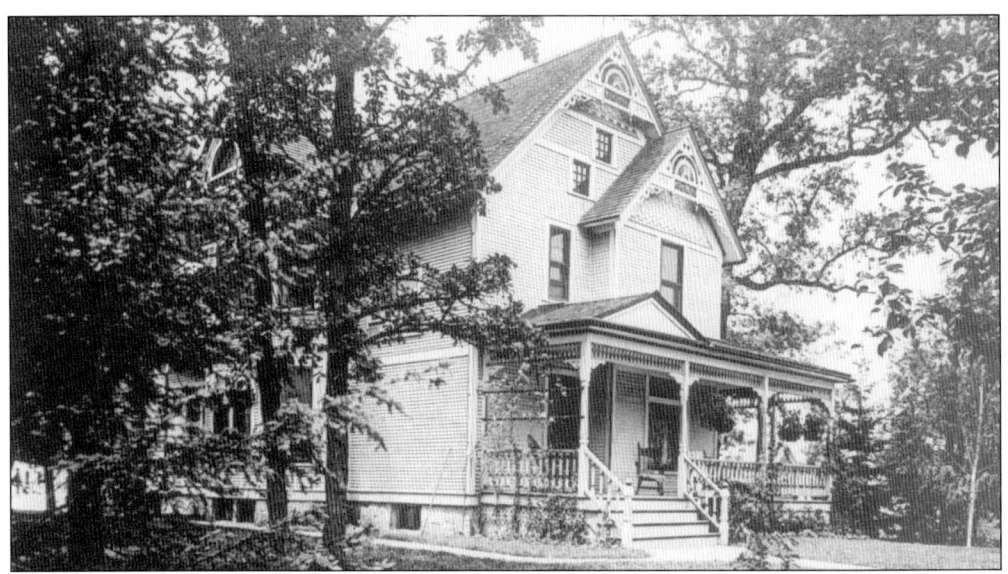

Lumberman F. C. Wilbur is responsible for this large frame house at 146 Westerfield Place. For a period of time it contained an apartment, and the front porch has been modified. A large carriage barn stands at the rear of the lot. (Courtesy of Grayslake Historical Society.)

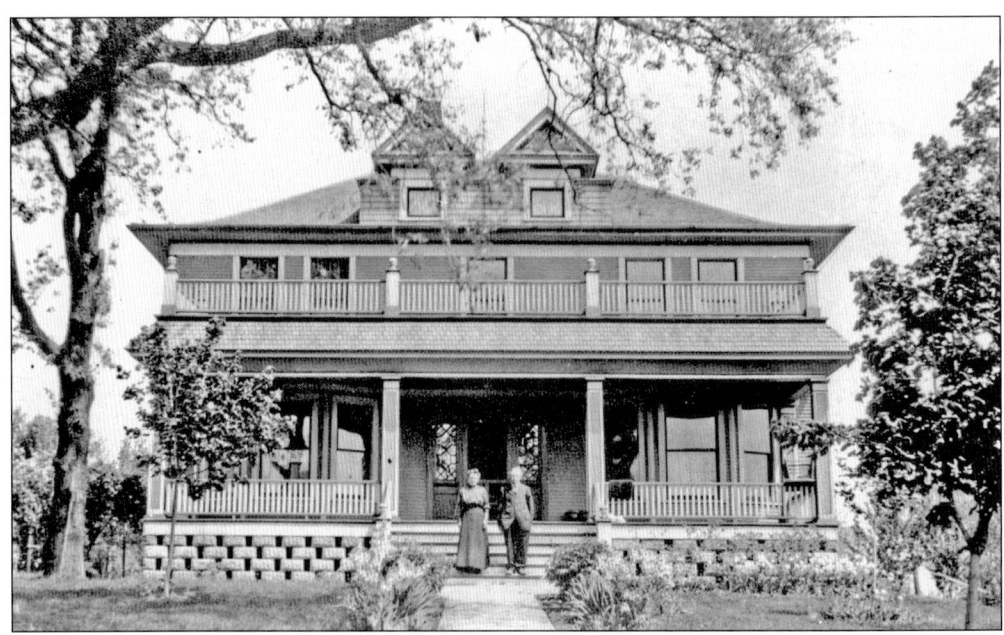

Charles F. and Mary Kuebker moved from their farm to their newly completed house on present-day Center Street in 1910. Mary took in roomers while Charles tended a cow, a horse, and chickens.

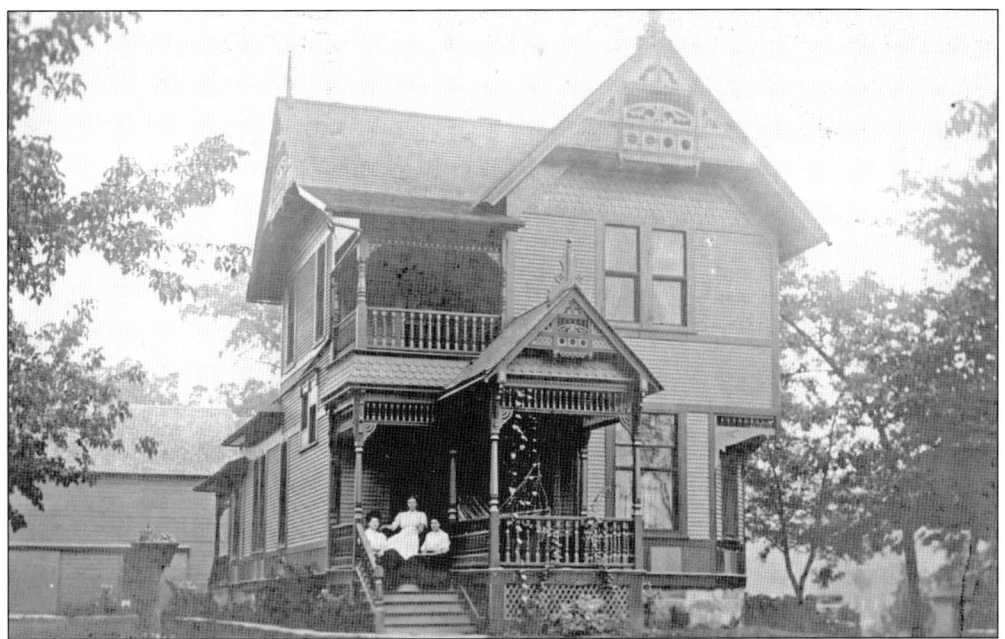

Dates in Grayslake's history were also eventful in the life of George Thomson. In 1886, the year the subdivision of Grays Lake was documented, he married C. Louisa Frazier. In 1895, the year of Grays Lake's incorporation, he became the first mayor and had this house built at 151 Park Avenue. (Courtesy of Grayslake Historical Society.)

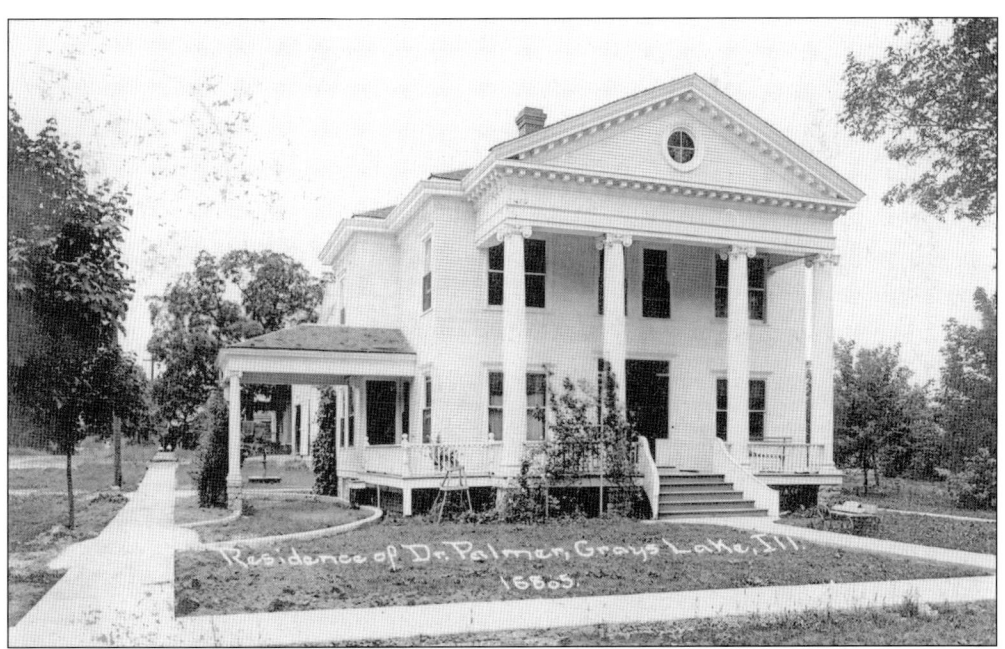

Dr. John M. Palmer had his home and office built in 1904 at the corner of George and then Center Streets. Grayslake druggist Phil Hildebrandt later lived here and bottled Coca-Cola in the carriage house in 1923.

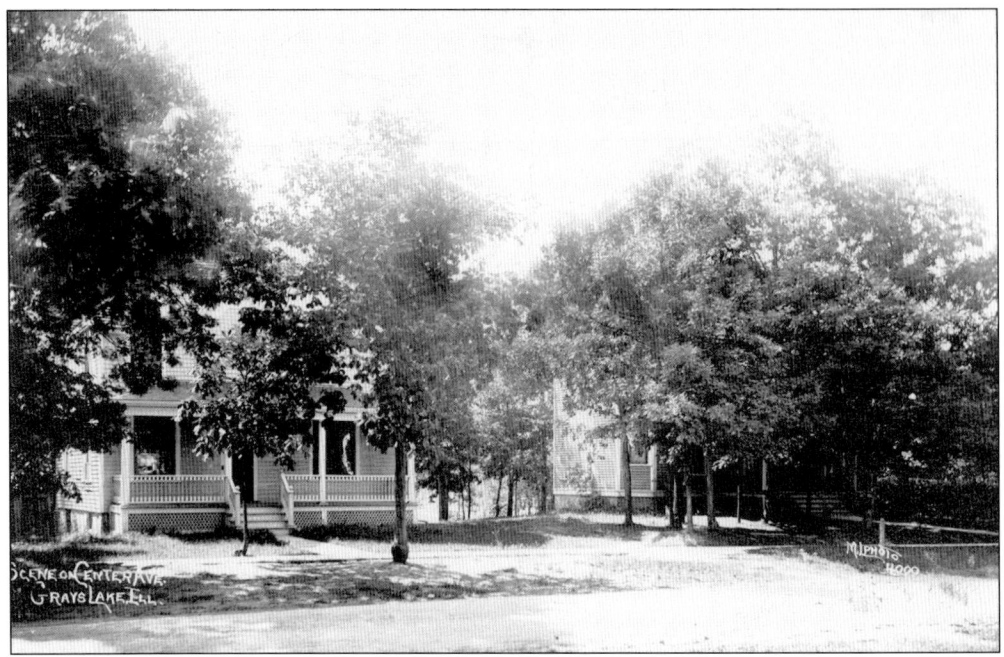

The Rich brothers, descendants of the pioneer David Rich family, built many fine houses and great barns in the Grayslake area. Charles Rich lived in this house at 126 South Lake Street for many years. There is no longer a front porch on this house.

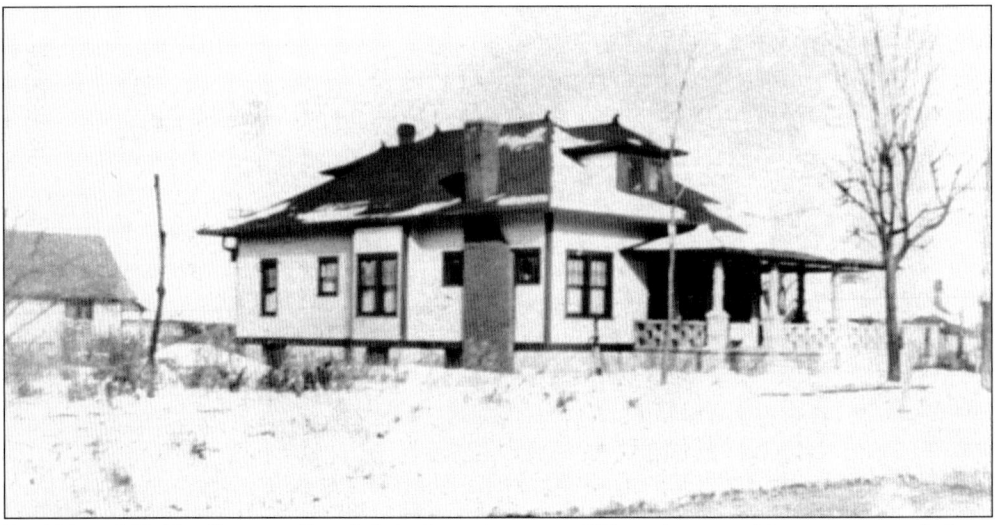

Dr. Edward F. Shaffer was Grayslake's first physician. When his son Marquis married Aura Battershall, he had this house at the northwest corner of Seymour and Park Avenues built for them. It is believed to be a catalog house. Druggist Cecil Hook lived here in the 1940s. (Courtesy of Grayslake Historical Society.)

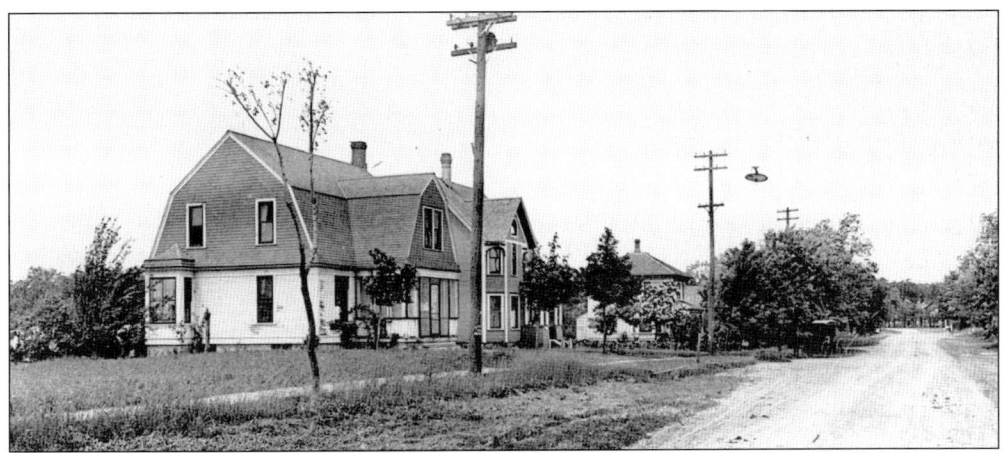

David G. and Amy Morse White lived in this house on Westerfield Place. He was a local barber, and she was postmistress from 1893 to 1898. The third house, a foursquare, was moved by house mover Clarence Ritta. He moved it to a lot to the west and turned it to face Seymour Avenue.

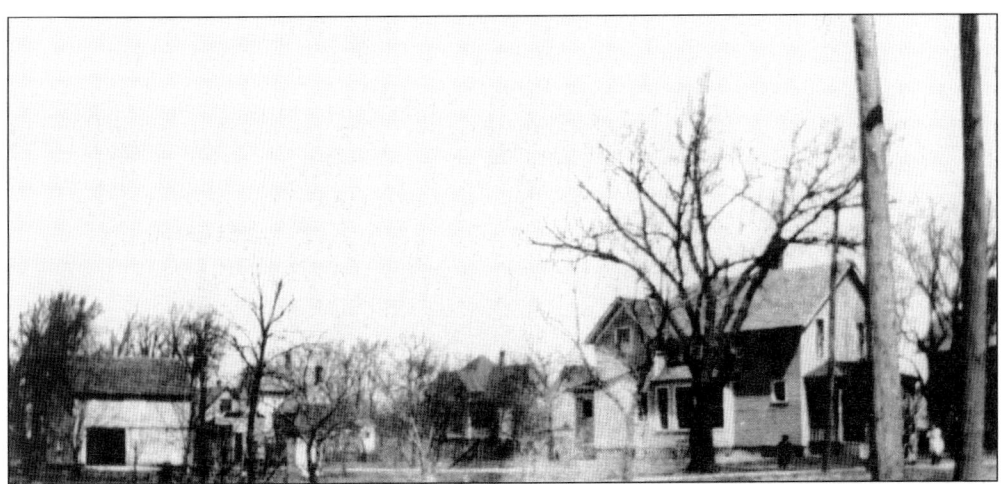

Almost every house in early Grayslake had a barn or carriage house for the family's horse and carriage. The Edwards residence in the 1930s had such a structure. Later the Clemens family lived here. It is now the site of Hawley Manor, a seniors residence at Hawley and Lake Streets. (Courtesy of Grayslake Historical Society.)

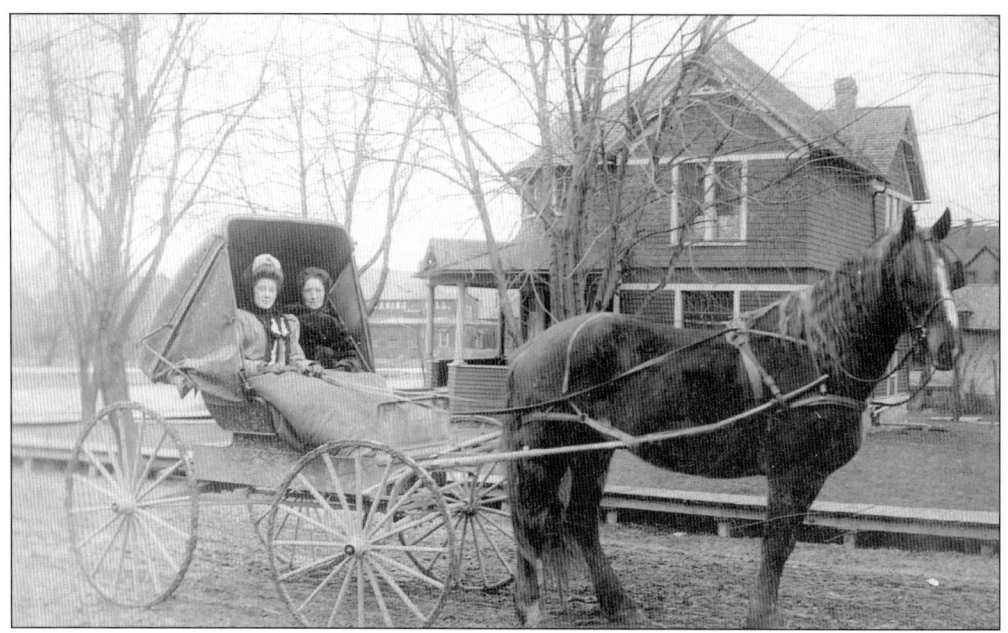

This postcard was addressed to Roberta Harvey and signed Lee. Lee Williams was a photographer who married Roberta in 1910. The buggy is stopped in front of Buck Shute's house at the corner of Seymour and Park Avenues. (Courtesy of Grayslake Historical Society.)

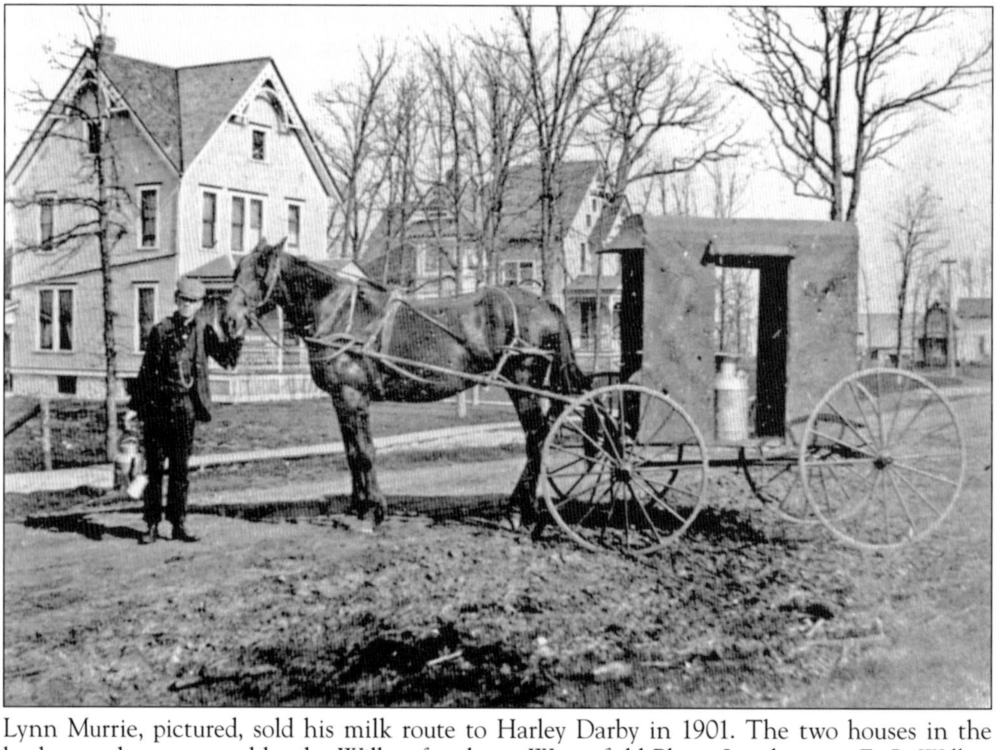

Lynn Murrie, pictured, sold his milk route to Harley Darby in 1901. The two houses in the background were owned by the Wilbur family on Westerfield Place. Lumberman F. C. Wilbur lived in the house on the right. His sister Delia Wilbur lived in the house on the left. (Courtesy of Grayslake Historical Society.)

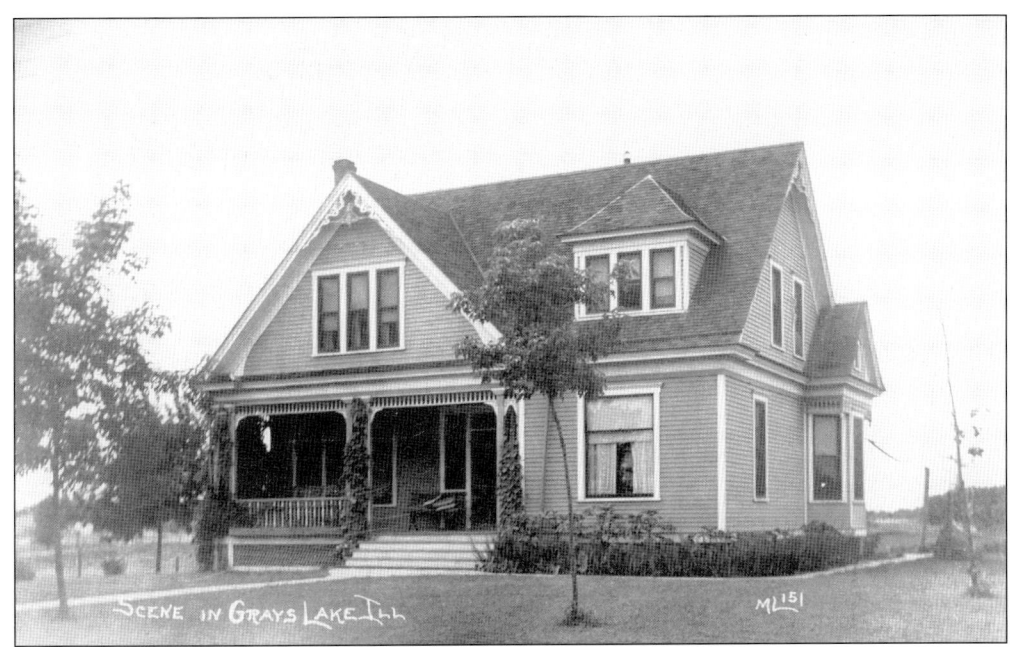

The picture above shows the Benjamin J. Loftus house. The same building is seen below. In 1937, Alvin J. "Peg" Behning opened Peg's Arena, a tavern near the northeast corner of Routes 120 and 83. He promoted boxing matches at this location. Peg left the business in 1945. Later Chet Cozy had a Key Club at this location. At the present time, no building stands on the former Loftus property. (Below, courtesy of Grayslake Historical Society.)

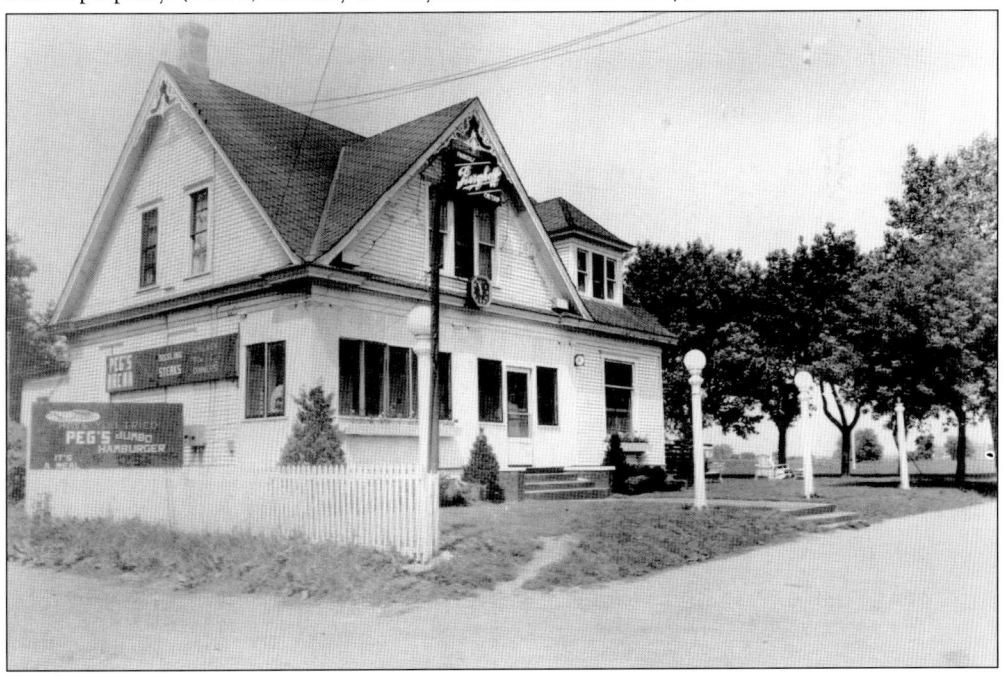

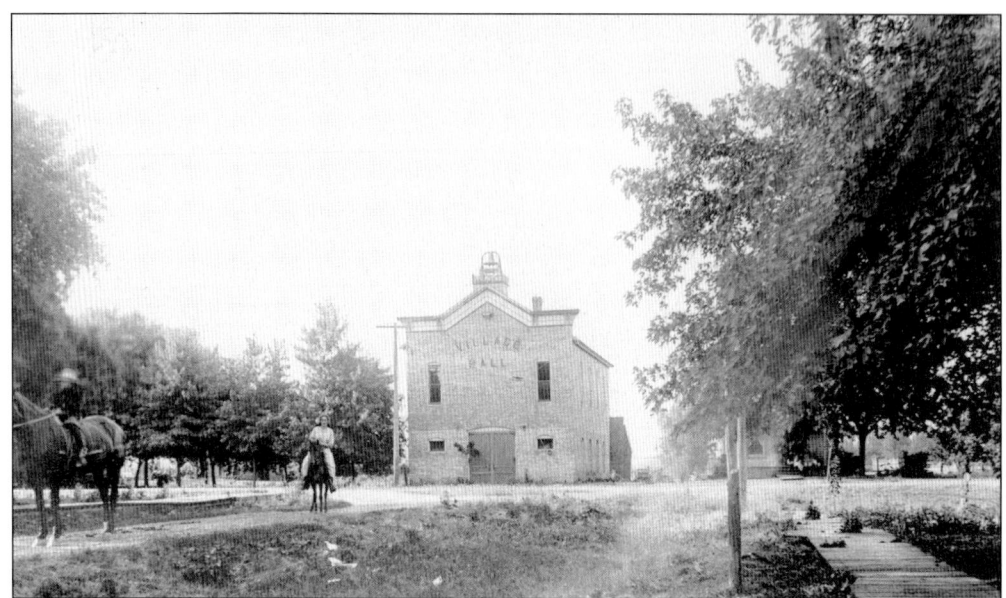

In 1895, a one-room frame schoolhouse was moved to Hawley Street, raised 10 feet, and bricked in order to become Grayslake's village hall. The structure has housed wrestling meets, high school classes, a jail, the local library, church services, the volunteer fire department, and the Grayslake Chamber of Commerce. The structure has continued to serve the community as the home of the Grayslake Municipal Historical Museum since 1993. (Courtesy of Grayslake Historical Society.)

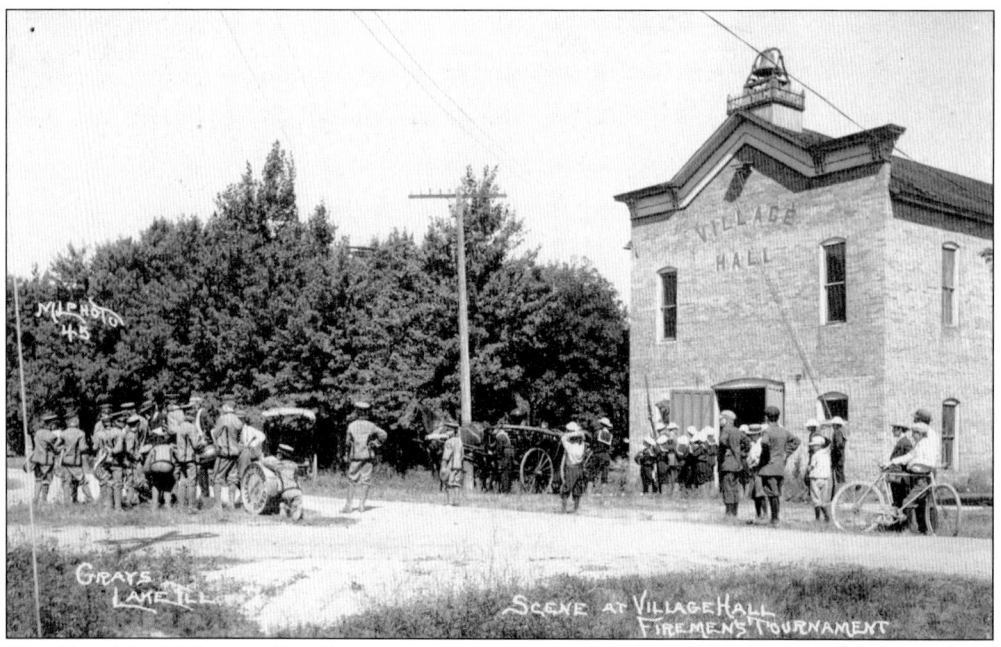

The Grayslake Volunteer Fire Department was organized in late 1899. In its early years, it held tournaments, which often included a parade. In this scene, the Allendale Farm Band of Lake Villa is taking part in such a parade. (Courtesy of Grayslake Historical Society.)

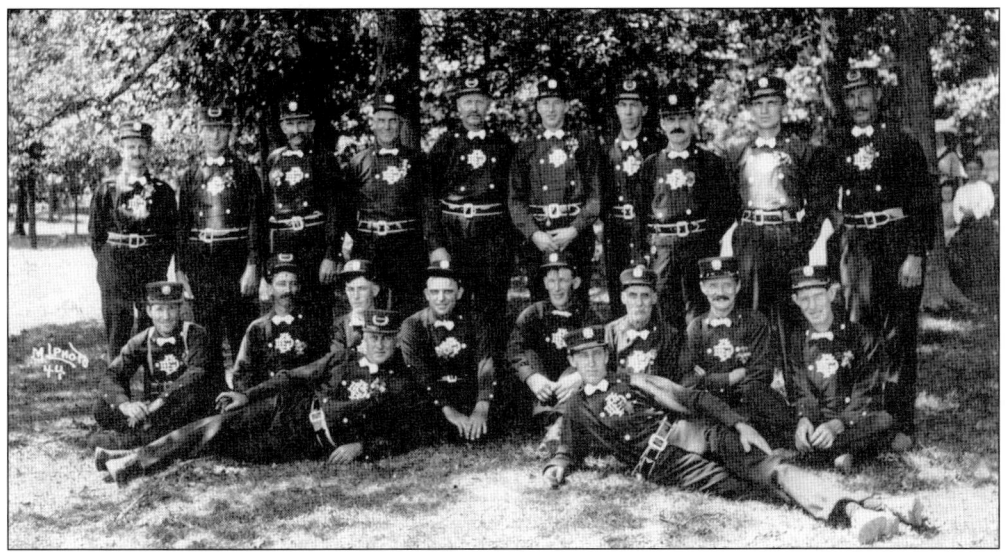

The members of the Grayslake Volunteer Fire Department around 1910 included these men. They are (first row) Arthur Rich, O. F. Washburn, Harold Cleveland, William Springer, James Hershberger, Justin Baldwin, William Jahns, Harry Rich, John Washburn, and Louis Grosvenor; (second row) William E. Moore, Paul Tobey, Louis Lobdell, William Kapple, Allen McMillen, George Brandstetter, John Mason, Earl Harvey, Ole Holmes, and Jacob Pech Sr. (Courtesy of Grayslake Historical Society.)

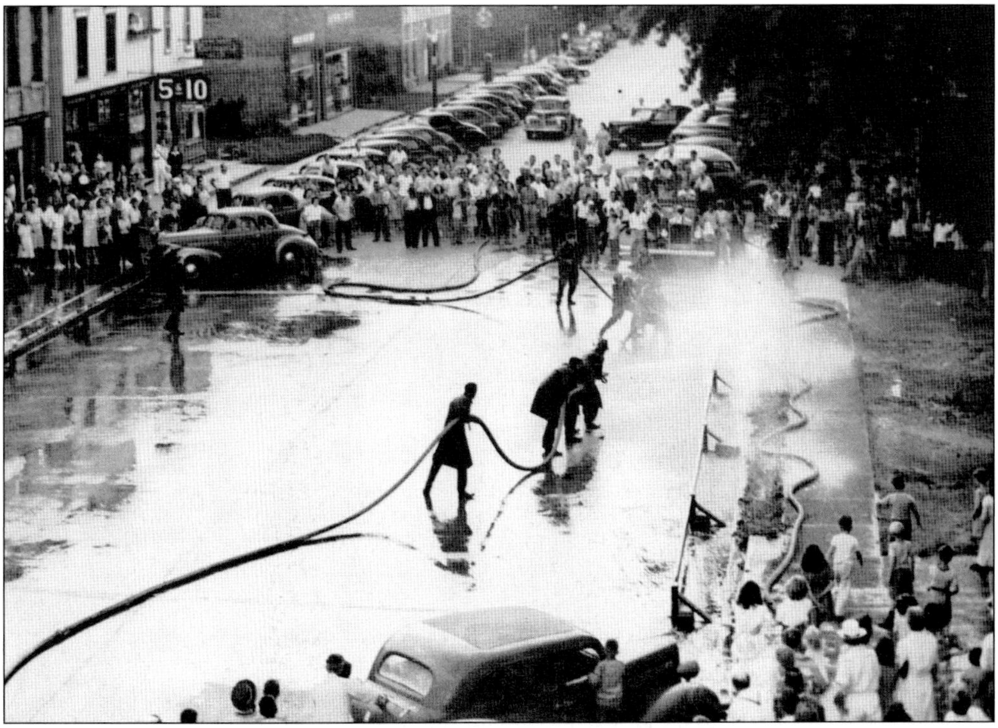

The Grayslake Volunteer Fire Department raised funds by hosting dances, sponsoring picnics, and having carnivals. This 1940s water fight was probably held during a carnival. The Grayslake Fire Protection District was formed in 1976. (Courtesy of Grayslake Historical Society.)

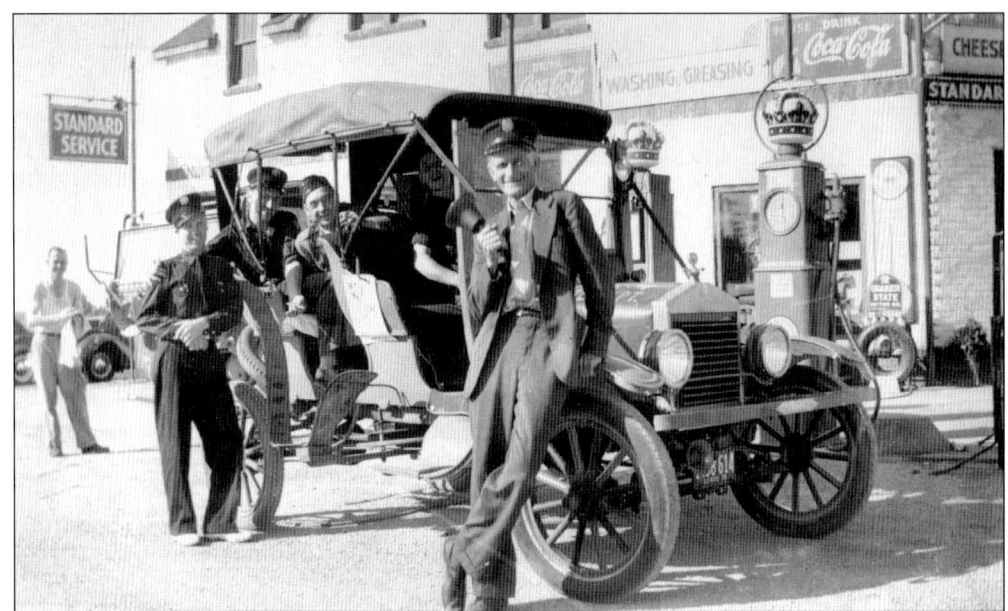

These Grayslake firemen are posing with a Ford Model T at the Cheeseman and Behning service station at Routes 83 and 120 around 1940. Identified are Fred Wendelkin in the foreground, Mike Reimers leaning against the car, and owner Harold Cheeseman standing with a towel. Reimers later became a mayor of Grayslake. The corner of Routes 83 and 120 was locally called High's Corner. (Courtesy of Grayslake Historical Society.)

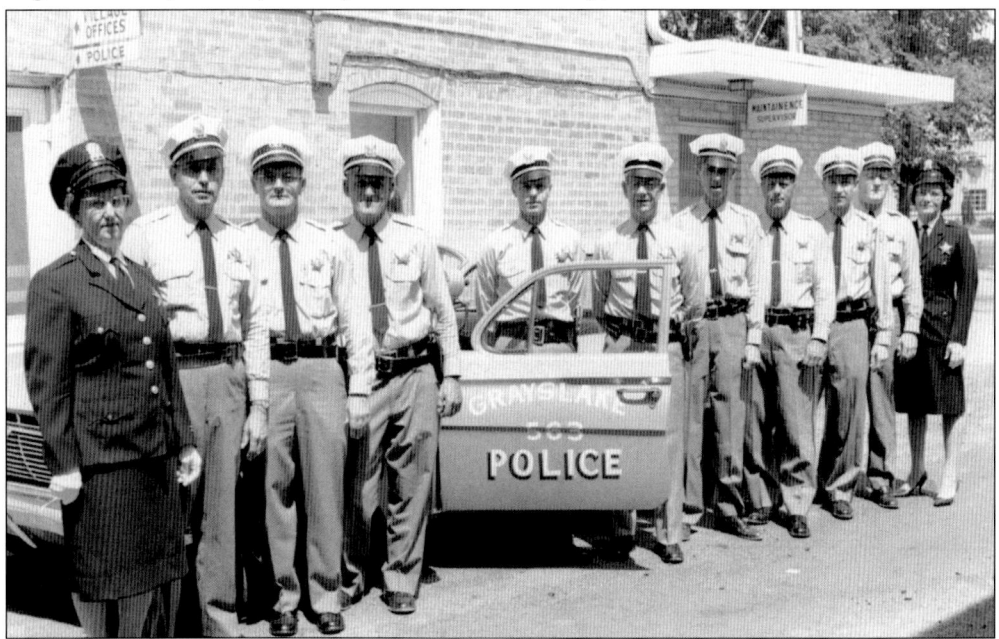

In the early 1960s, police matrons were added to the police department. Included in the picture are Chris Gohr, Richard Whittington, Chester Levandowski, Ralph Fenzel, Jack Callanan, Joe Sonn, Chief David Lees, Dick Stang, Gordon Shattuck, Willard Richards, and Elsie Phillips. At that time, the police station was in the village hall, now the Grayslake Municipal Historical Museum. (Courtesy of Grayslake Historical Society.)

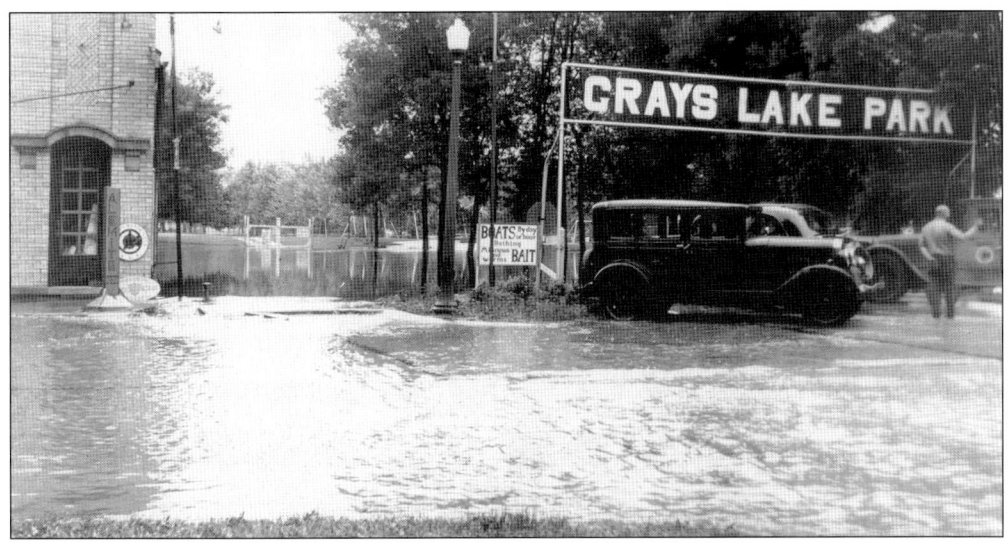
Grayslake and much of the surrounding area experienced a major flood in 1938 as Grays Lake overflowed its banks. This scene is on Lake Street, with Brandstetter's Garage on the left and the Grays Lake Park on the right. (Courtesy of Grayslake Historical Society.)

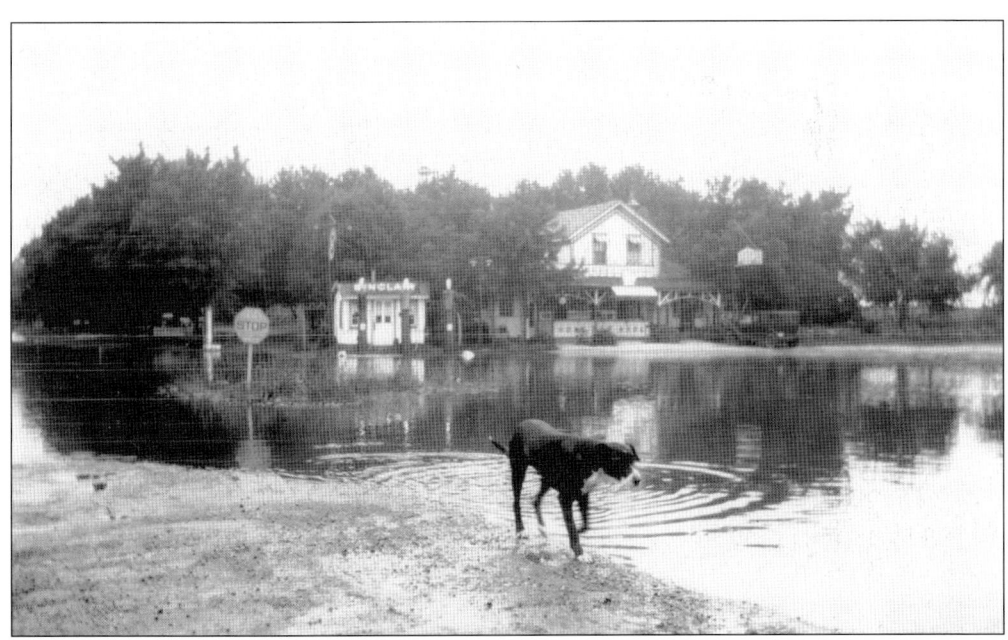
During the 1938 flood, the Avon-Fremont drainage ditch also overflowed. The stop sign is at Barron Boulevard and Center Street. A bank presently occupies the site of the former filling station and restaurant. (Courtesy of Grayslake Historical Society.)

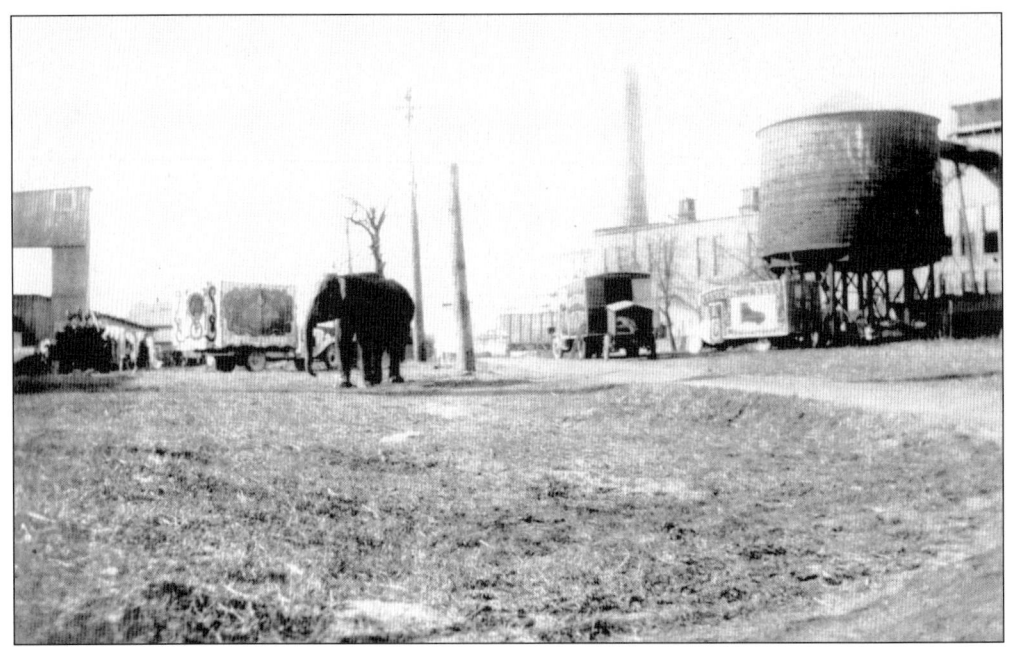
In the fall of 1932, the Seils Sterling Circus came to Grayslake to spend the winter. It was housed in the former canning factory buildings located at the end of Railroad Avenue and stayed only one winter.

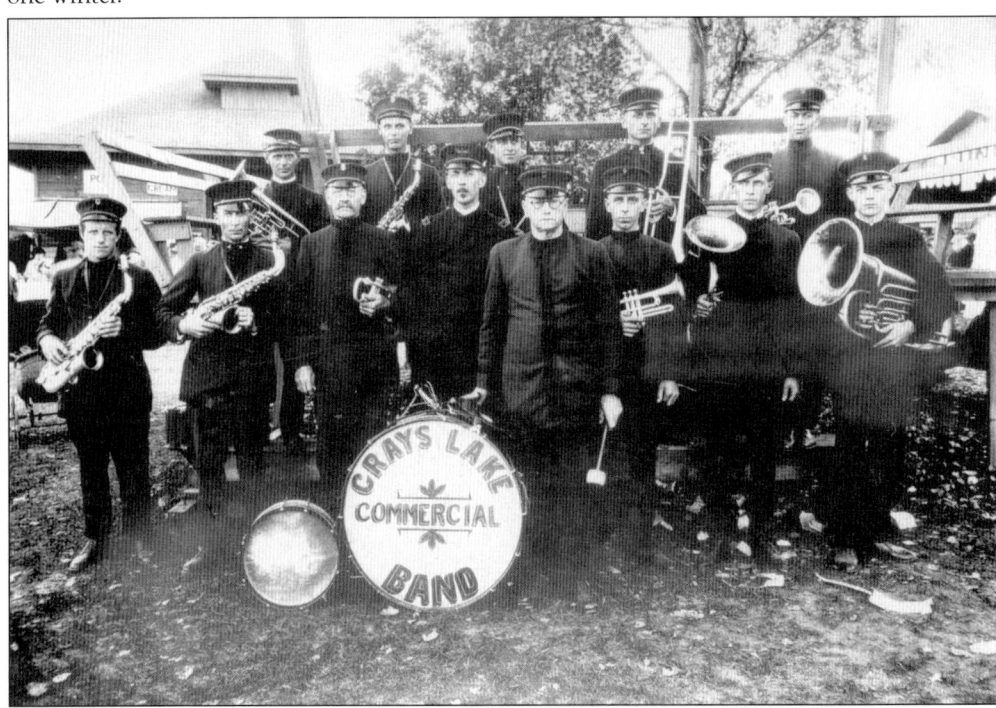
Little is known about the Grays Lake Commercial Band. Included in this undated photograph are William DeHaan, Albert Horton, John Mogg, Herman Meyers, Almond Lowell, Allen McMillan, Professor Nichols, Lou Frank, Roy McBride, and Pete DeHaan. (Courtesy of Grayslake Historical Society.)

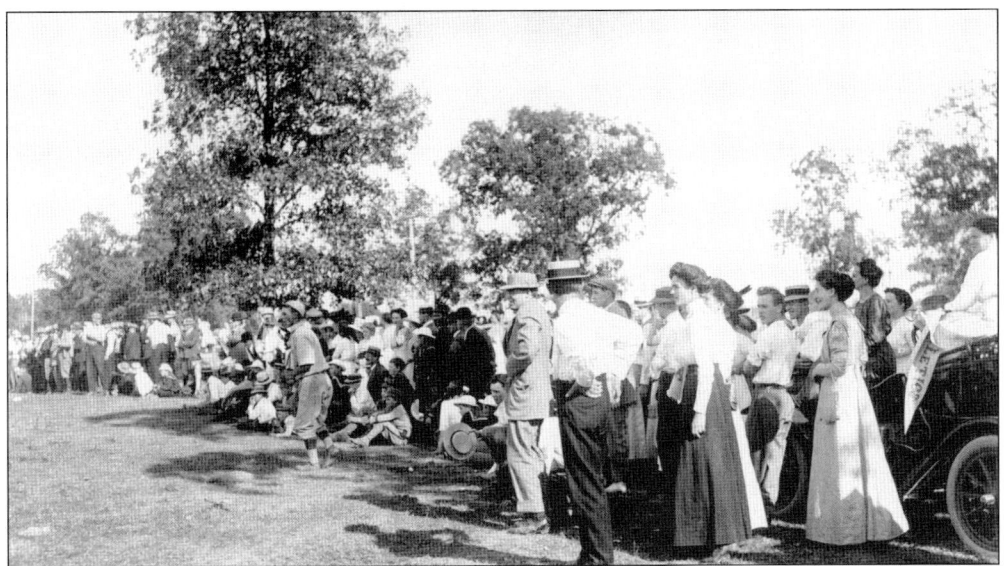

The Firemen's Tournament held in the early 1900s provided entertainment. In this photograph, the crowd is enjoying a baseball game. Other tournament activities included a parade, a trap shoot, and a band concert. (Courtesy of Grayslake Historical Society.)

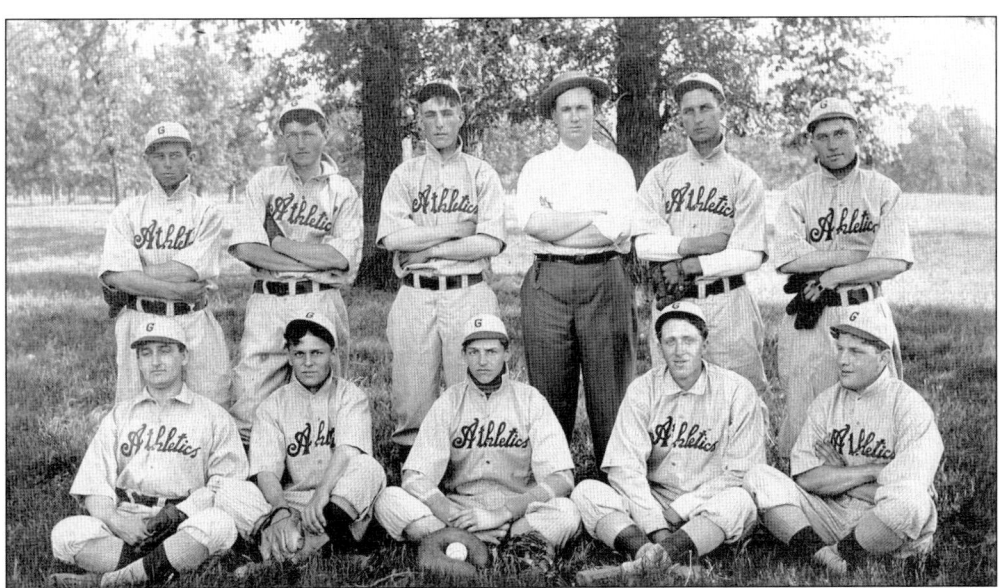

Grayslake had a baseball team as early as the 1890s. Around 1907, the local team, known as the Grays Lake Athletics, played in farmers' fields or on vacant village property. Pictured here from left to right are (first row) Jesse Longabaugh, Frank Winkel, Leonard Hook, Frank Cremin, and unidentified; (second row) Howard Murrie, Horace Kapple, Harold Cleveland, Marquis Shaffer, Gus Krumery, and Maurice Murrie. (Courtesy of Grayslake Historical Society.)

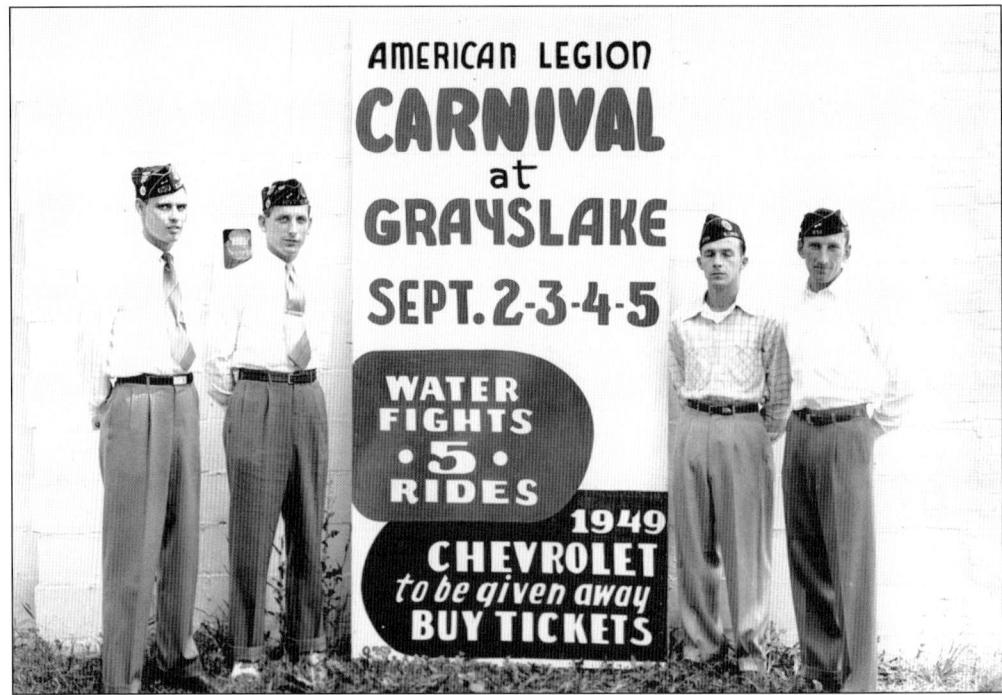

The American Legion was organized in Grayslake in 1920. To raise funds, it sponsored a carnival each year, held in the vacant lot at the northeast corner of Whitney and Center Streets. Suspense would be created as raffle ticket holders waited to learn who won the new car each year. In 1949, from left to right, legionnaires Doug Rockenbach, Jack Richardson, Wes Druce, and Clarence Collins are volunteer workers. (Courtesy of Grayslake Historical Society.)

Grayslake's World War II honor roll stood proudly in the vacant lot at the southwest corner of Whitney and Center Streets. Men from other Avon Township areas were included. War fatalities were noted with a star. Grayslake's downtown drugstore now occupies the site. (Courtesy of Grayslake Historical Society.)

Three

THE ROUND LAKE AREA

The Round Lake area is composed of four villages, with the Village of Round Lake being the first to be incorporated. Like Grayslake, the village of Round Lake can trace its early history to the railroad, but in this instance a branch of the Chicago, Milwaukee and St. Paul Railroad.

In 1899, the railroad's construction was nearing Hainesville. George Battershall, a merchant and landowner at Hainesville, set a high price on his land and would not negotiate with the railroad. Amarias White offered the railroad a free site for a station farther west. The offer was accepted on the condition that streets would be built leading to the new station. The railroad station was built, and in 1901, White filed a plat for the subdivision of Round Lake at the Lake County Court House. A post office opened that same year, and soon there were a lumberyard, hardware store, general store, and other businesses. When the railroad came, so did Armour and Company, which built a large icehouse, with a railroad spur, on the south shore of the lake. The Village of Round Lake was officially incorporated in 1908 with White being elected its first mayor in 1909.

Subdivisions were developed around the lake. Edwards Subdivision on the east shore was platted in 1904 and Porter Duell's Shorewood Subdivision began development in 1910. In 1921, George Renehan started subdividing his ancestral land along the south shore of the lake. L. B. Harris, who developed 1,700 acres of the Round Lake area, bought Oliver Hook's property and started the process in the mid-1920s. Shorewood Estates was platted in 1929. Many of the first homes in these subdivisions were built as summer cottages and later winterized.

In 1936, the Village of Round Lake Beach was incorporated and John J. Lynch elected its first mayor. It took Round Lake Park two referendums before incorporation in 1947, with Stuart McKecknie as its first mayor. After three tries, the area previously known as Indian Hill was incorporated as Round Lake Heights in 1960. William McDonald was the new village's first mayor. Parts of the Round Lake area villages have expanded beyond the borders of Avon Township.

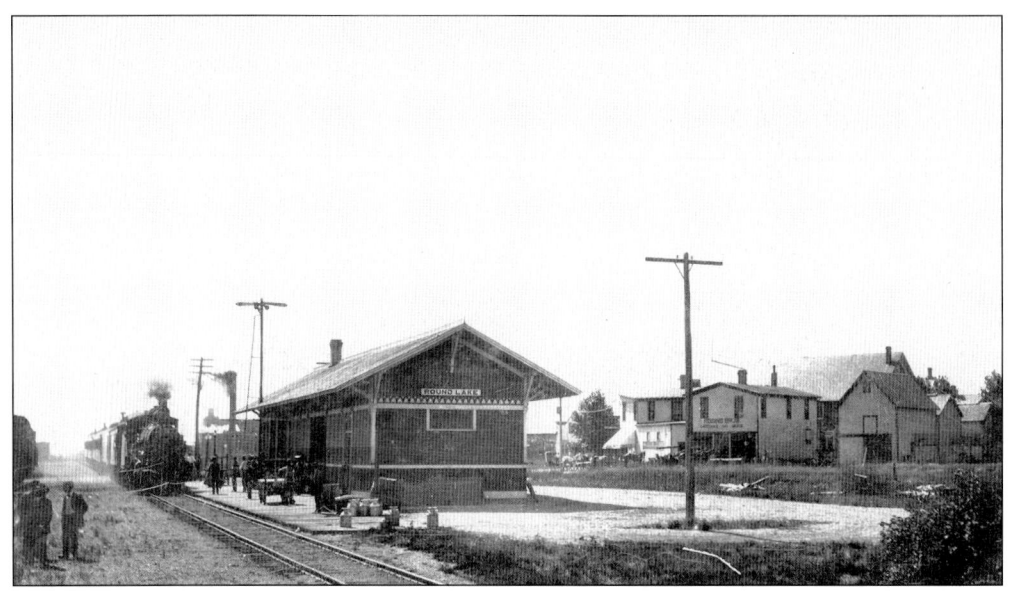

A month after the Chicago, Milwaukee and St. Paul Railroad came to Round Lake in 1901, Amarias White filed the original plat of the village at the Lake County Court House. This postcard is postmarked 1910.

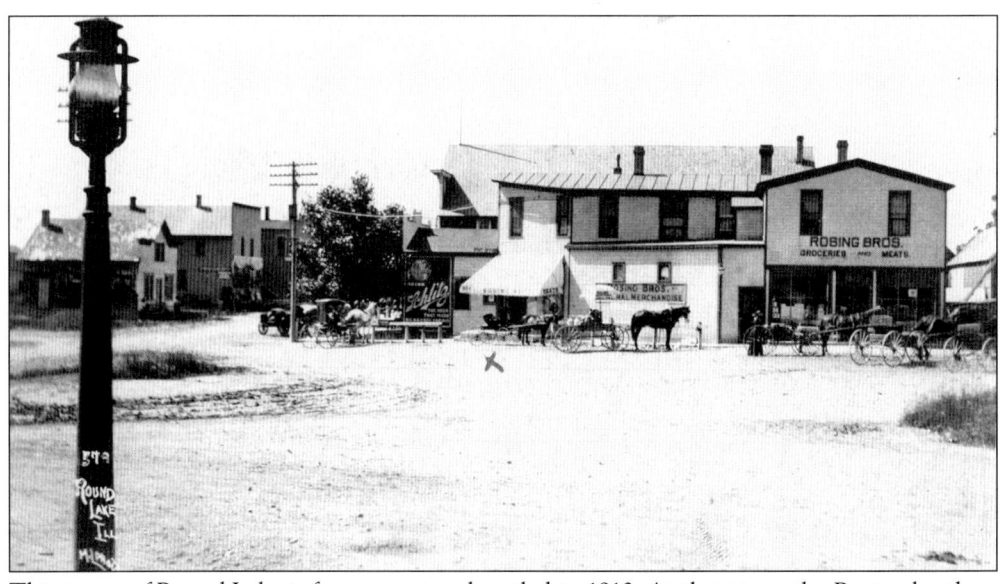

This image of Round Lake is from a postcard mailed in 1910. At that time, the Rosing brothers had a general merchandise store in the building facing the railroad. The building facing Cedar Lake Road was the location of a store run by Henry Gieseke and later E. C. Webber. This group of buildings can still be seen at the corner of Cedar Lake Road and Route 134.

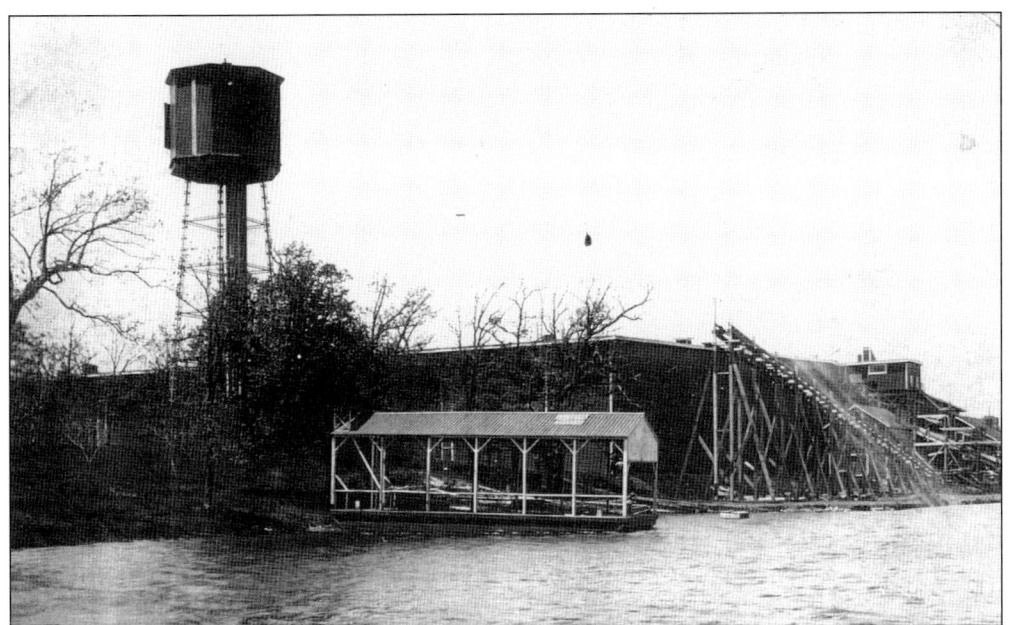

The Armour and Company icehouse was built in 1901 along the south shore of Round Lake. The building covered five acres and was reported to be the largest icehouse in the world. More than 100,000 tons of ice were harvested each winter and sent by train to Armour's Chicago processing plants. The icehouse burned in 1917 and was not rebuilt. (Above, courtesy of Lake County Discovery Museum.)

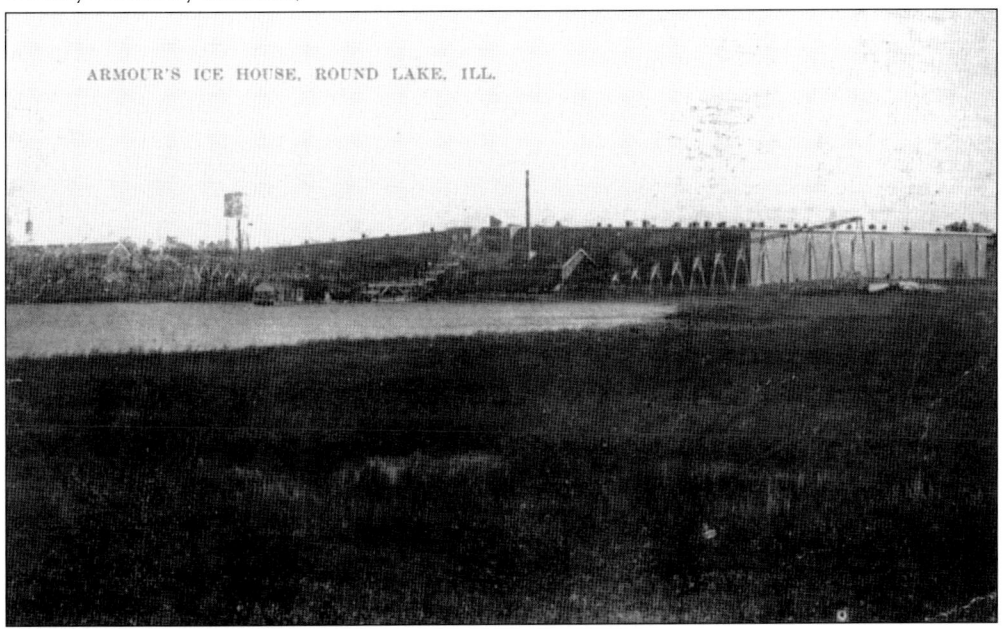

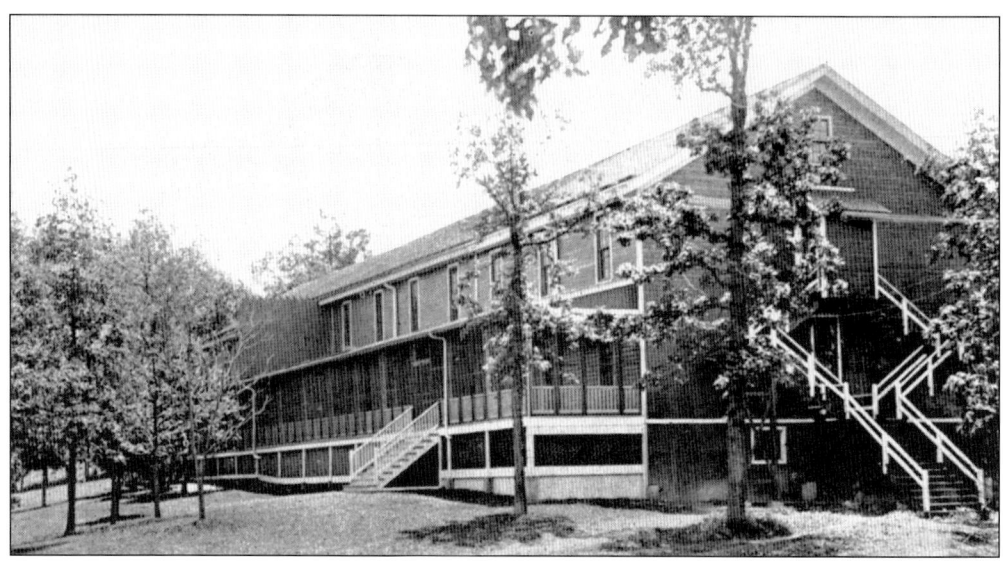

The boardinghouse for Armour employees seen in the photograph above accommodated 300 workers. After the 1917 icehouse fire, it was remodeled by a Mrs. Armour and became a private resort, known as the Oval Lodge, for women employees of Armour's Chicago plant. In 1928, the Alpine Gun Club, seen in the photograph below, purchased the property. Originally trap shooting was allowed over the lake.

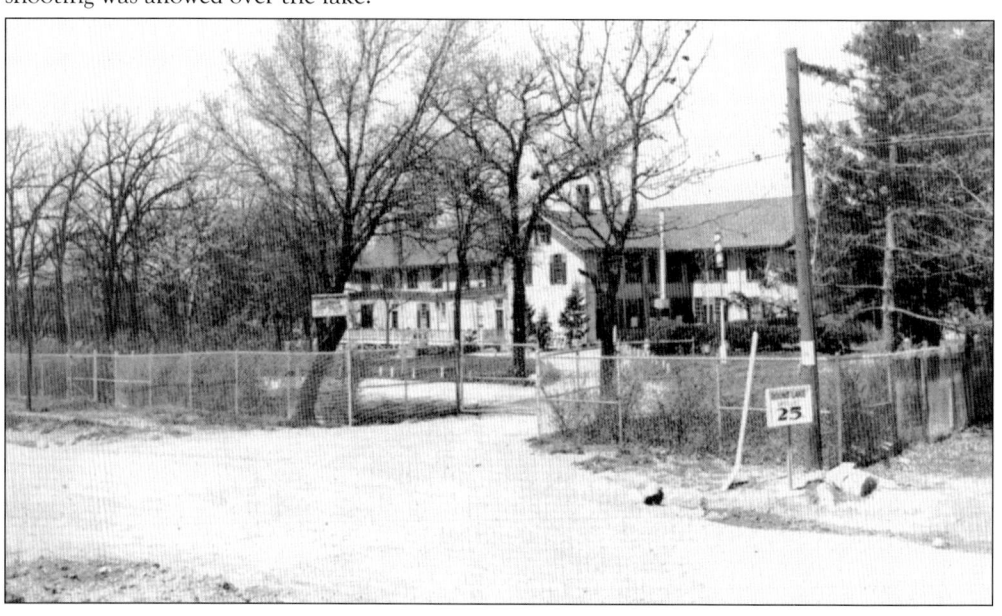

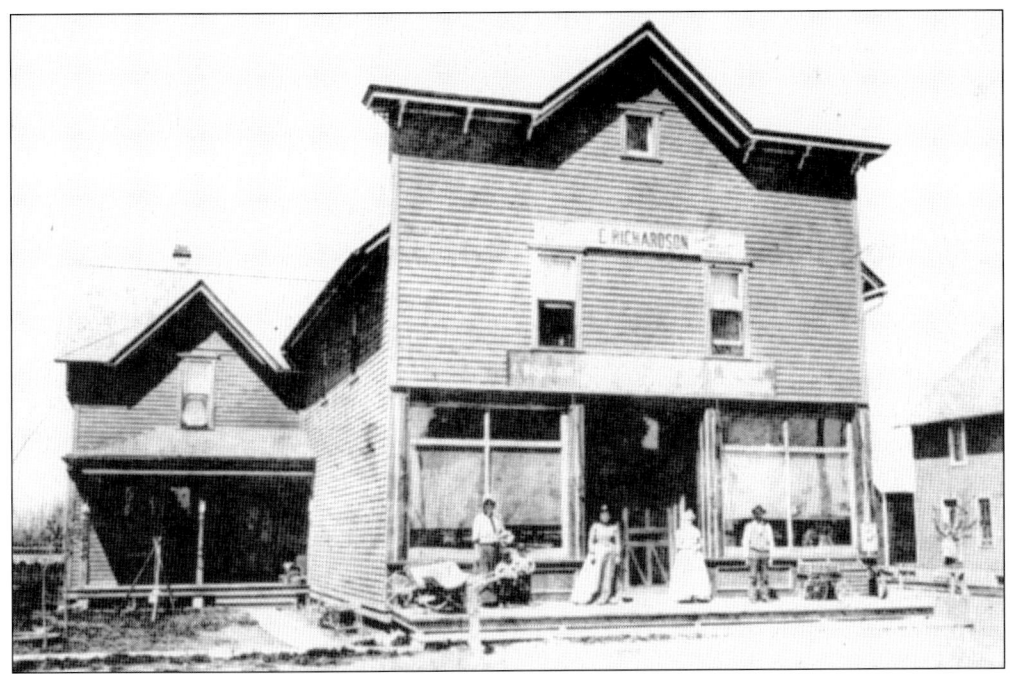

Elijah Richardson moved his business from Hainesville to this building in Round Lake. In later years, a Mr. Bendulls had a department store here. The structure, seen here in an image from *50 Years, Golden Jubilee, 1908–1958, Round Lake*, remains standing at the southwest corner of Avilon Avenue and Cedar Lake Road.

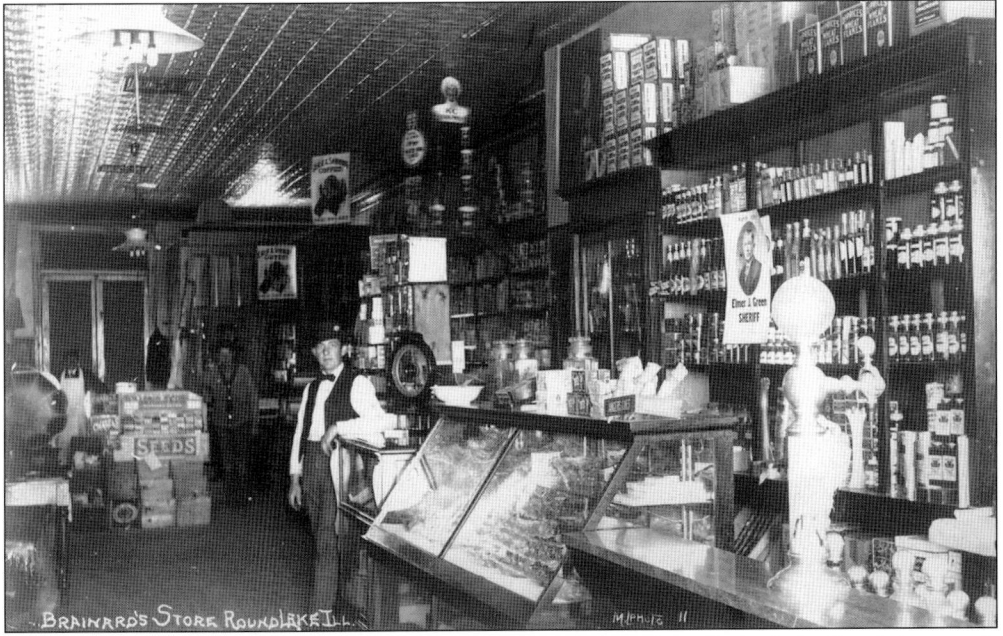

Charles Brainard started his Round Lake grocery store in 1905 on Cedar Lake Road, just south of the Richardson store. The local post office was in this location for several years with Brainard as postmaster. He also served a term as mayor of Round Lake. (Courtesy of Lake County Discovery Museum.)

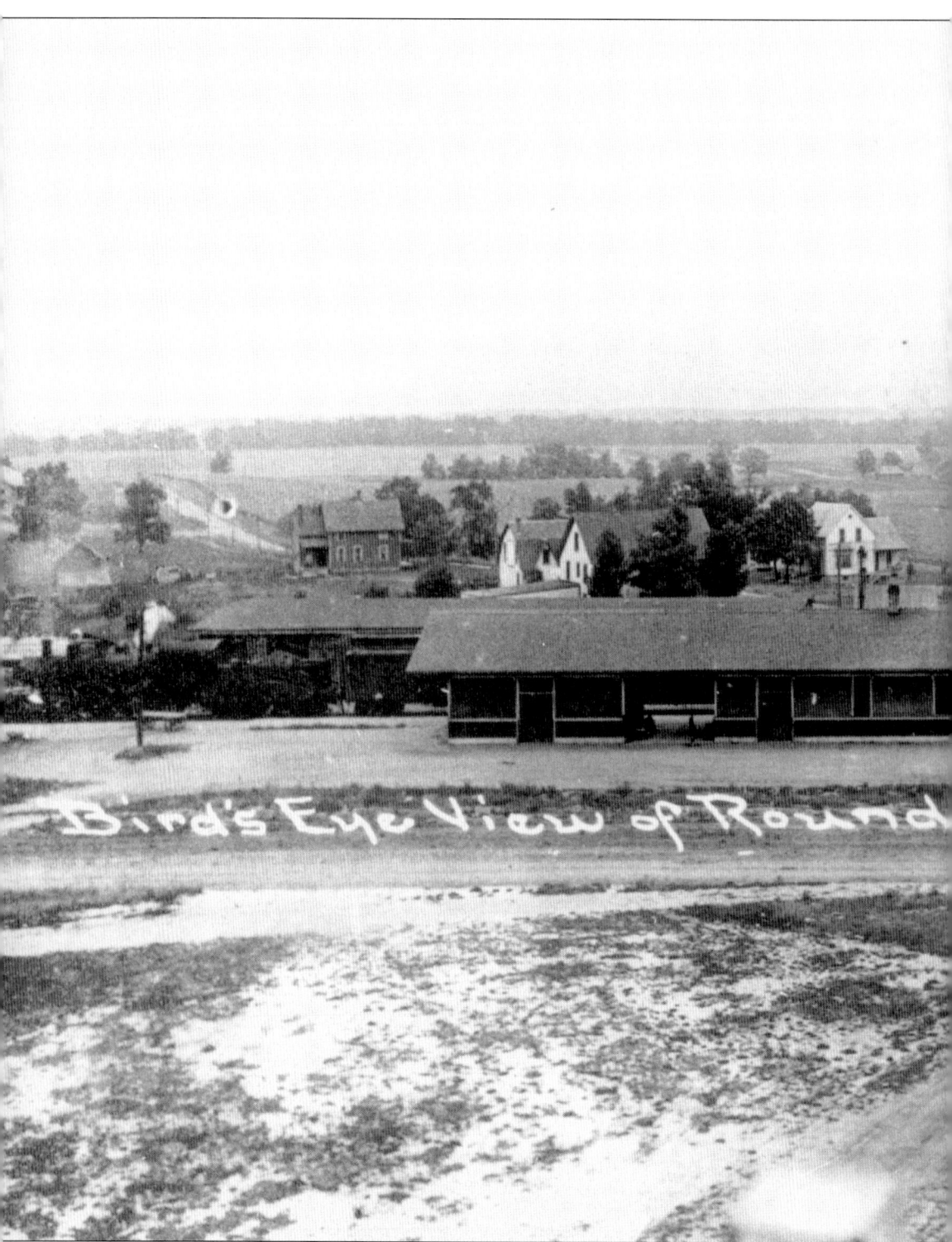

A bird's-eye view of Round Lake, from around 1908, shows the area from Goodnow Boulevard north to the lake. Included in the photograph are Armour's water tower, the railroad depot, the

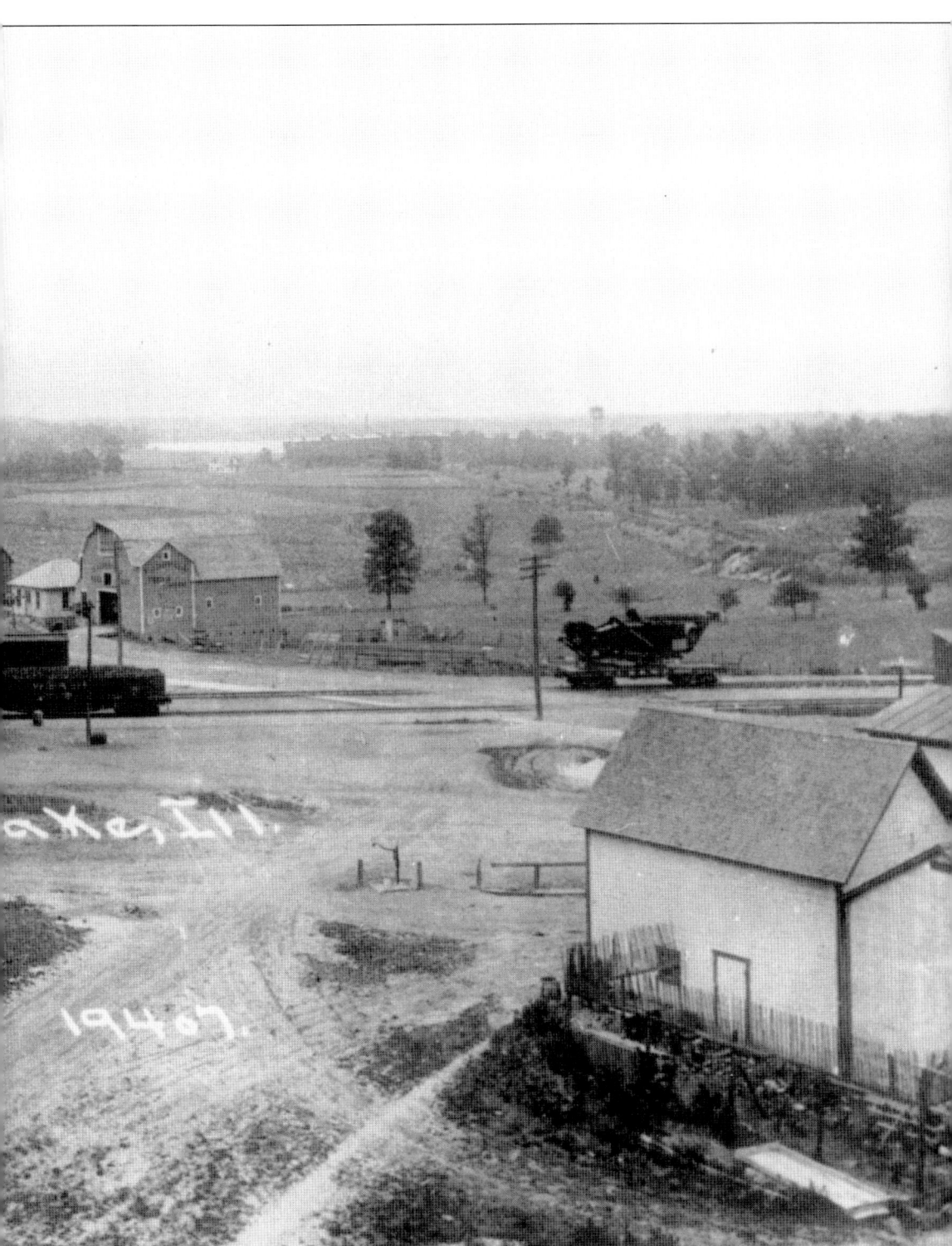
jail, a livery barn, and various other structures.

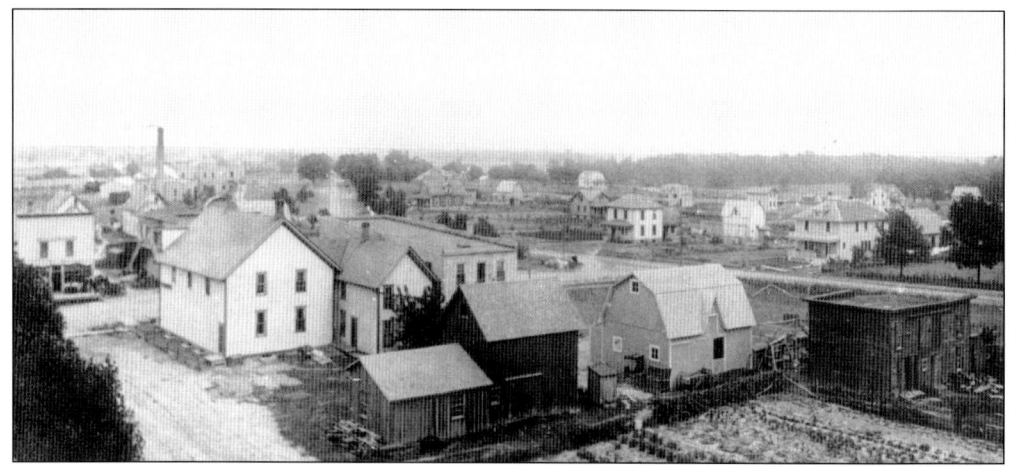

This bird's-eye view of Round Lake was taken from the corner of Goodnow Boulevard and Avilon Avenue. The rear of the former Richardson building, which faces Cedar Lake Road, is to the left. In the background is the smokestack of the former creamery at 314 West Nippersink Road. (Courtesy of Winnie Frost Cox.)

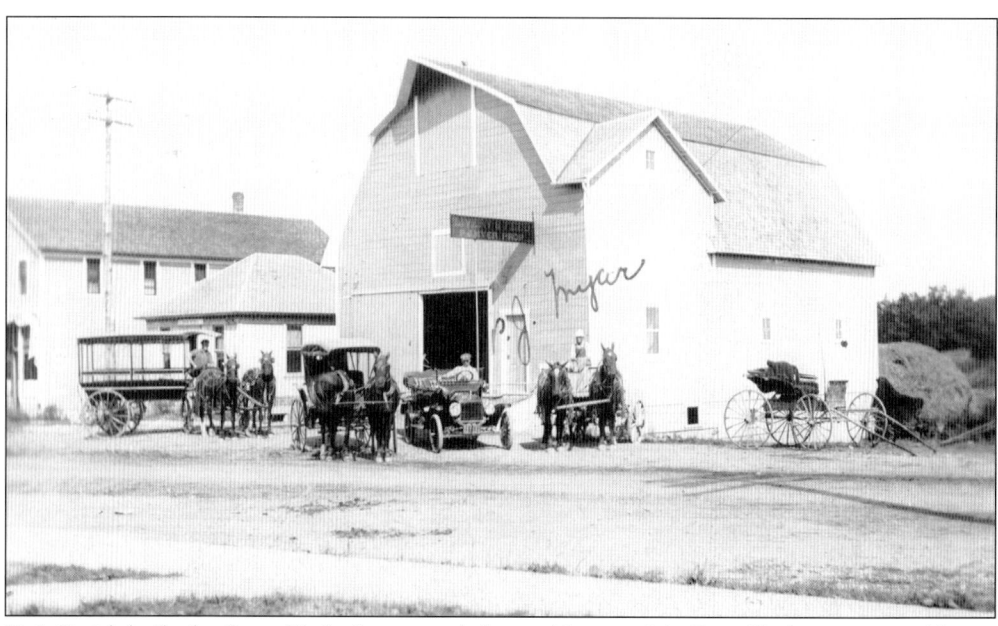

O. J. Smith built the Round Lake Livery and then sold it to a Mr. Dowell who in turn sold it to Martin Thelen. At the time of this photograph, Pete J. Myer was the proprietor. An automotive accessories business presently occupies the site. The small building to the left of the livery was the village jail.

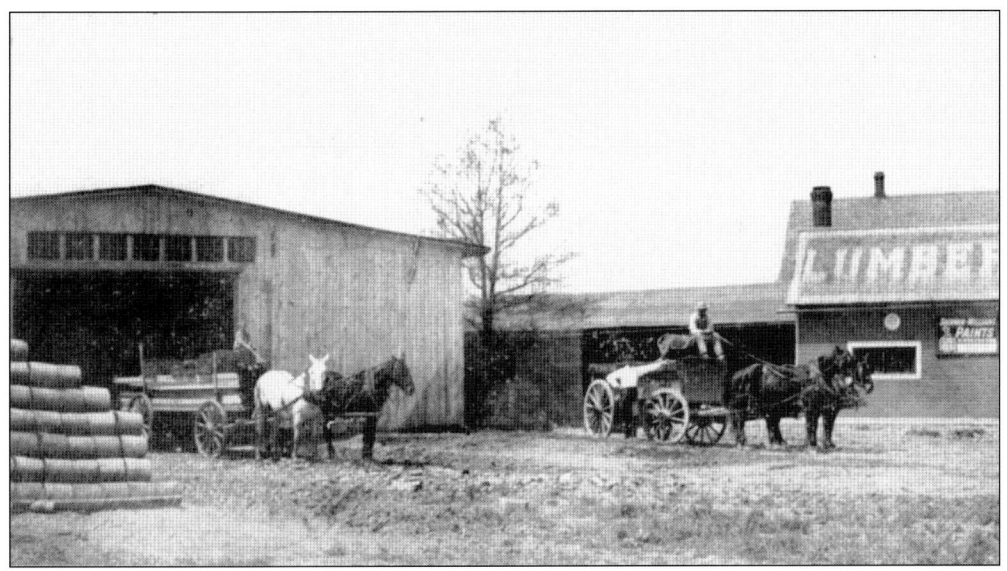

The railroad was the impetus for growth in Round Lake. J. C. Pratt built a lumberyard next to the tracks. By 1907, the lumberyard was the Tibbits Cameron Lumber Company.

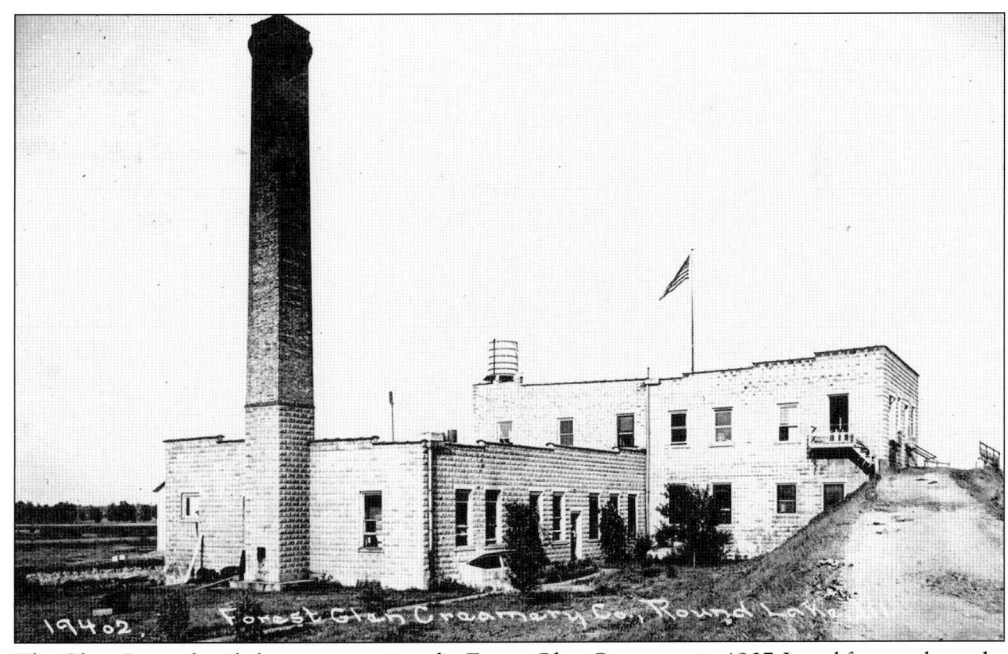

The Claus Junge family began operating the Forest Glen Creamery in 1907. Local farmers brought their milk to the factory, which employed 25 to 30 full-time workers. The workers prepared the milk to be shipped by train to Chicago. Parts of the former creamery, seen in this postcard dated 1908, are still visible at 314 West Nippersink Road.

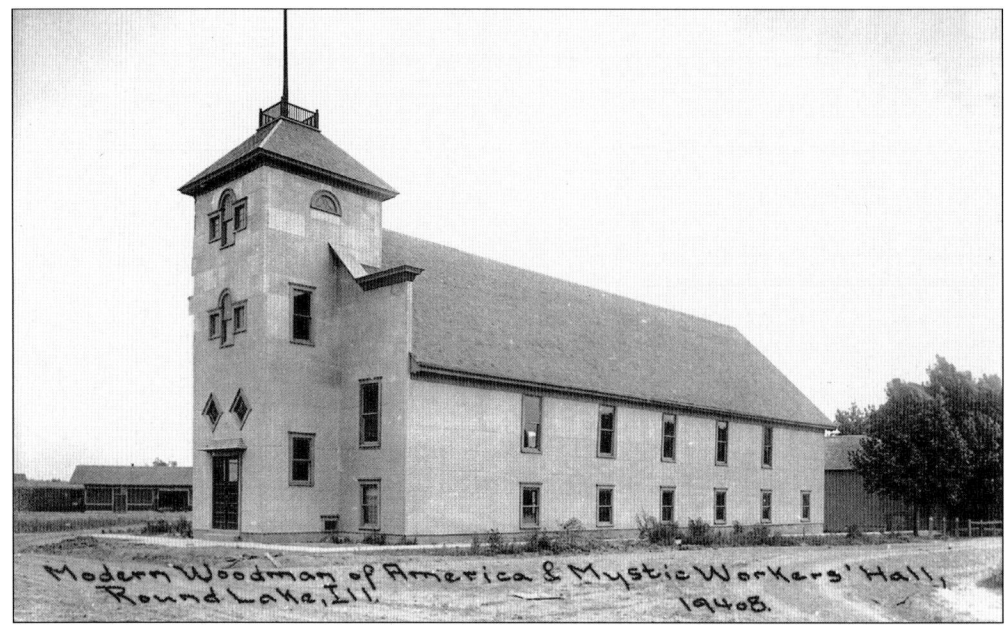

The Modern Woodmen of America, a fraternal organization, built this hall at the corner of Goodnow Boulevard and Avilon Avenue. The Modern Woodmen of America, Mystic Workers, and others used the second-floor meeting room for dances, benefits, parties, and vaudeville shows. The two-story, 40-by-80-foot frame building burned in the mid-1920s following a New Year's Eve gathering. (Courtesy of Lake County Discovery Museum.)

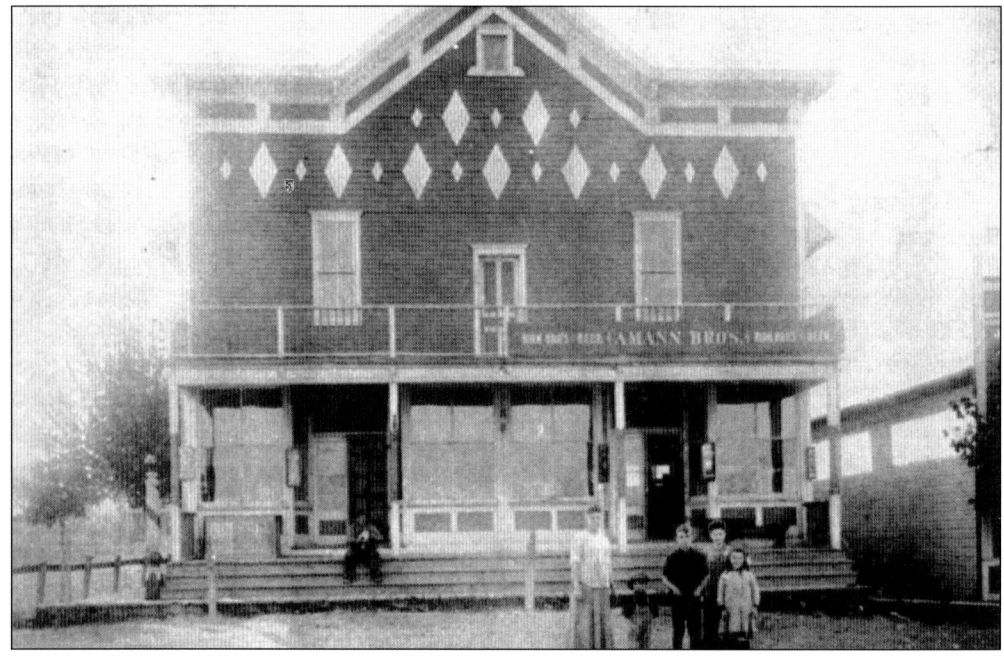

Amann Hall, seen here in an image from *50 Years, Golden Jubilee, 1908–1958, Round Lake*, was built in 1901 for Joseph and Frank Amann. There was a saloon on the first floor and a dance floor on the second. Later Charles Mason had a barbershop in the basement. Before the building burned in 1986, it was the Brass Wheel Restaurant. As of 2007, the property is vacant.

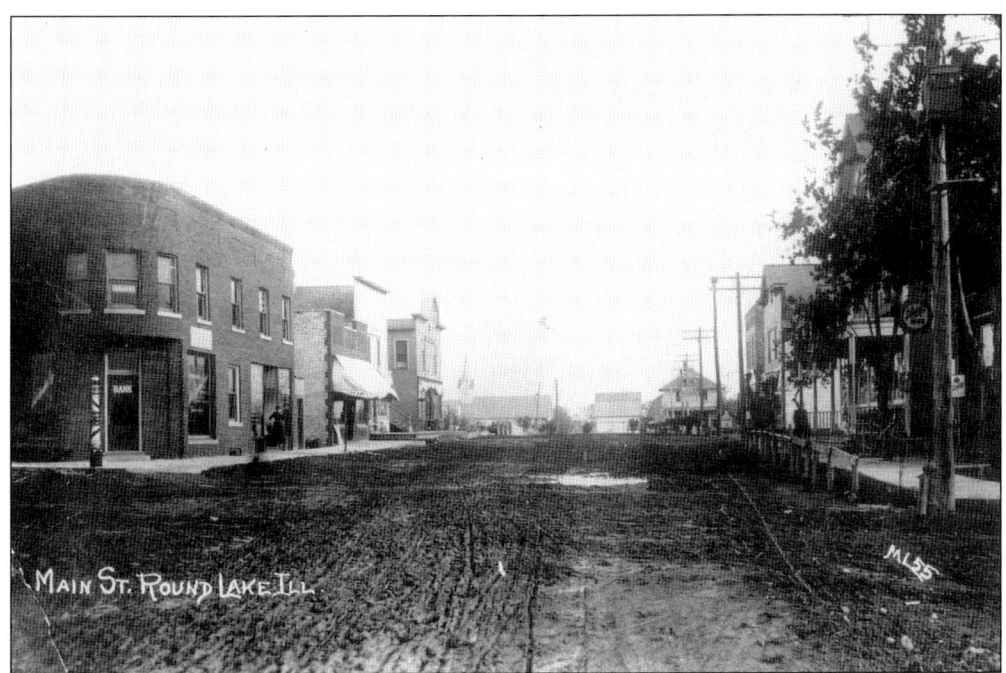

There are two major differences in the two photographs on this page. The photograph above shows the main street of Round Lake with an unpaved surface. The photograph below, postmarked 1941, shows motorized vehicles and a paved Cedar Lake Road. The Bank of Round Lake, viewed at the left, was chartered as a private institution in 1918 with John Hart as president. It closed in 1939. For many years, Dr. G. A. Goshgarian had his office in the former bank building. Presently an insurance agency occupies the site. (Above, courtesy of Winnie Frost Cox.)

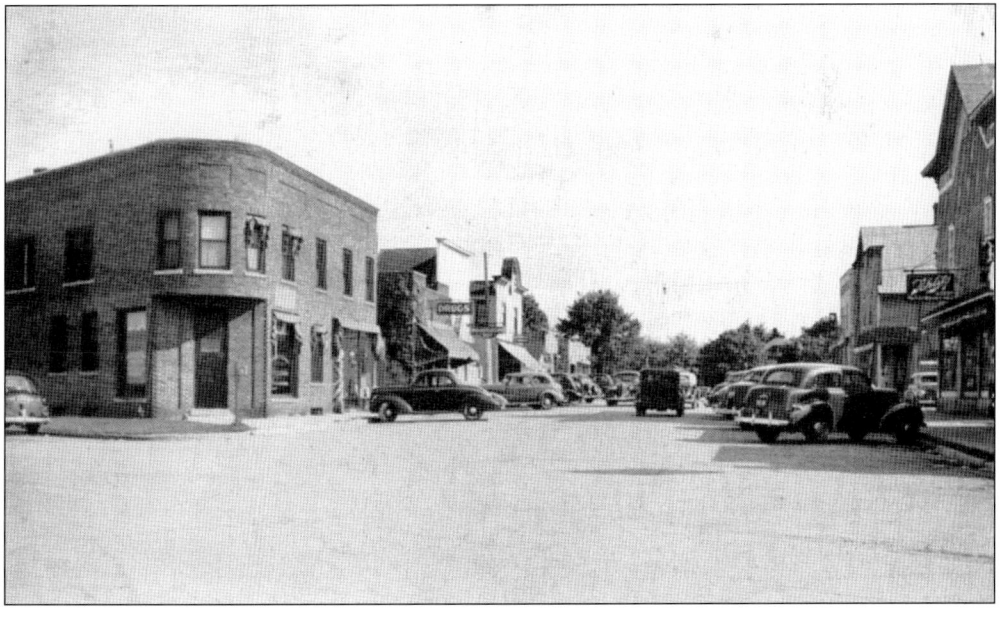

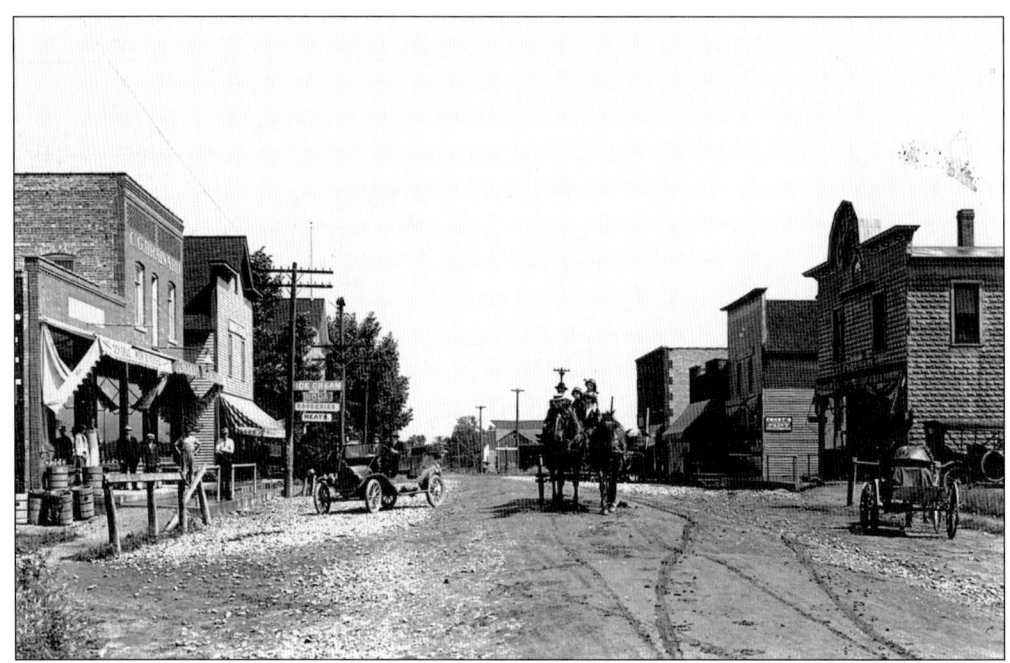

In both of these photographs, the photographer's lens is looking north from near the corner of Avilon Avenue and Cedar Lake Road. In the photograph above, the street is unpaved, and ice cream, soda, groceries, and meats are advertised. In the photograph below, the street is paved, and the billboard in the center of the image is advertising Renehan's Resort. (Above, courtesy of Lake County Discovery Museum.)

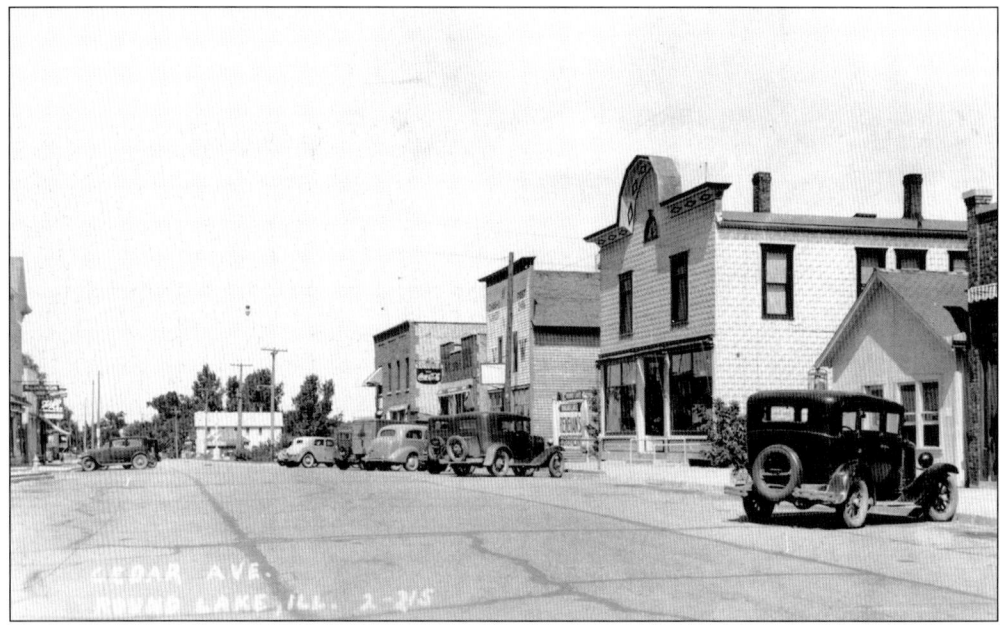

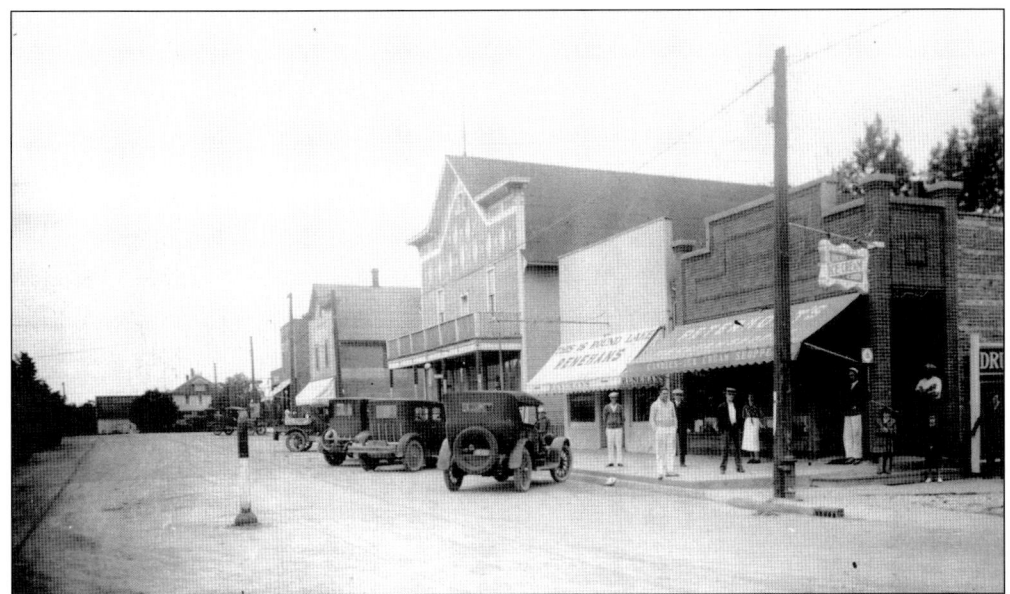

These images are quite similar, viewing Cedar Lake Road looking south from Avilon Avenue. The image above is from the 1920s and the image below from the 1930s. In both views, Ben Peterkort's business is to the right. The Joseph Peterkort family had a hotel in Grayslake in the early 1900s. Son Ben moved to Round Lake where he served a term as mayor and had a business. In the image above, he is selling candies and ice cream, while the image below shows that his business became a tavern. (Below, courtesy of Lake County Discovery Museum.)

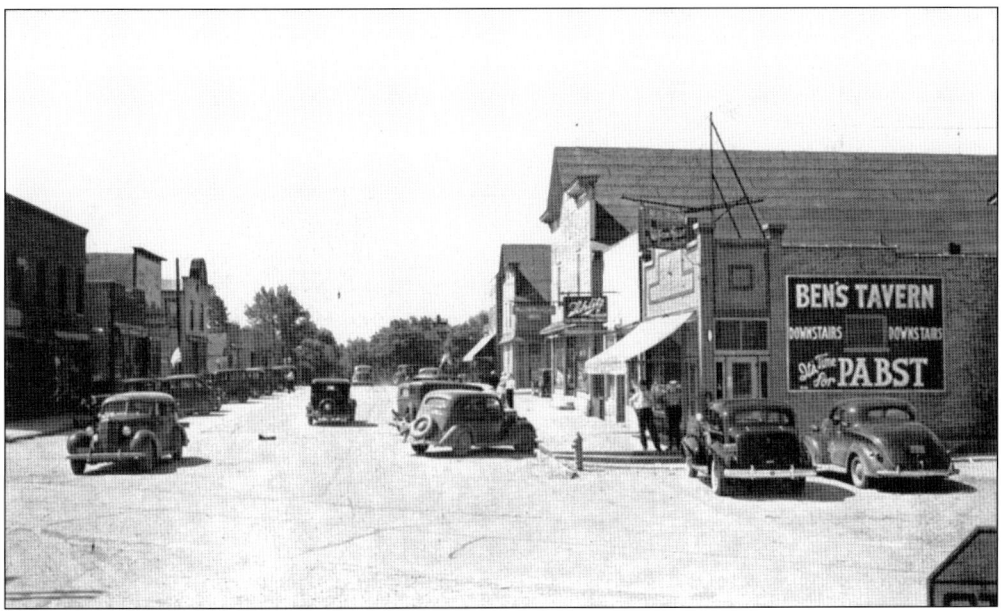

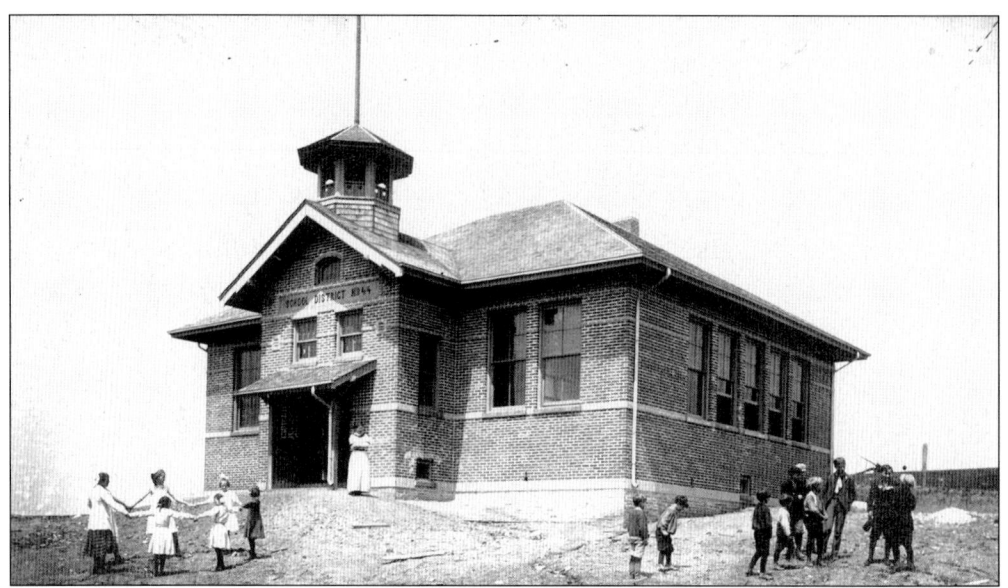

The first consolidated school in Lake County was formed in 1910 when the Meade and Gilbert one-room schools closed and became part of the Round Lake School District. Meade School had been located at 403 West Rollins Road, and Gilbert School was at the end of Hart Road by Fairfield Road. This postcard is dated 1914.

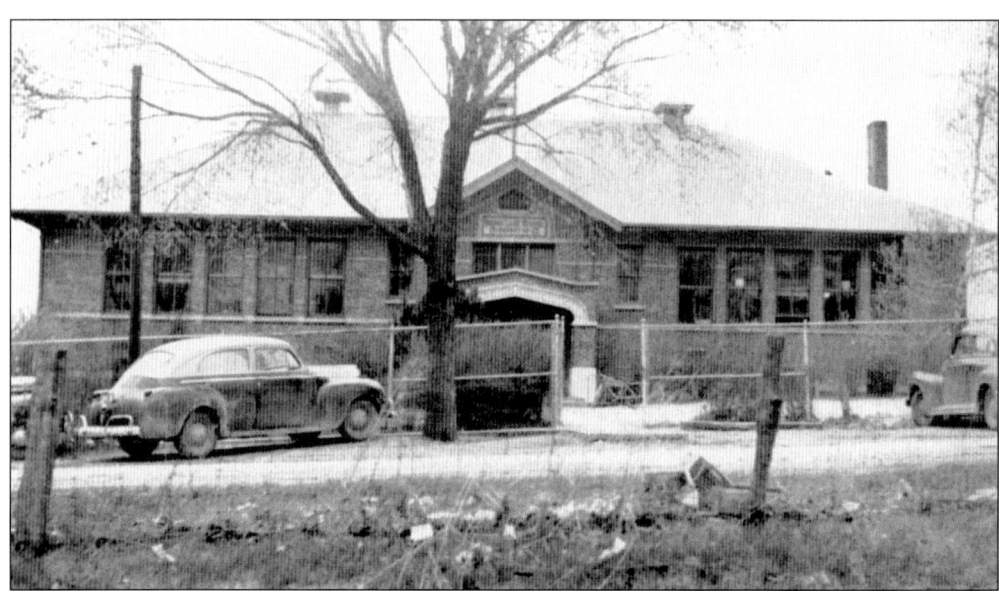

This image of the Round Lake Grade School was taken after the 1910 building was doubled in size. Later it held classes for the lower grades, and more recently, it was used for other educational purposes before closing.

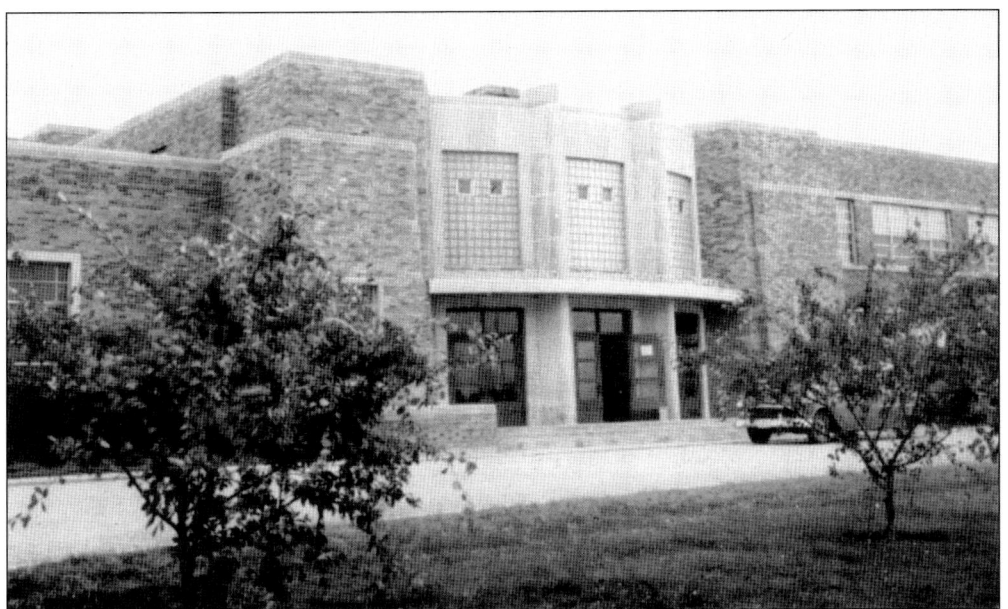

The building at 500 North Cedar Lake Road was built in 1950 for the Round Lake Grade School system. It later became the Magee Middle School, in honor of John T. Magee, an Avon Township assessor and Round Lake school board member. The building closed in 2004 for renovation.

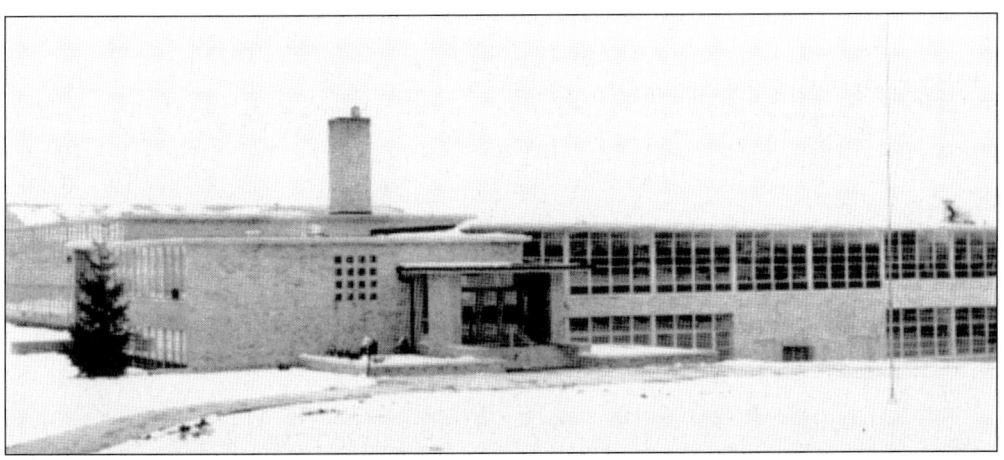

Round Lake High School opened in 1954 with only freshman and sophomore classes. Other classes continued to attend other area high schools for another year. This view is of the high school before any additions were made. (Courtesy of Round Lake High School Library.)

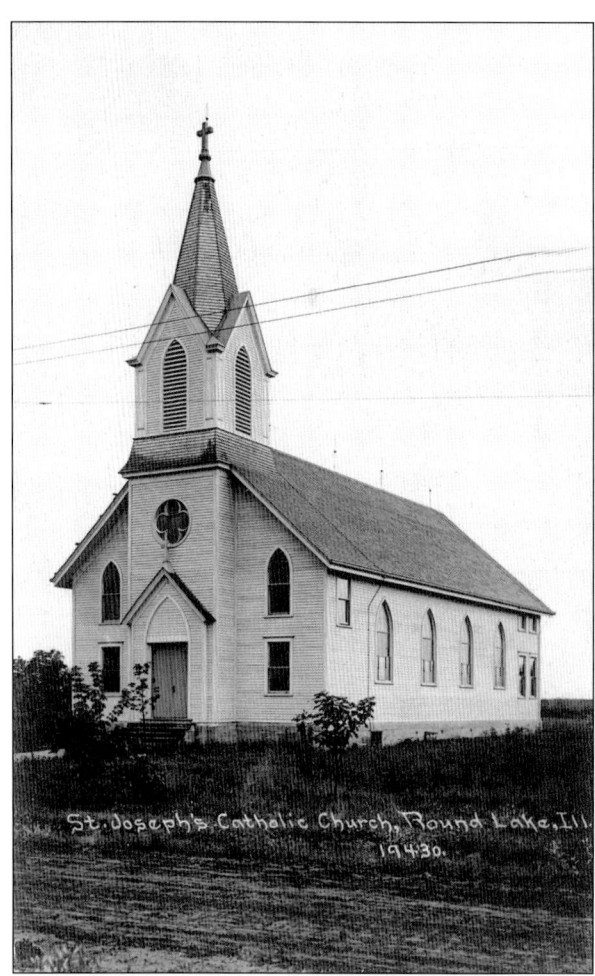

In 1912, the first mass was said in Round Lake's St. Joseph Catholic Church on Lincoln Avenue. A new brick church was built next door in 1952. The photograph to the left shows the original frame church, which is still used by the parish. The photograph below shows the interior of the original church. (Left, courtesy of Lake County Discovery Museum.)

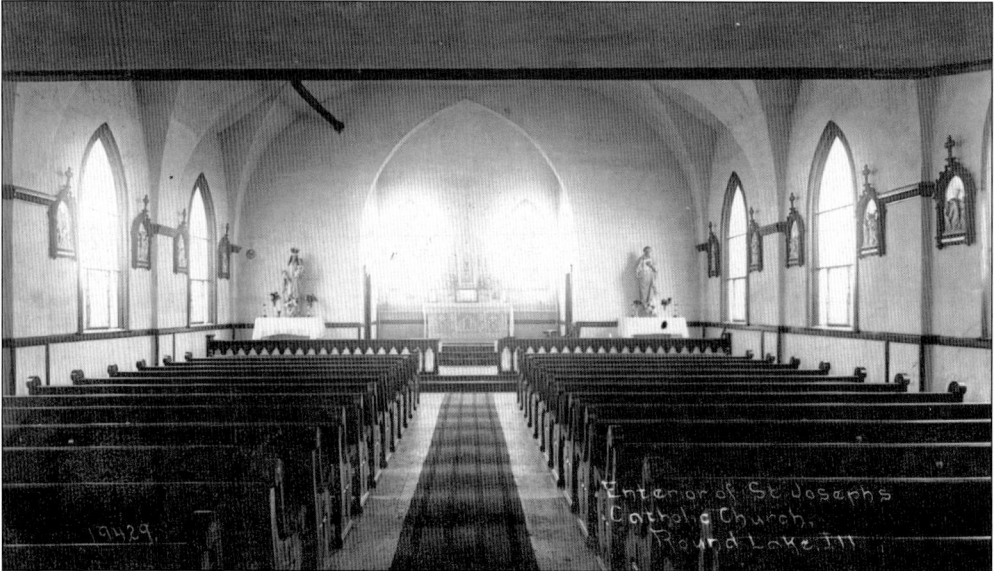

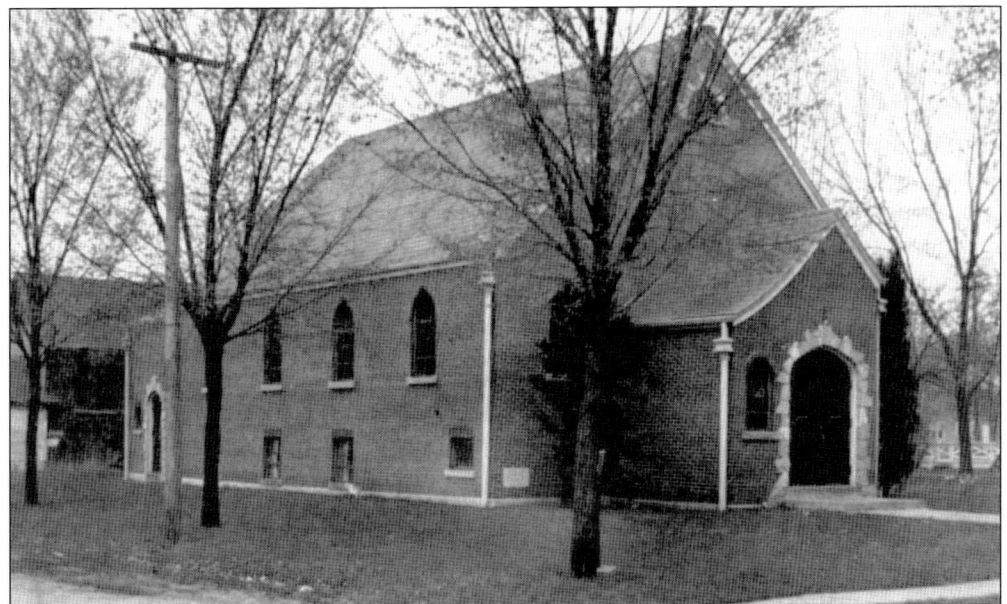

The Round Lake Community Church was an outgrowth of the Union Sunday school. It met in several locations until 1932 when this building at the corner of Avilon Avenue and Goodnow Boulevard was dedicated. The structure is presently being enlarged.

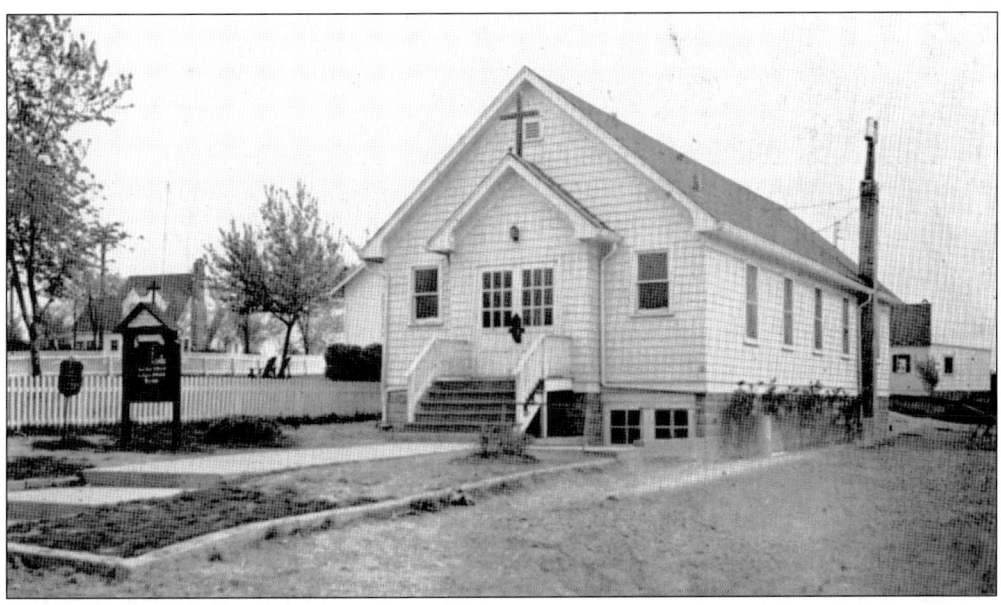

The first building of St. Paul Evangelical Lutheran Church, dedicated in 1940, shown above, is now the Church of Jesus Christ of the Apostolic Faith. St. Paul Evangelical Church is presently at 420 Greenwood Avenue. The first building was located at the corner of Greenwood Avenue and Renehan Road, now Washington Street. Washington Street from Lake Street in Grayslake to Cedar Lake Road in Round Lake was known as Renehan Road until 1968.

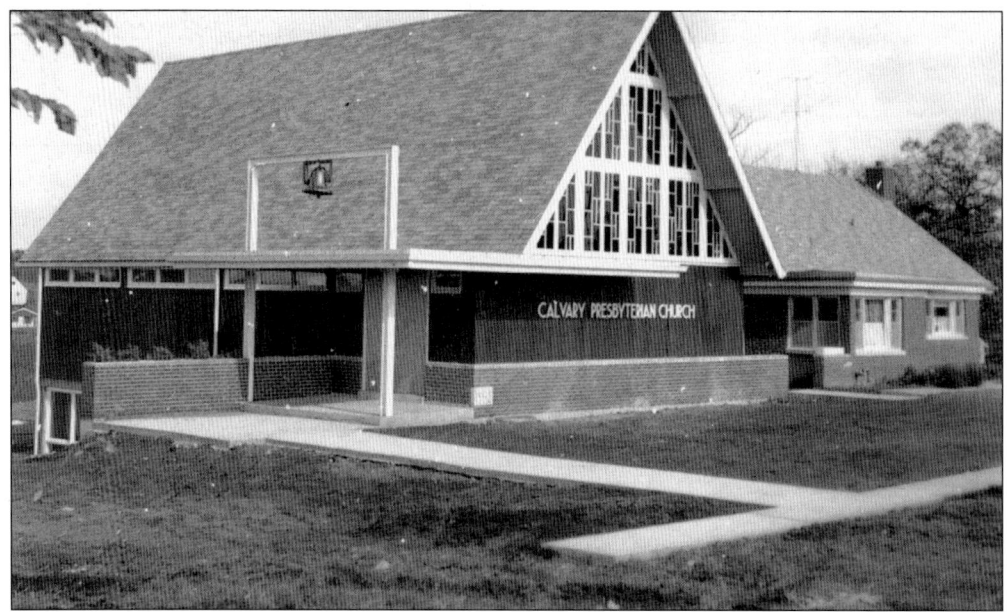

Calvary Presbyterian Church was organized in 1953. The congregation moved into its manse, attached at the right, in 1955. The cornerstone for the church was set in place in 1958, and this image was taken soon afterward. The former manse is now used for church offices. (Courtesy of Calvary Presbyterian Church.)

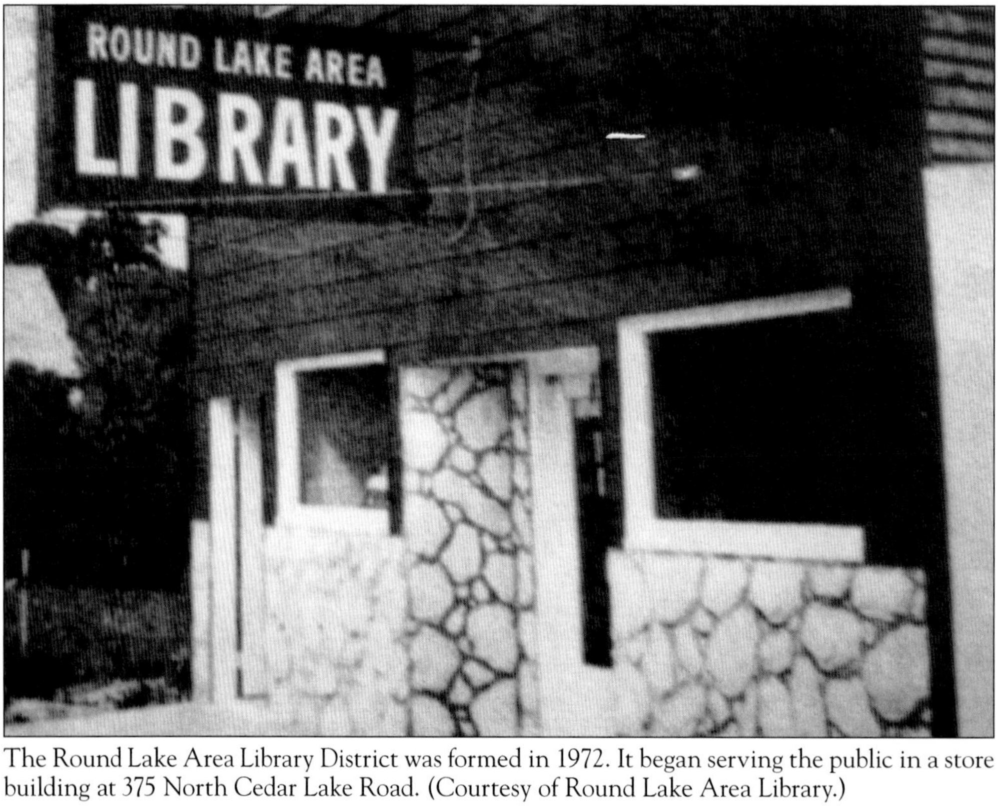

The Round Lake Area Library District was formed in 1972. It began serving the public in a store building at 375 North Cedar Lake Road. (Courtesy of Round Lake Area Library.)

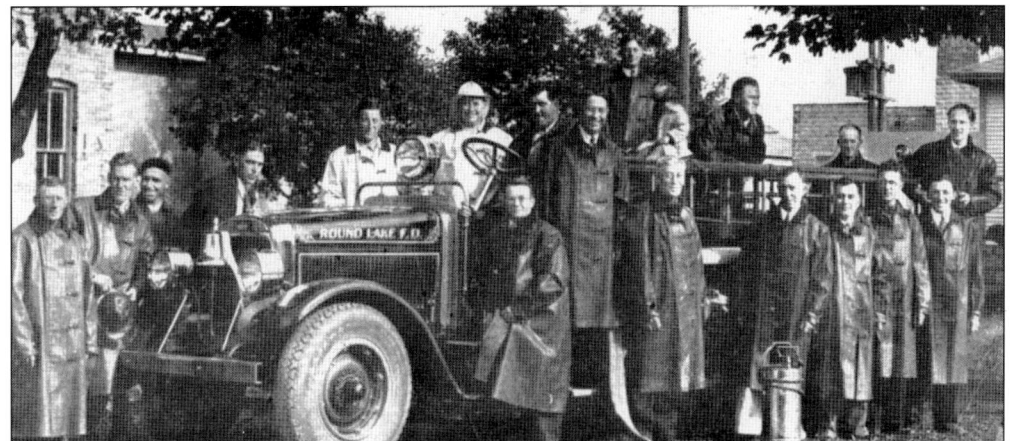

The fire truck in this c. 1934 photograph was called "Old Pete." Standing in front are Tony Leonard, Nels Hoigaard, Mike Luby, Bill Frost, Jim Luby, and Ray Rippberger. Pictured in the back row with Old Pete are Clint Hendee, Bill Harrison, Joe Molidor, Pooch Smith, Bill Hironimus, Reverend Schmitz, Bus Luby at the wheel, John Dick, Elmer Hendee, young Donald Hendee, Harry Litwiler, Floyd Renehan, and George Orth. (Courtesy of Greater Round Lake Fire Protection District.)

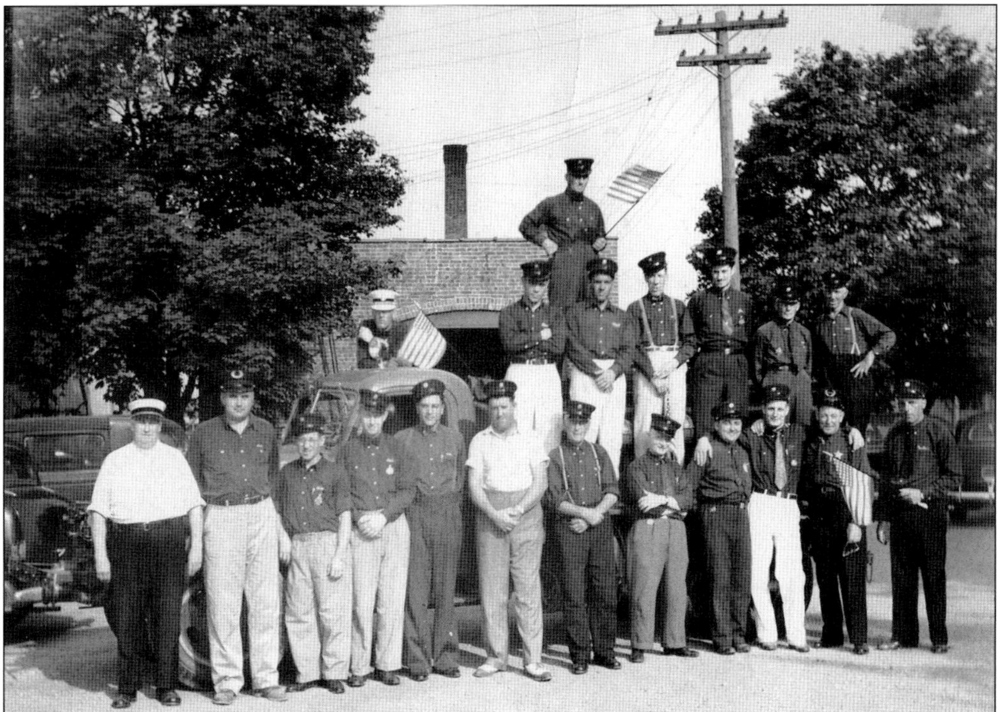

In this image, firemen pose in front of the old firehouse. Edward Hendee is holding the flag. The others are Bill Harrison, Owen Litwiler, Milt Litwiler, "Joker" Adamson, Don Luby, Clint Hendee, Mike Luby, Reverend Schmitz, Bud Amann, Bill Redman, Ralph Orth, Ed Amann, Bus Luby, Nels Hoigaard, Lester Dolph, Frank Vogt, Jim Ness, Bill Hironimus, and Walter Rosing. (Courtesy of Greater Round Lake Fire Protection District.)

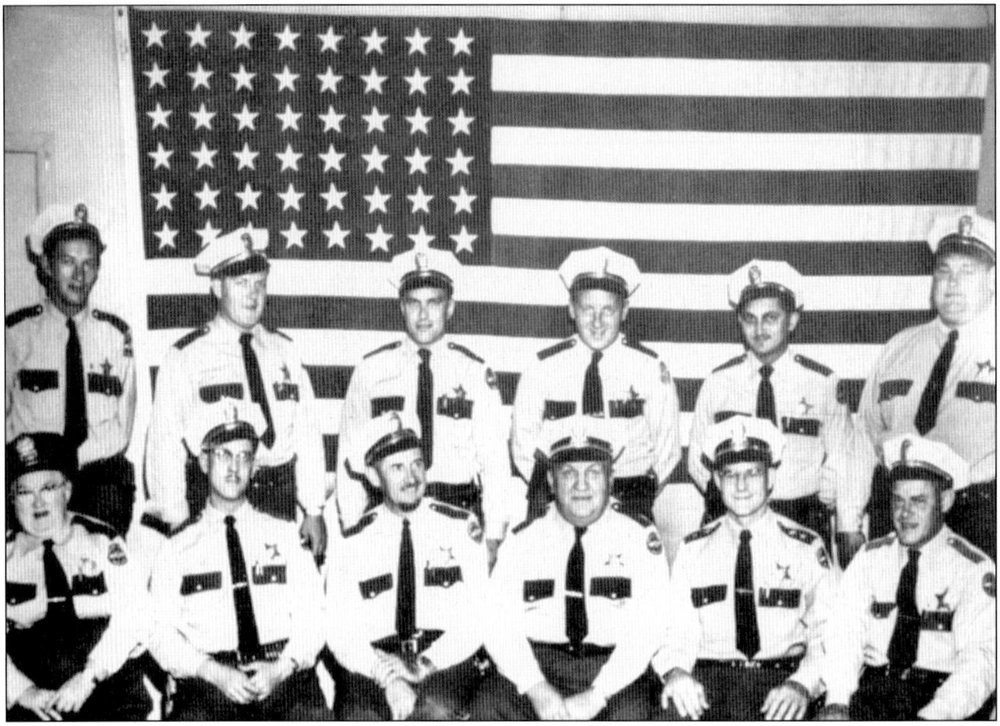

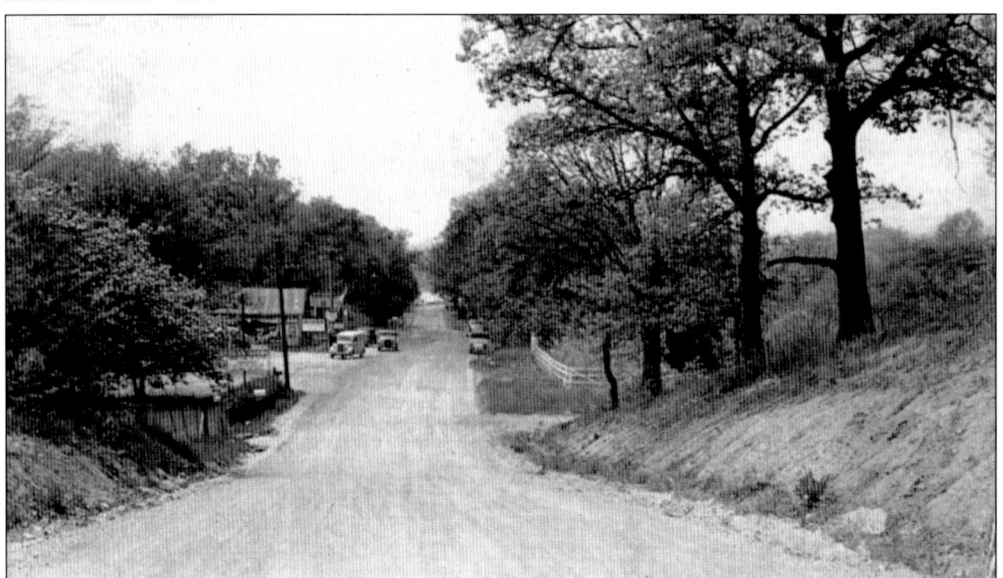

Pictured here, in an image from *50 Years, Golden Jubilee, 1908–1958, Round Lake*, is the Village of Round Lake Police Department in 1958: Chief M. J. Hoellen, Capt. Jack Murphy, Lt. Albert Mueller, Sgt. Charles Akers Jr., patrolmen John Wayne Craig, George Wold, Alphonse Prewara, Walter Pfannenstiel, Frank Skowronski, Donald Nicoline, and C. "Tiny" Williams, and police matron Helen Wake.

Parts of Fairfield Road formerly had different names. One section was known as Fort Hill Road, while another part was called Grub Hill Road. Pictured here is Grub Hill Road. The three roads were joined with one name about 1975. (Courtesy of Lake County Discovery Museum.)

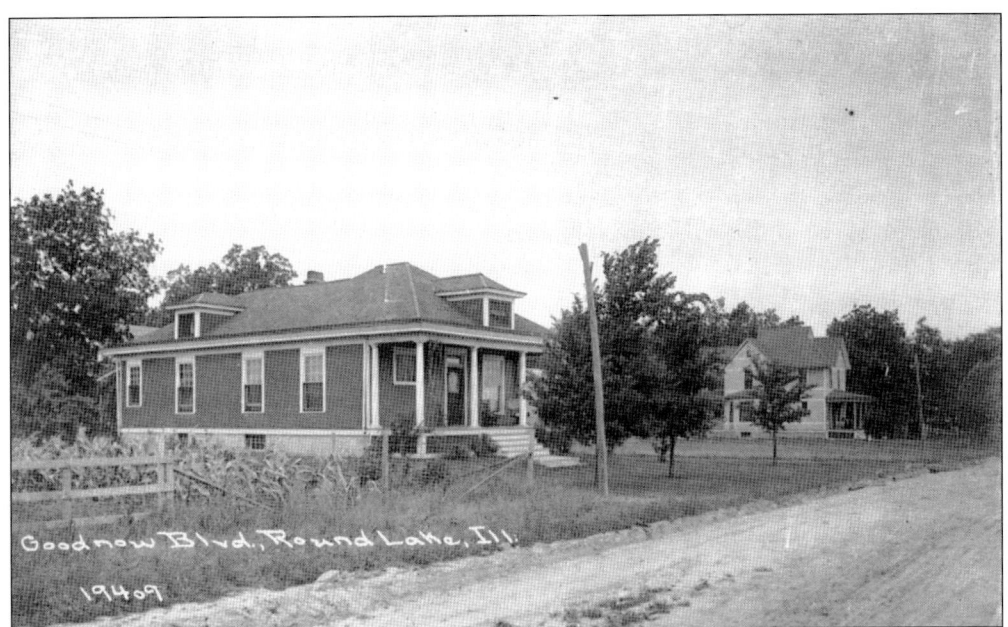

In the foreground at 218 Goodnow Boulevard is a former Amann house. In the background, a former Rosing house has been replaced by a gravel parking lot. Goodnow Boulevard is named for A. C. Goodnow, head of the Lake, Cook and McHenry Counties Railway Company and later a vice president of the Chicago, Milwaukee and St. Paul Railroad. (Courtesy of Lake County Discovery Museum.)

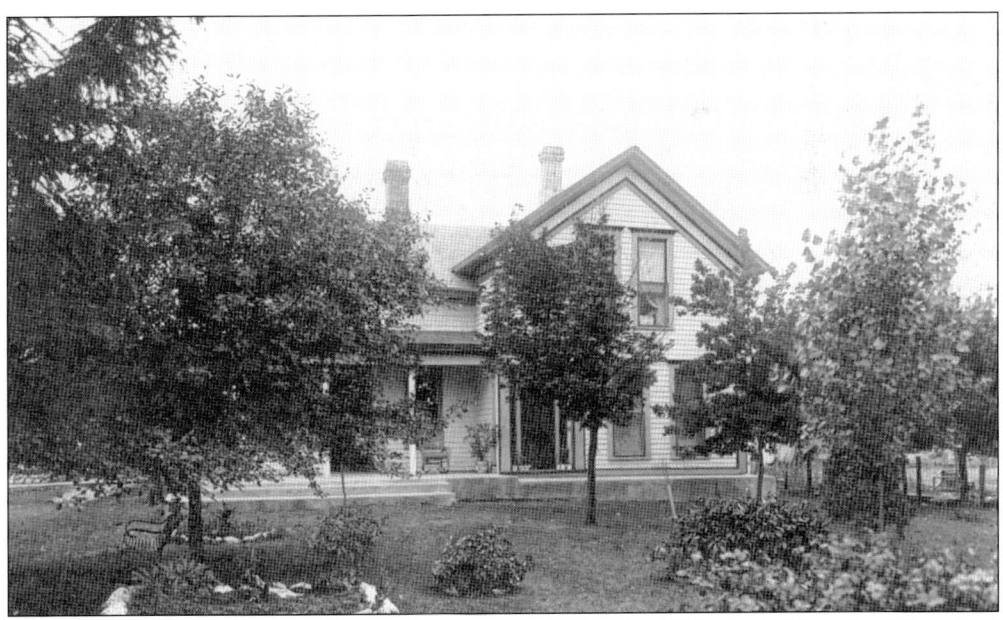

This postcard view is of White's Sanitorium at Round Lake. Walter and Nicholas White had property along the eastern shore of Long Lake. Brother Amarias's property was west of the original plat of Round Lake. Amarias was instrumental in getting the railroad to have a station in Round Lake and was elected the village's first mayor. (Courtesy of Grayslake Historical Society, Ruth Mogg Collection.)

ROUND LAKE BEACH

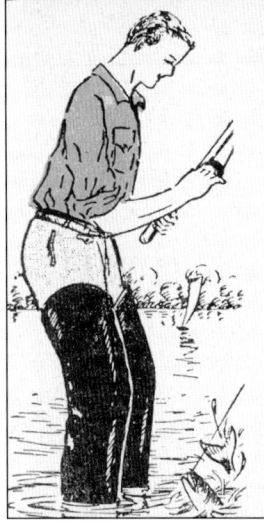
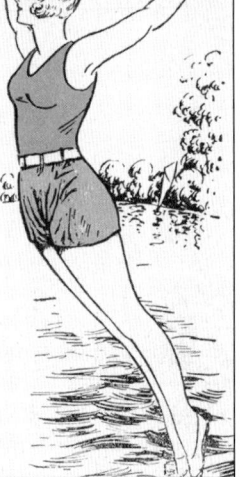

On Beautiful ROUND LAKE
IMPROVED LAKE LOTS
40 x 125 Feet
TOTAL COST
Only $2.00 Down **$195.00** Pay $2.00 A Week

Mail This Card Now—No Postage Necessary

Gentlemen:
☐ Please send me Free Booklet, Road Map and descriptive literature of Round Lake Beach.
☐ Please Send Free Round-Trip Tickets for .... persons.
☐ Please drive us out in one of your private cars.

Date ....
It is understood that the above request will not cost me anything, nor obligate me in any way.

Name ....
Address ....

ROUND LAKE BEACH
IN THE CHAIN O' LAKES REGION

A Summer or Permanent Homesite at the Lake

WITH EVERY CONVENIENCE OF THE CITY

35 MILES FROM CHICAGO
CONCRETE ALL THE WAY

NO ASSESSMENTS
COMMUNITY PARKS—PLAYGROUNDS—WELLS
GRAVELED STREETS—PIERS—TREES
NATURAL SAFE SANDY BEACHES

TWO FEE GOLF COURSES ADJOINING PROPERTY

BATHING BOATING FISHING
HUNTING

FOUR BLOCKS TO STORES, CHURCHES, SCHOOLS
and R. R. STATION

65 MINUTES TO THE LOOP BY TRAIN
26½ CENTS COMMUTATION FARE

An Investment in
PLEASURE plus PROFIT

TRUSTEE: FOREMAN TRUST & SAVINGS BANK
Titles Guaranteed by Chicago Title & Trust Co.

L. B. HARRIS CO.
Resort Lake-Shore Developers
1062-67 FIRST NATIONAL BANK BLDG.
33 SO. CLARK STREET   CENTRAL 5950
CHICAGO, ILLINOIS.

In early 1926, Louis B. Harris, a Chicago businessman, purchased land along the west shore of Round Lake from Oliver Hook. Doing business as the Resort Lake-Shore Developers, he sold property to mostly Chicago people, who built vacation homes. He subdivided over 1,700 acres in the Round Lake area. The L. B. Harris Company incorporated in 1946. The two images are part of a double-fold postcard that Harris mailed to potential buyers.

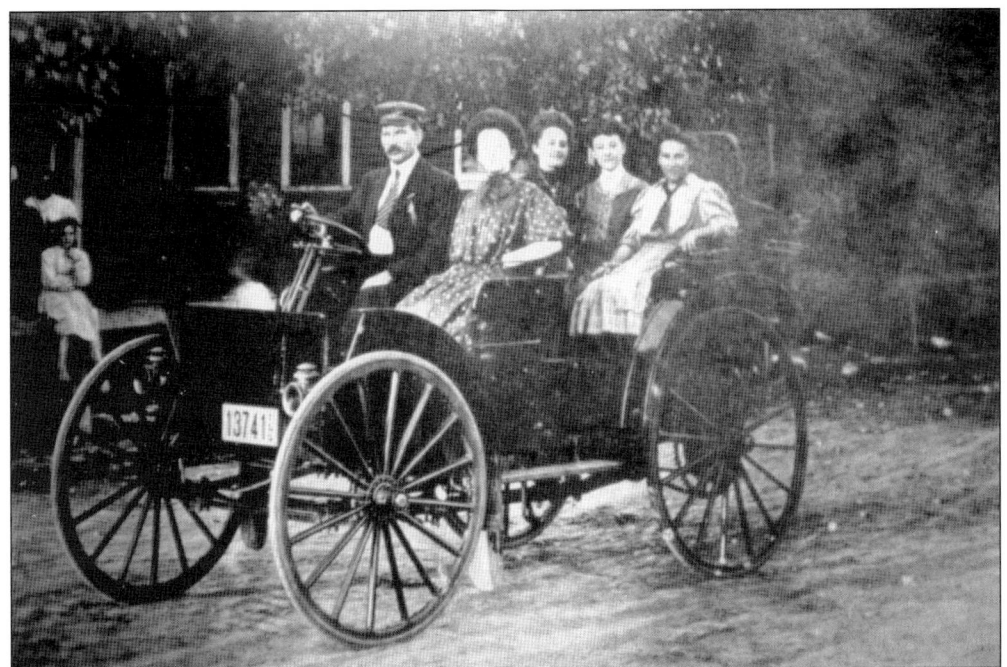

Joseph Amann had the first car in Round Lake, a 1908 International Harvester. The second car in the village, a Ford, was owned by Martin Thelen. Thelen was a blacksmith who became an automobile mechanic. (Courtesy of Round Lake Area Library.)

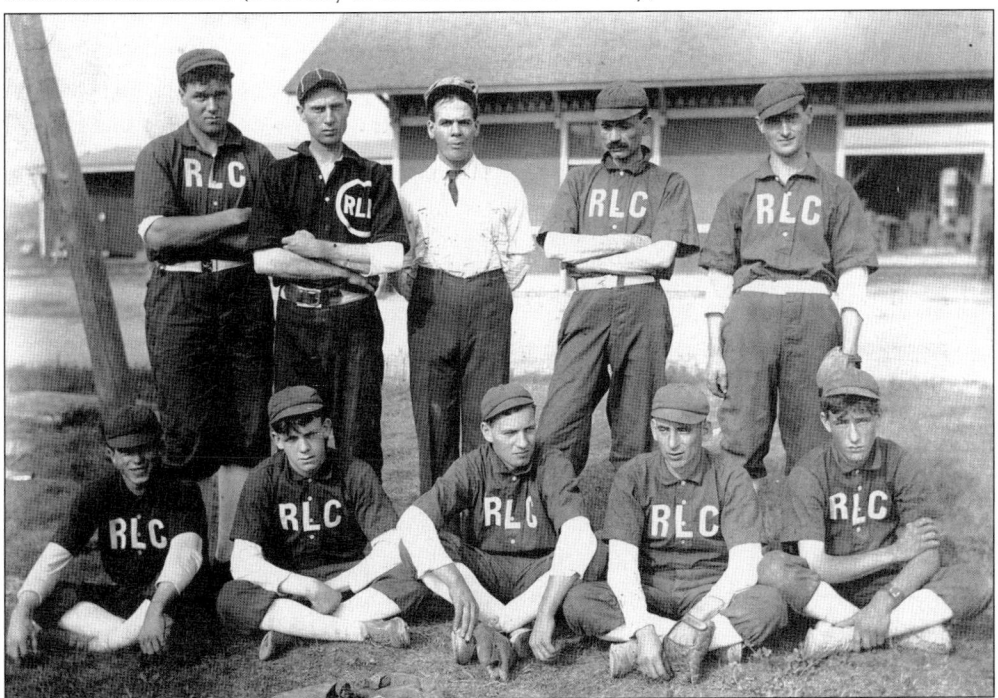

Avon Township and nearby communities had baseball teams as early as the 1890s. The Round Lake team, known as the Maroons, is pictured here in front of the Round Lake depot around 1910. (Courtesy of Grayslake Historical Society.)

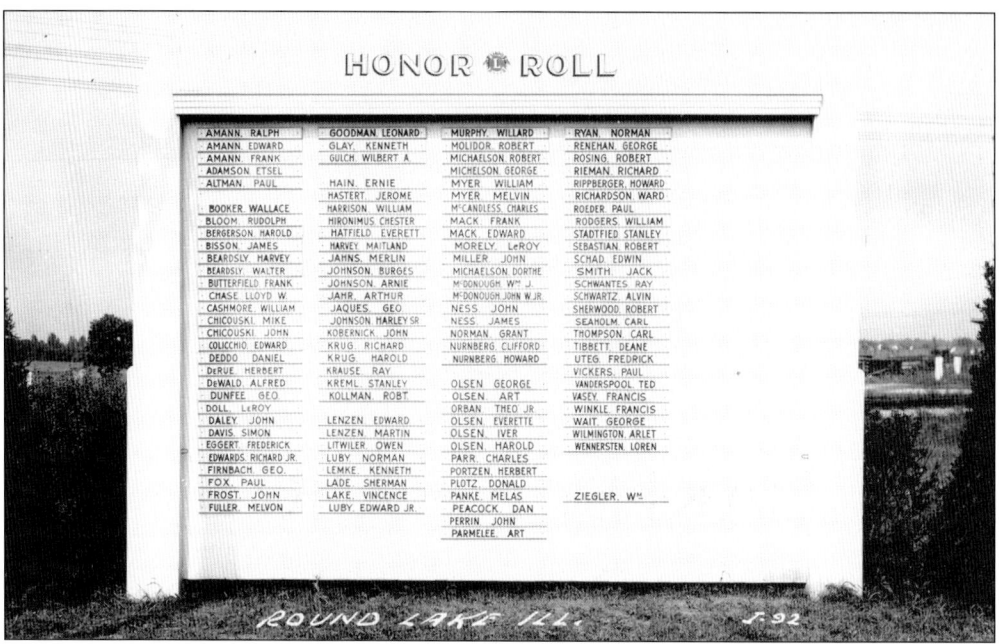

Round Lake's World War II honor roll stood at the northeast corner of Cedar Lake Road and Route 134. There are many siblings and cousins listed.

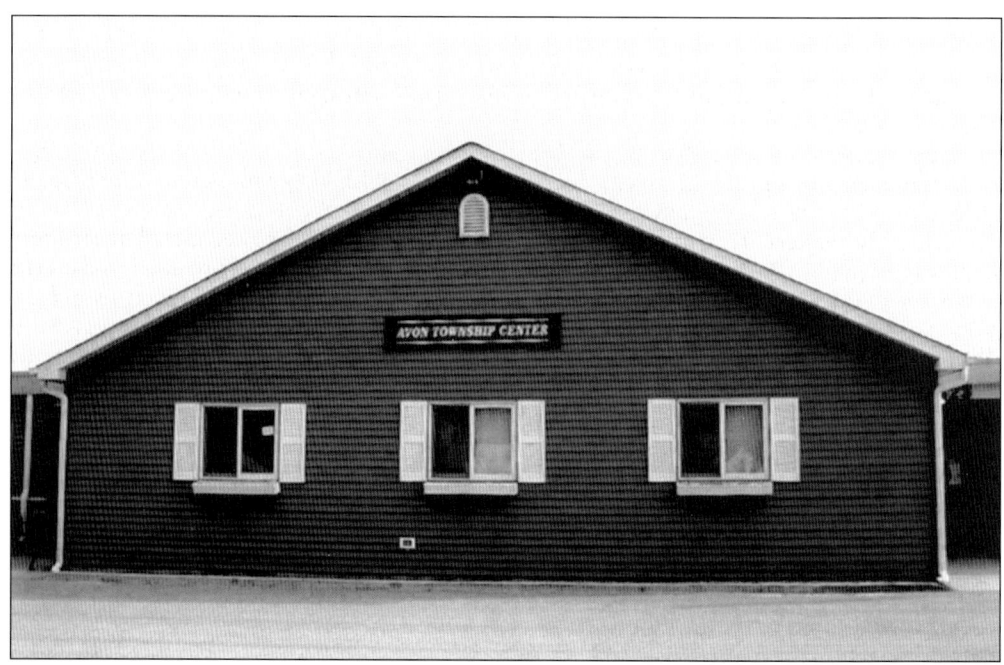

The Avon Township offices are located at 433 East Washington Street, Round Lake Park, on property that was purchased in 1978. This building is the first permanent home for the township. Previously the township supervisors used storefronts as offices. Additions to the structure were made in 1981 and 1993.

Four

LAKES, RESORTS, AND RECREATION

There are several lakes in Avon Township. Grays Lake and Round Lake have already been referenced but there are others. Some of the lakes have had their names changed.

Highland Lake was originally Taylor's Lake. The Taylor's Lake name started in the 1830s when a man by the name of Taylor was a squatter on property by the lake. He is credited with being the first resident of Avon Township even though he soon left the area.

Cranberry Lake, located along Hainesville Road, derives its name from the cranberries that were once abundant there.

There are First, Second, Third, and Fourth Lakes. First Lake is today known as Gages Lake and is located in Warren Township. It is named for John Gage, who came to the area in 1836. Druce Lake was once known as Second Lake. The eastern part of the lake is in Warren Township, the western in Avon Township. It is named for early settler Alexander Druce. Third Lake was originally Chittenden Lake. Myron Chittenden, from Vermont, purchased land on the north side of the lake. The Village of Third Lake was incorporated in 1959 and is partly in Lake Villa Township. Fourth Lake and Lake Miltmore were once considered one lake and in Avon Township. Today they are two lakes in Lake Villa Township. The Aaron F. Miltimore family came to the area in 1839.

Elijah Haines, in his writings, references a Slough Lake. For several years, it was commonly known as Duck Lake. This lake has been in Lake Villa Township since 1912 and is presently called Douglas Lake.

The eastern part of Long Lake is in Avon Township, the rest in Grant Township.

With so many lakes in the area, it is not surprising that resorts, summer hotels, and camps were established. Some of the farmers took in summer guests. Other recreational opportunities found in Avon Township before 1940 included a swimming pool, a roller rink, and sport clubs.

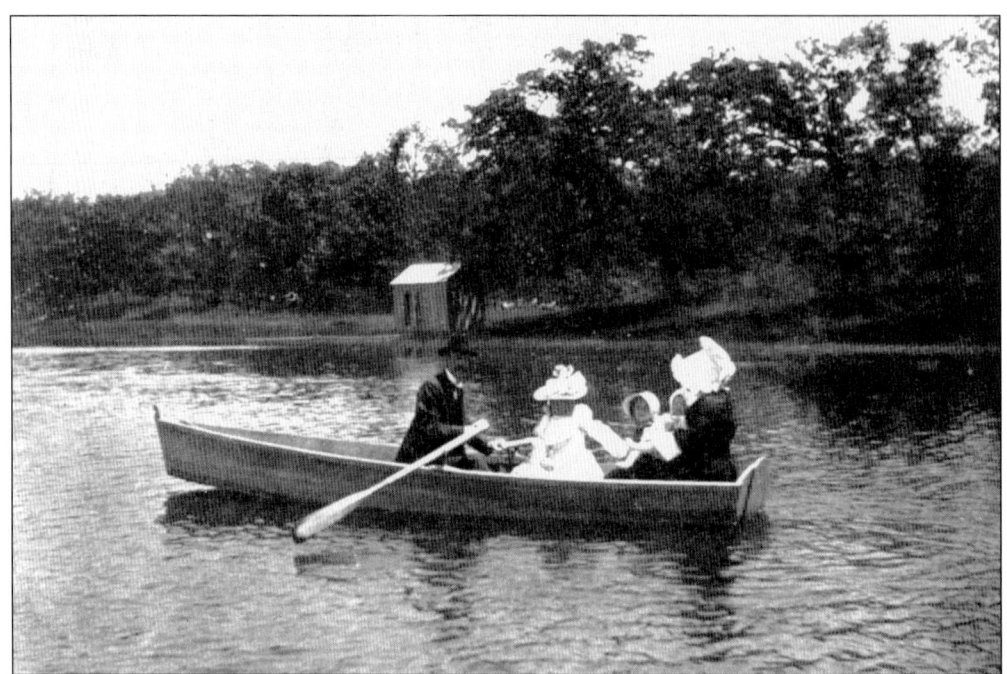

Although this 1906 postcard is labeled "Round Lake Hotel, P. O. Hainesville," it could have pictured any Avon Township lake during that time frame.

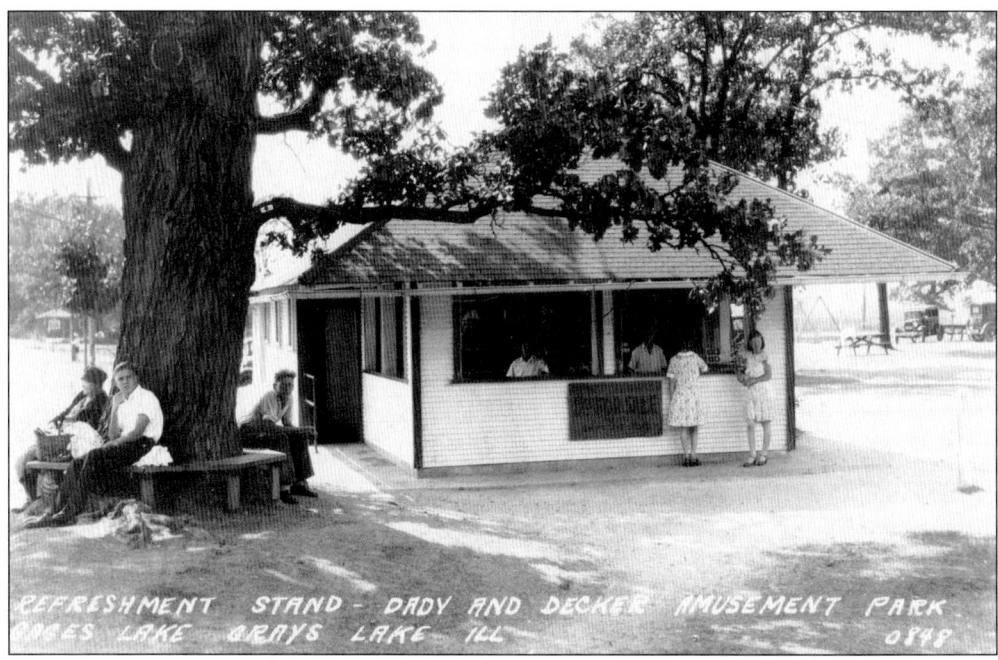

Dady and Decker Picnic Park was on the northwest shore of Gages Lake. The property now has townhomes. Gages Lake was named for John Gage, who came to the area in 1836. Gages Lake is in Warren Township with parts of it within the Grayslake village limits.

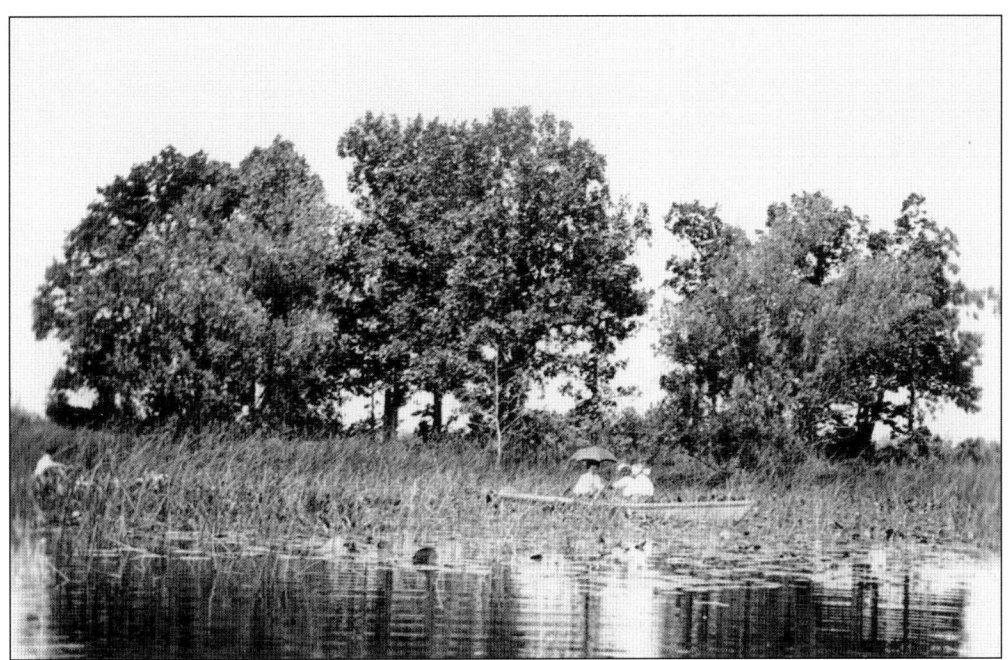

Druce Lake is named for Alexander Druce, who came from New York and settled on the south bank of the lake. On early maps, Druce Lake is often referred to as Second Lake. Part of Washington Street was once called Druce Lake Road.

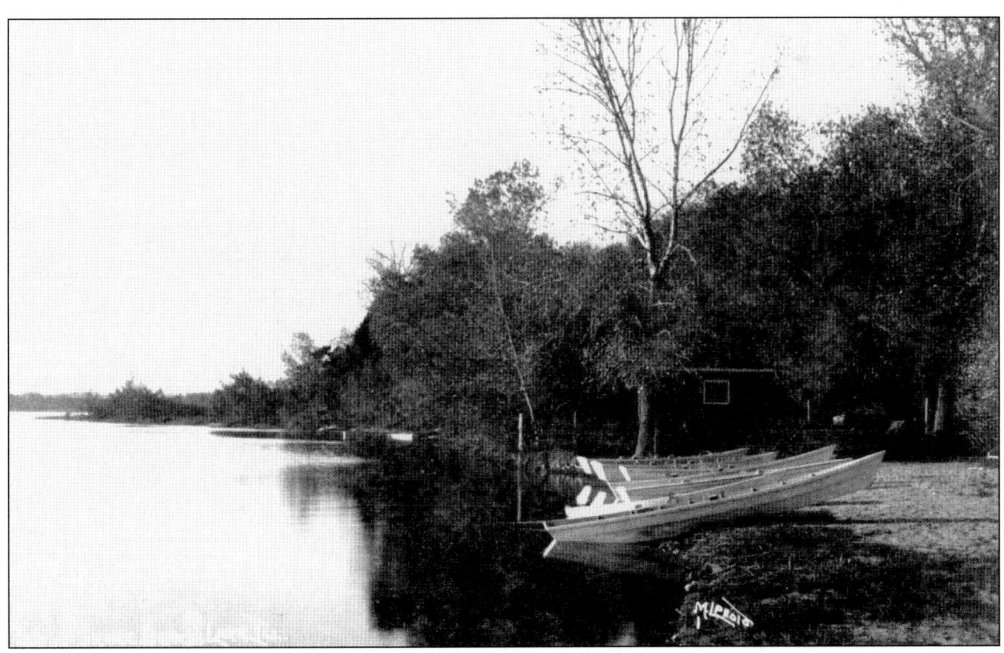

Druce Lake is bisected by a township line. The west shore, seen here, is in Avon Township. The east shore is in Warren Township. Some parts of Druce Lake have a Lake Villa address.

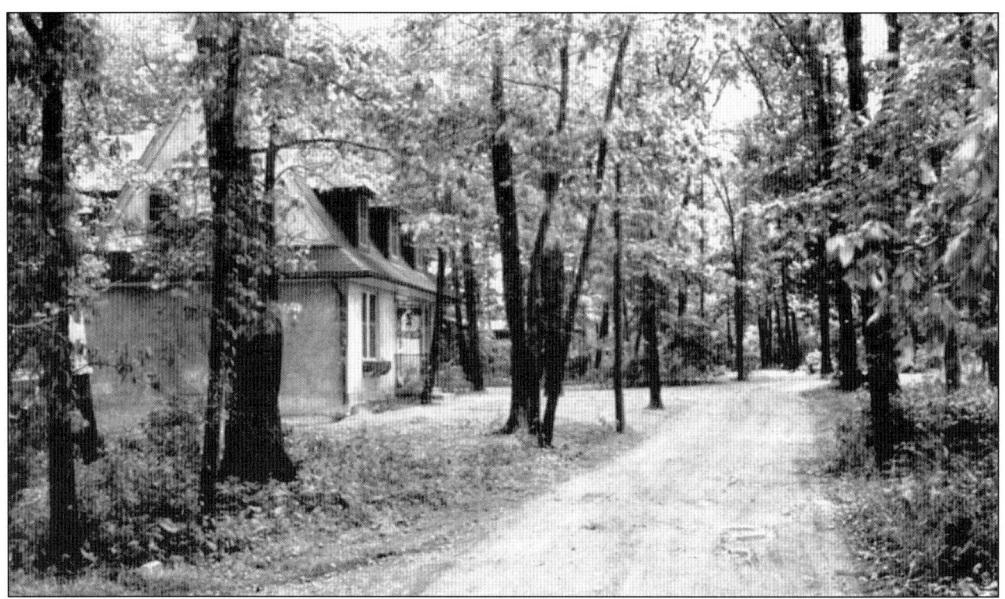

Association House started acquiring property in 1914 and added land in 1922. The postcard image above shows the entrance to its Druce Lake Camp. In the view below, a screened-in, open-air cabin is in the foreground. A larger cottage is hidden behind the trees. These views date from around 1940.

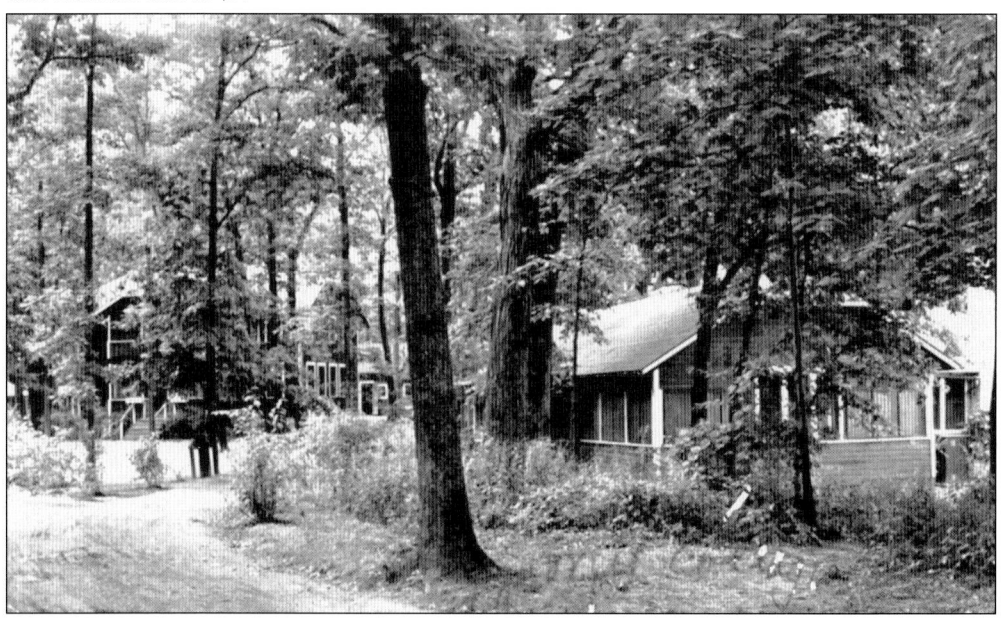

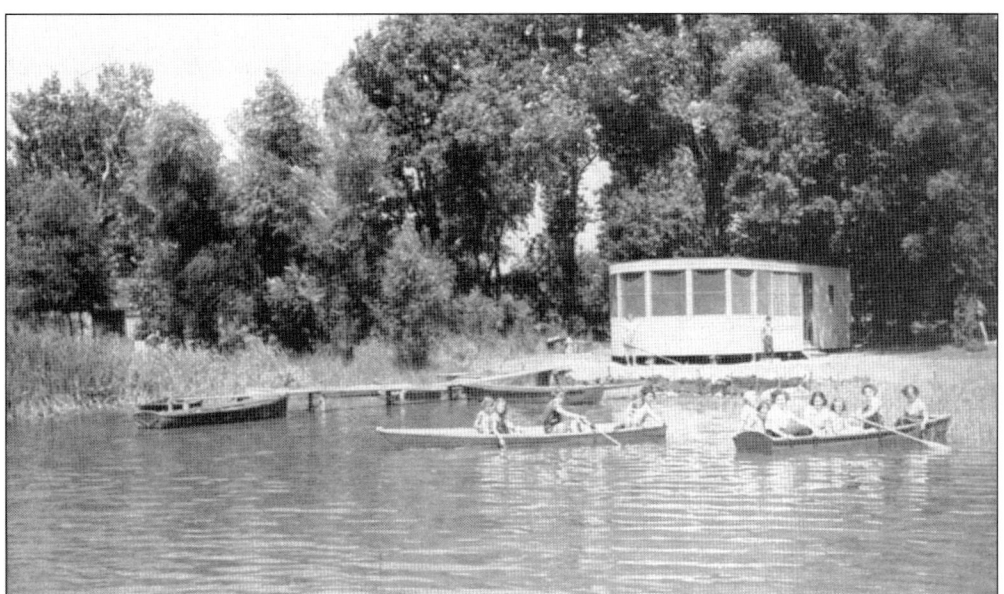

In 1926, the Druce Lake Association House Camp was incorporated. Documents tell that it was formed to do settlement work among the poor people of Chicago. This included maintaining summer camps and playgrounds for their benefit. The image above shows the camp's boathouse on Druce Lake, while the image below shows the campers enjoying the camp pool. (Courtesy of Lake County Discovery Museum.)

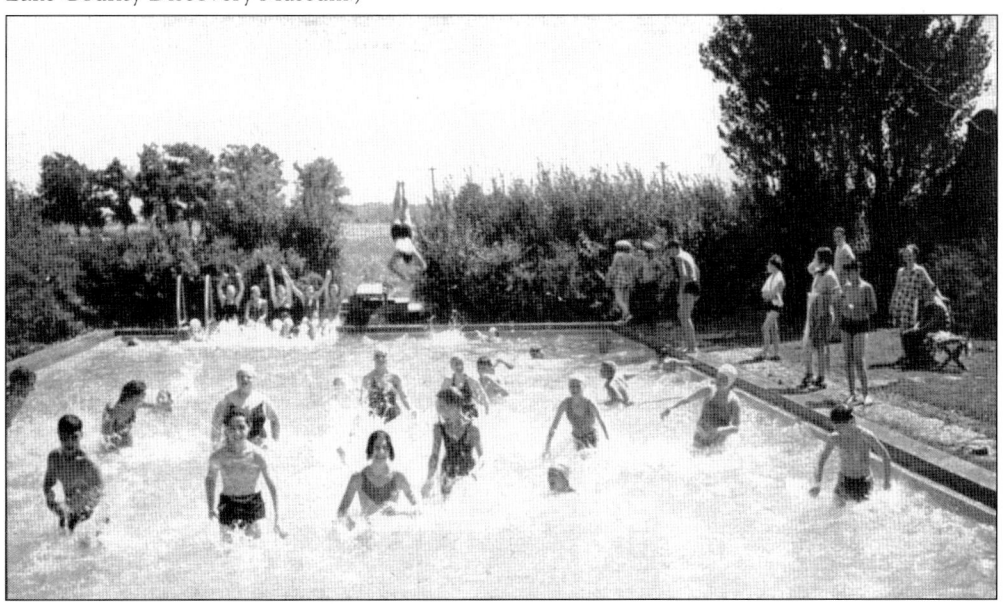

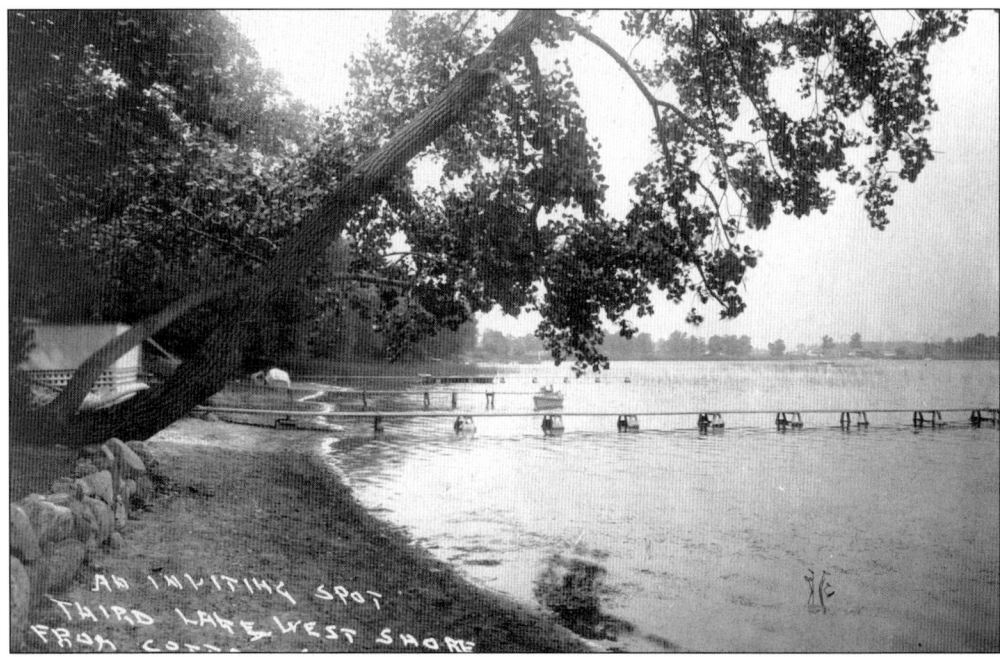

On early maps, Third Lake is often referred to as Chittenden Lake, named for the Chittenden family. Myron Chittenden purchased land on the north side of the lake in the 1840s. The photograph above is the west shore of Third Lake, while the image below is the east shore.

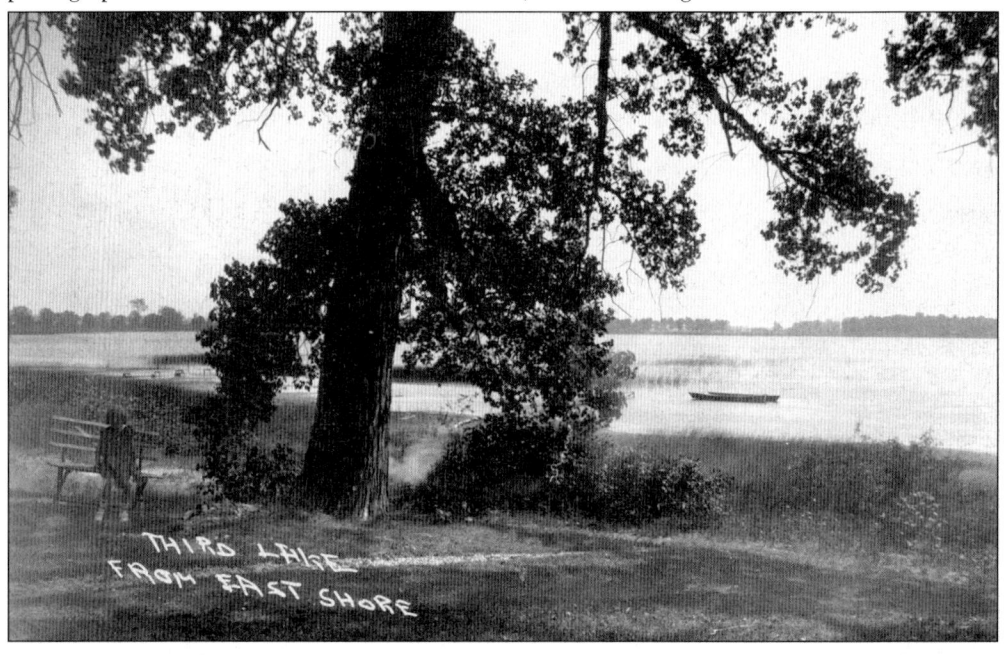

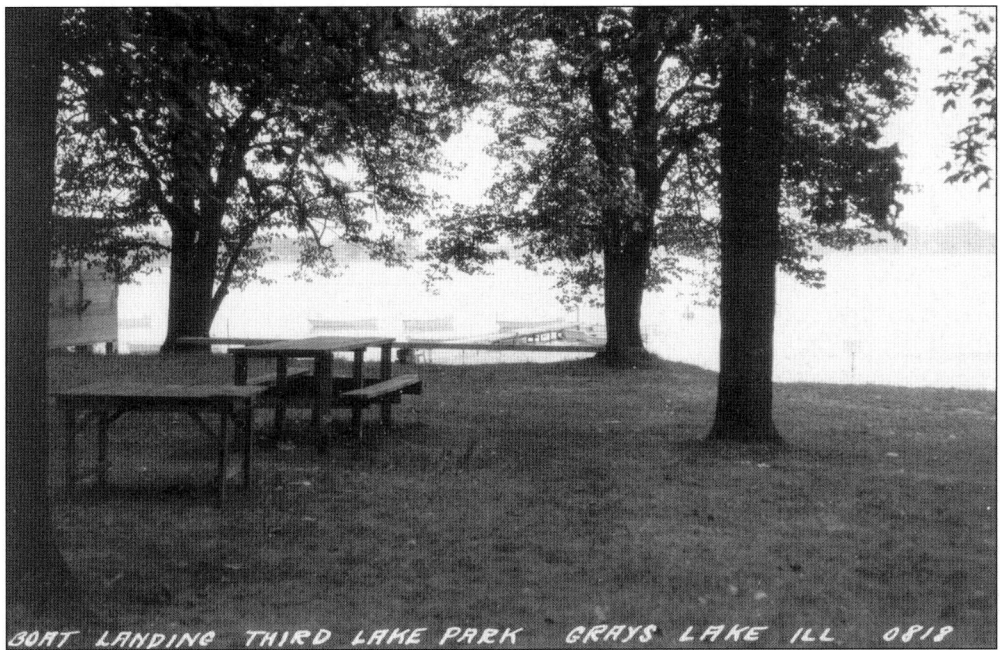

Third Lake Park was located on the south shore of the lake with an entrance off Linden Lane. During its years of operation, the owners have included Porter Duell, Ed Hall and his two brothers-in-law, and Leonard DeGraff. The land is now controlled by the Lake County Forest Preserve.

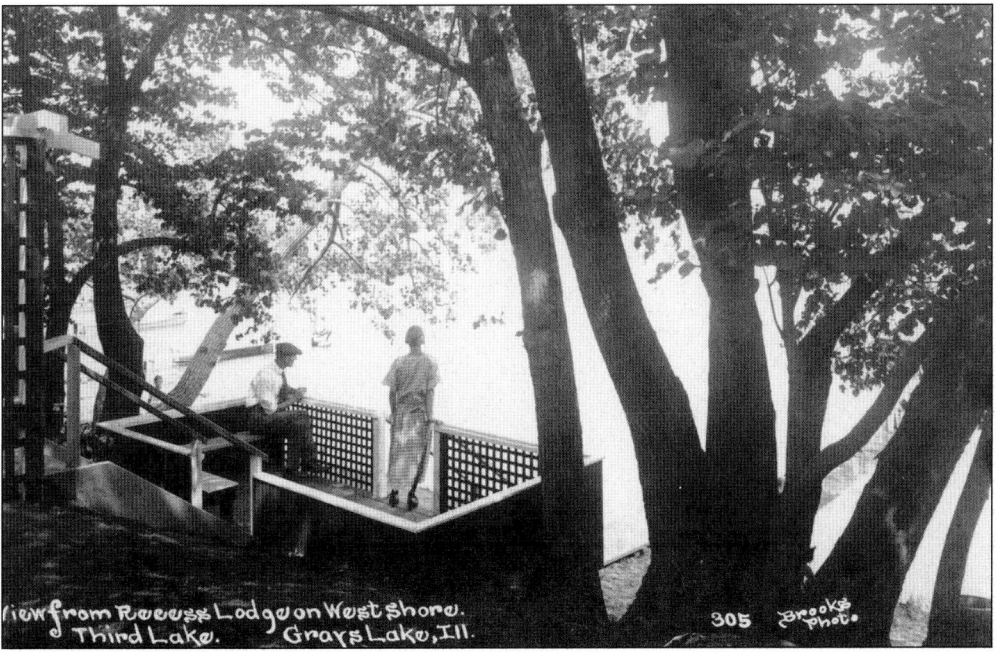

This lake overlook was on the property of one of the many lodges and summer cottages located along the shore of Third Lake. The lodges and cottages have been replaced with permanent residences.

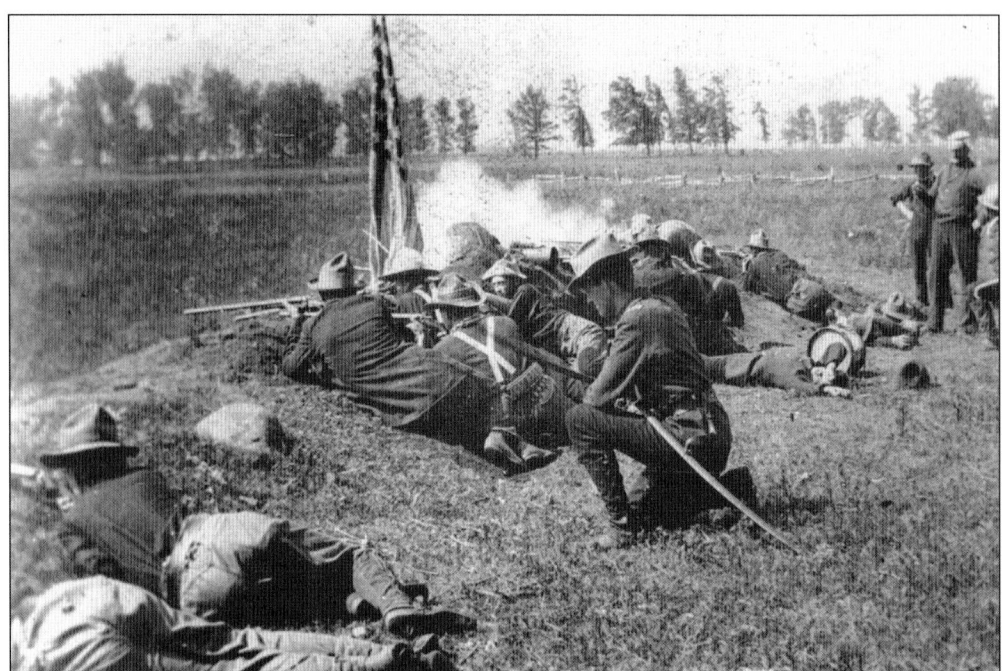

With the outbreak of the Spanish-American War in 1898, inventor and film producer Edward Amet of Waukegan re-created the war as reported in newspapers. Using friends and family as the actors, Amet reenacted the Battle of San Juan Hill at Third Lake as seen in this still. (Courtesy of Lake County Discovery Museum.)

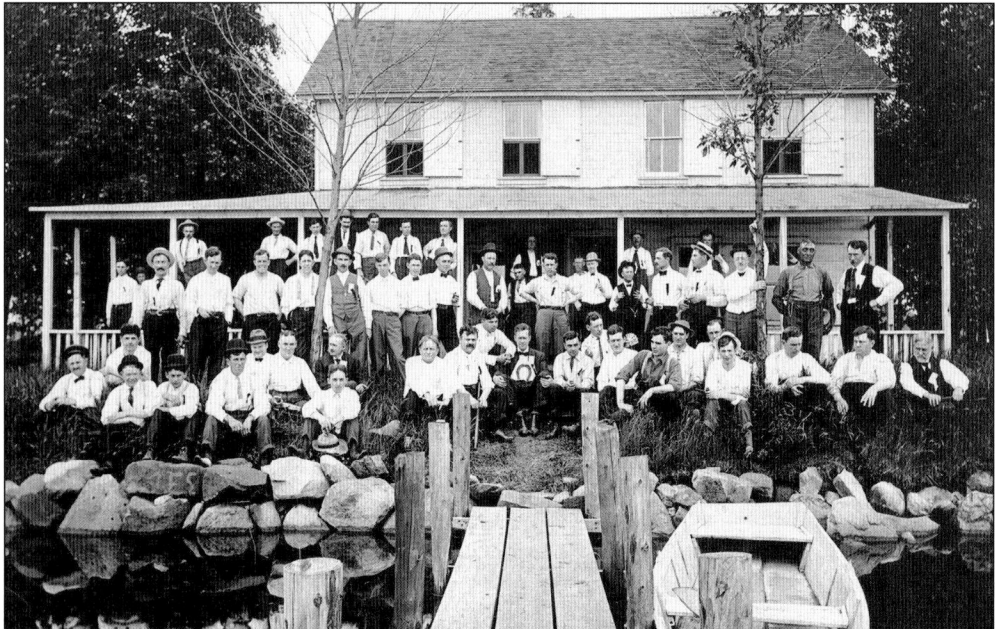

The Waukegan Bachelor Club, an elite male social group, was incorporated in 1891. It was composed of 25 men who purchased property and erected a clubhouse overlooking the east shore of Third Lake. Each year, opening day was a celebration, as seen in this 1908 photograph. In the early 1920s, the property was subdivided. (Courtesy of Waukegan Historical Society.)

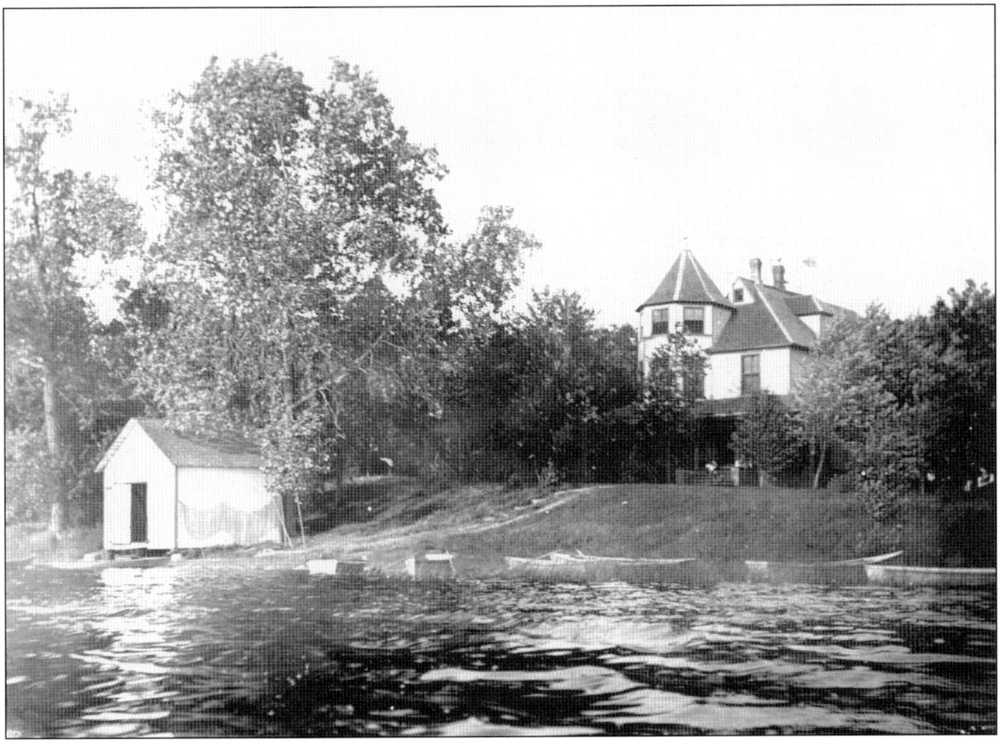

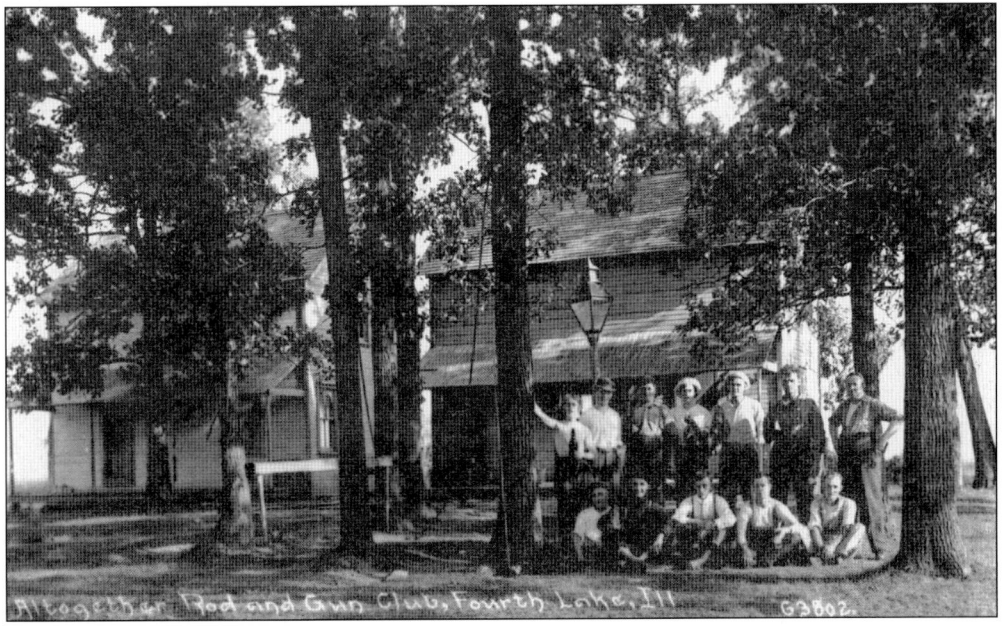

Pictured here is the Prospect Bluff Hotel, which was in operation around 1907. It was located on Fourth Lake, which was formerly in Avon Township but now is in Lake Villa Township.

In addition to private residences and summer hotels, various clubs had property on the lakes. A rod and gun club had a clubhouse on Fourth Lake in the early 1900s.

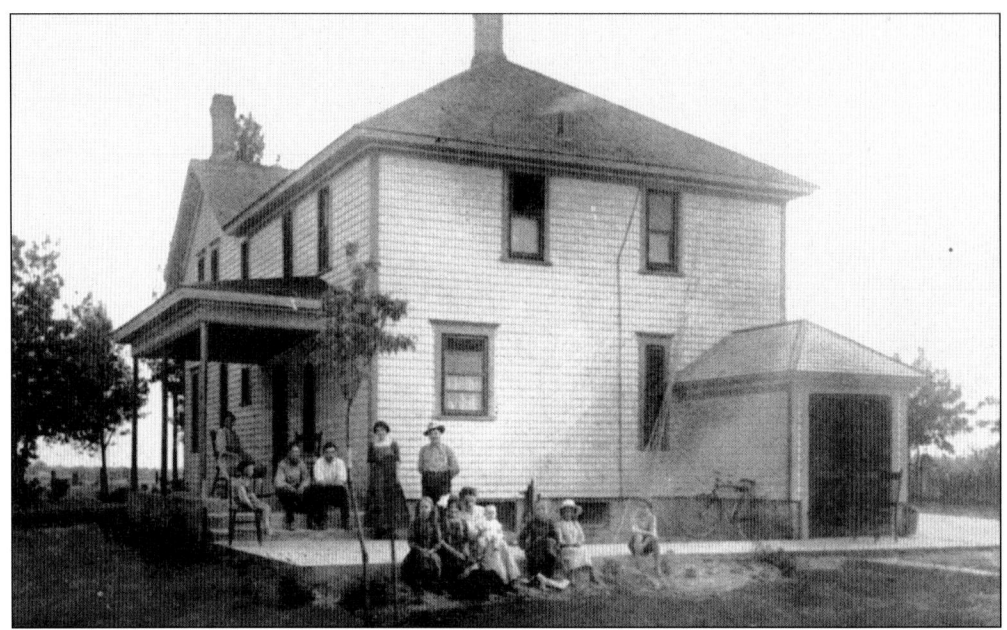

The Sheldon farmhouse at Fourth Lake became a boardinghouse in the summer months and catered to vacationers from the city.

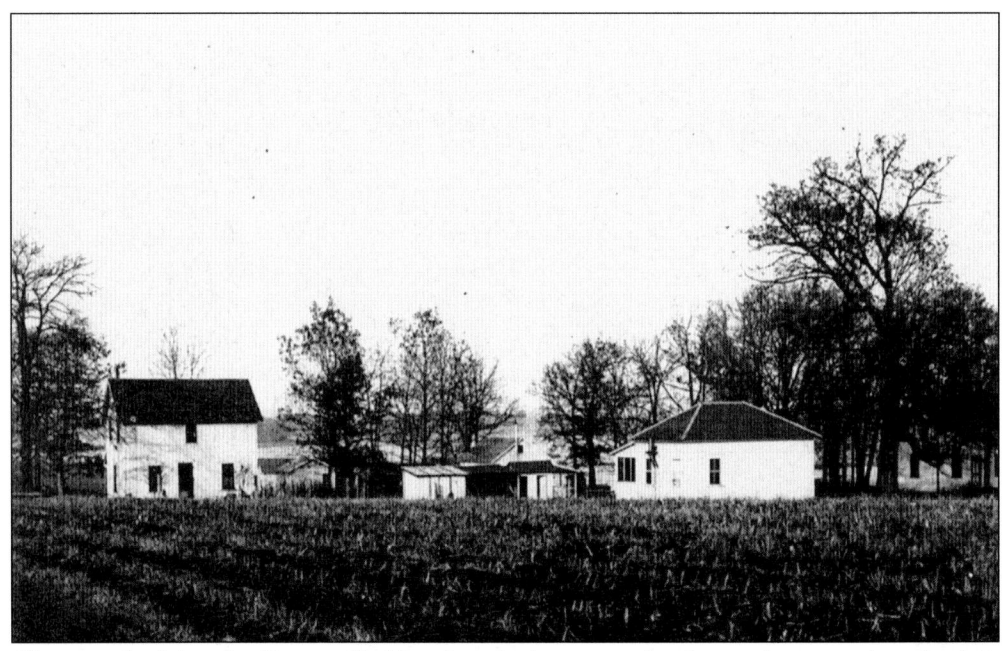

Closer to the lake, the George Sheldon farm had cottages for those who wanted to do their own housekeeping.

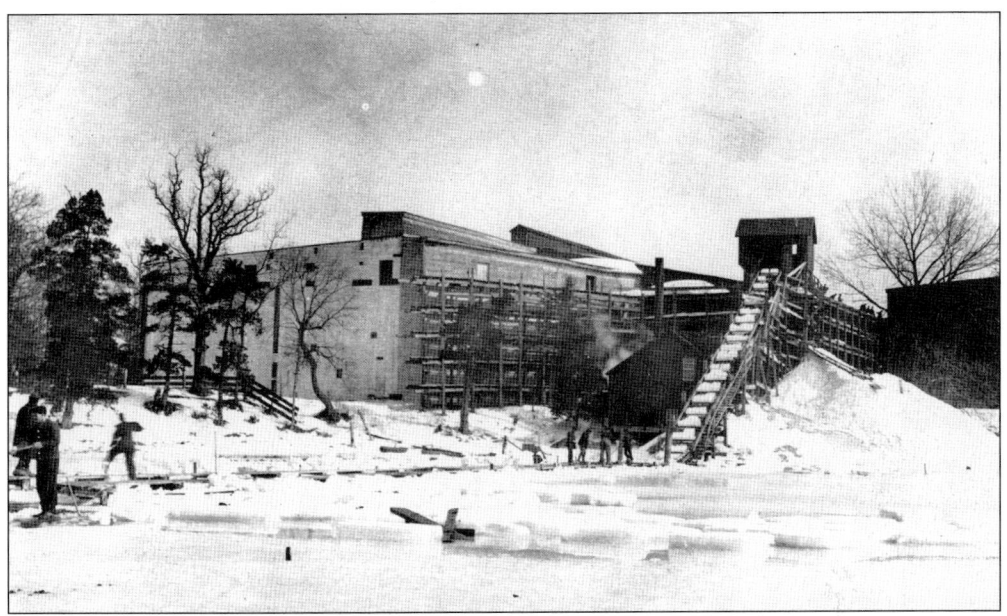

The icehouse on Taylor's Lake was built in 1886 by the Knickerbocker Ice Company and sold later to the Consumer Ice Company. It was constructed on eight acres along the east shore and had a railroad spur to the Wisconsin Central Railroad. (Courtesy of Grayslake Historical Society.)

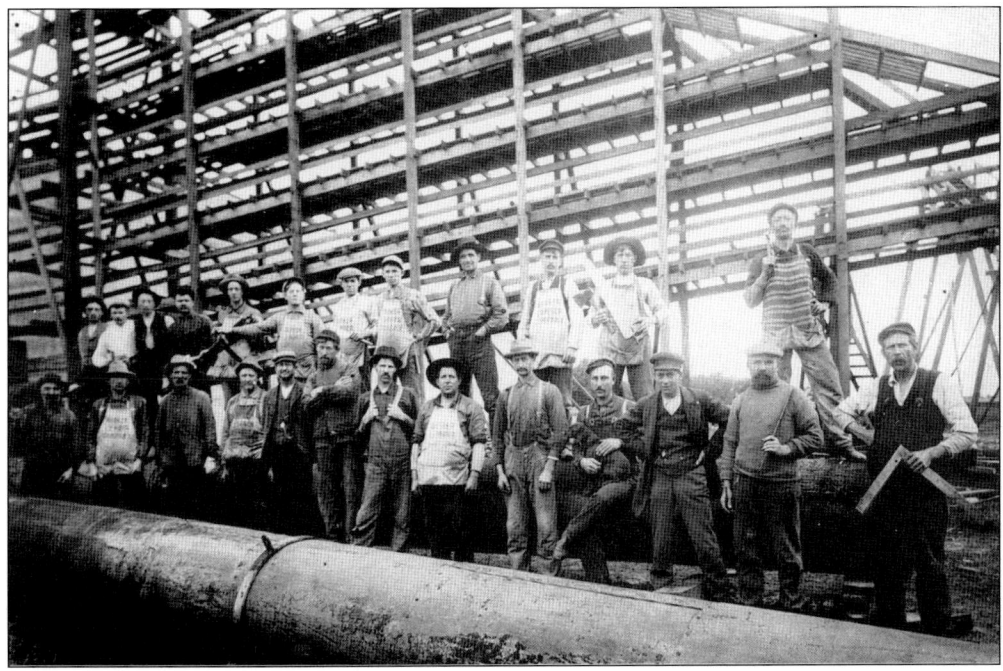

It took many men to build and maintain an icehouse. Pictured here are workers taking a break from their tasks. The date of this picture is around 1898. (Courtesy of Grayslake Historical Society.)

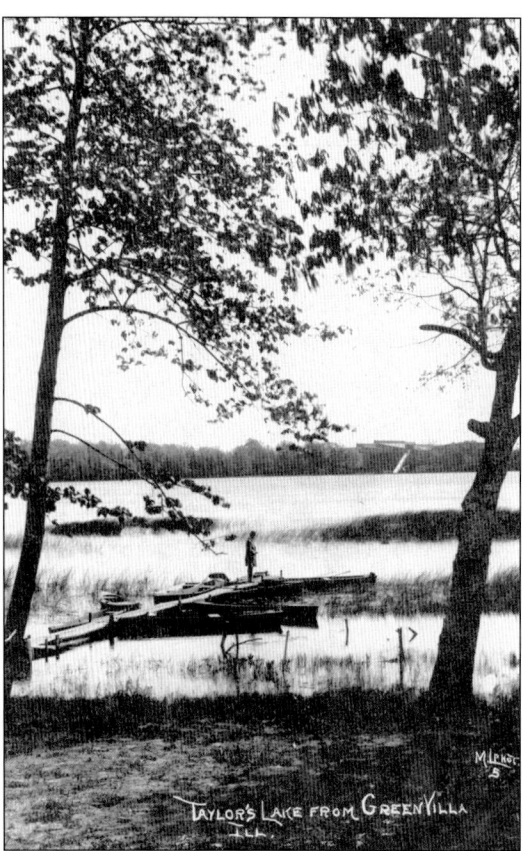

This image from a postcard dated 1912 was taken from a summer place on Taylor's Lake called Green Villa operated by a Mrs. L. Greene. The icehouse is visible across the lake.

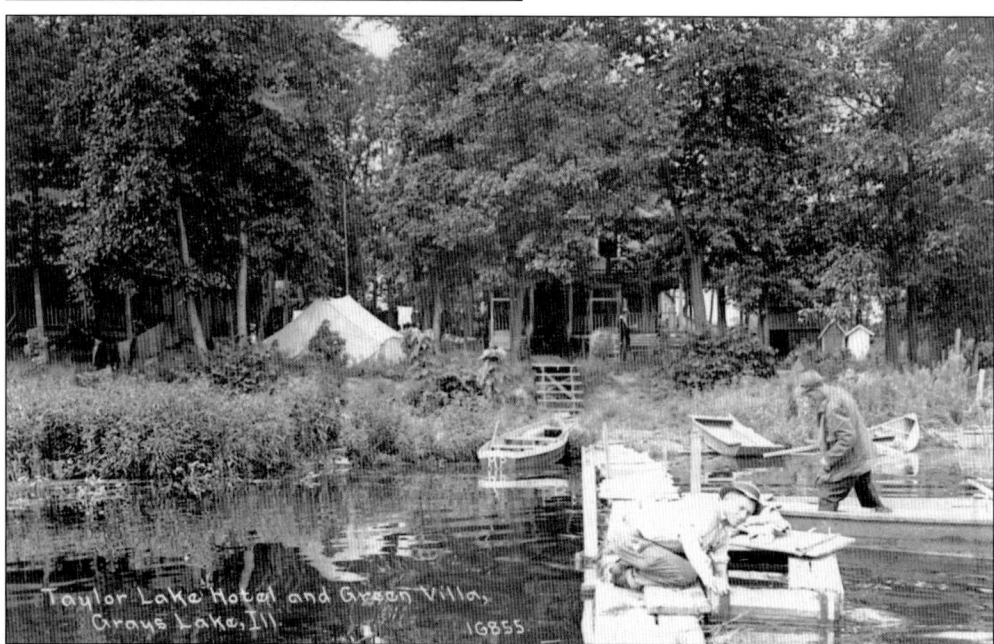

The Taylor Lake Hotel and the Green Villa summer hotel were located on the west shore of the lake. (Courtesy of Lake County Discovery Museum.)

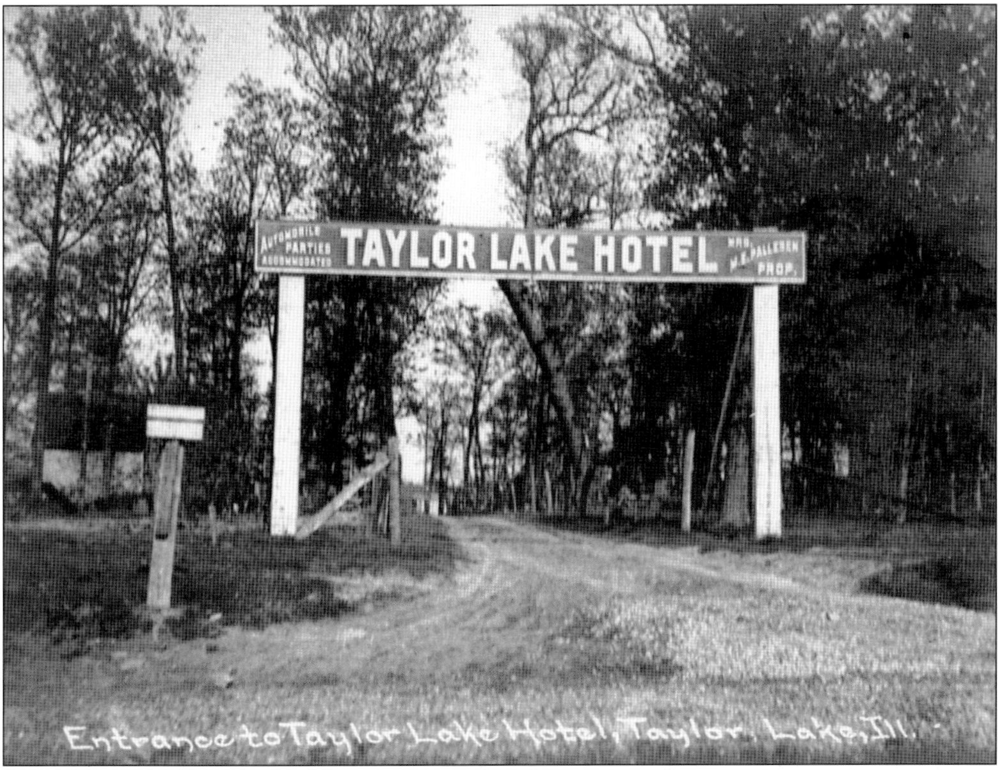

The image above documents that Mary E. Pallesen ran a summer hotel at Taylor's Lake. The hotel was a large two-story, foursquare house with a wraparound porch. The picture below illustrates that visitors enjoyed country life as well as lake activities. (Courtesy of Al Westerman.)

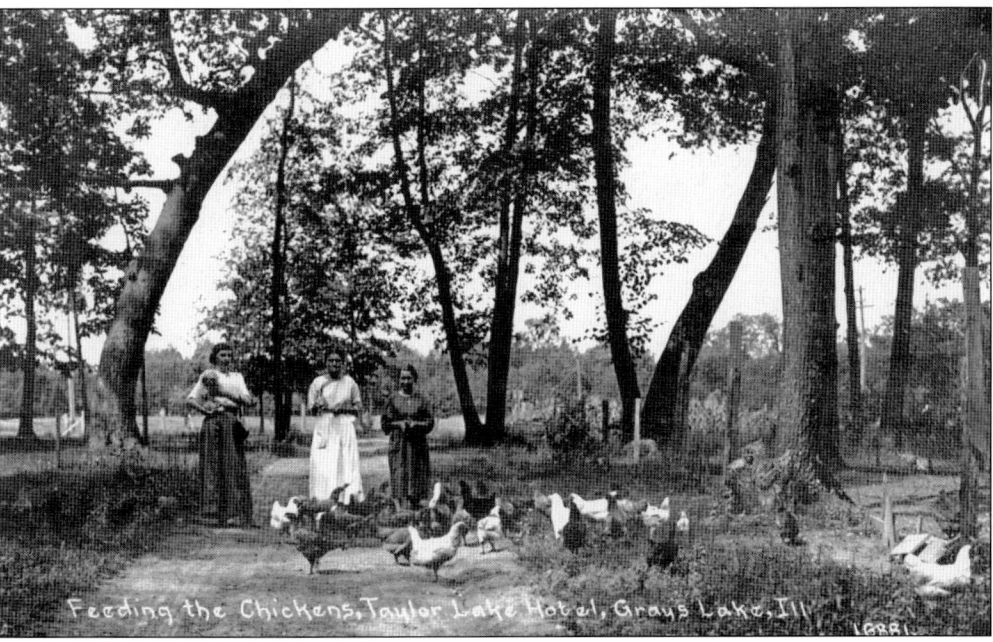

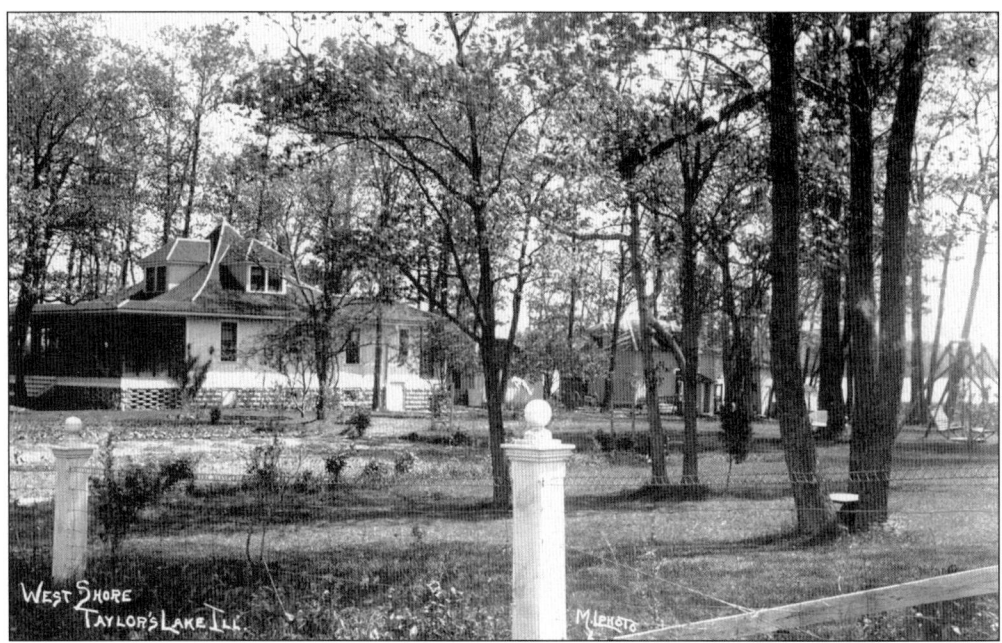

Taylor's Lake had private summer cottages as well as summer hotels. This scene is on the west shore. The summer cottages and hotels were owned by people who lived in Chicago and in suburbs the rest of the year.

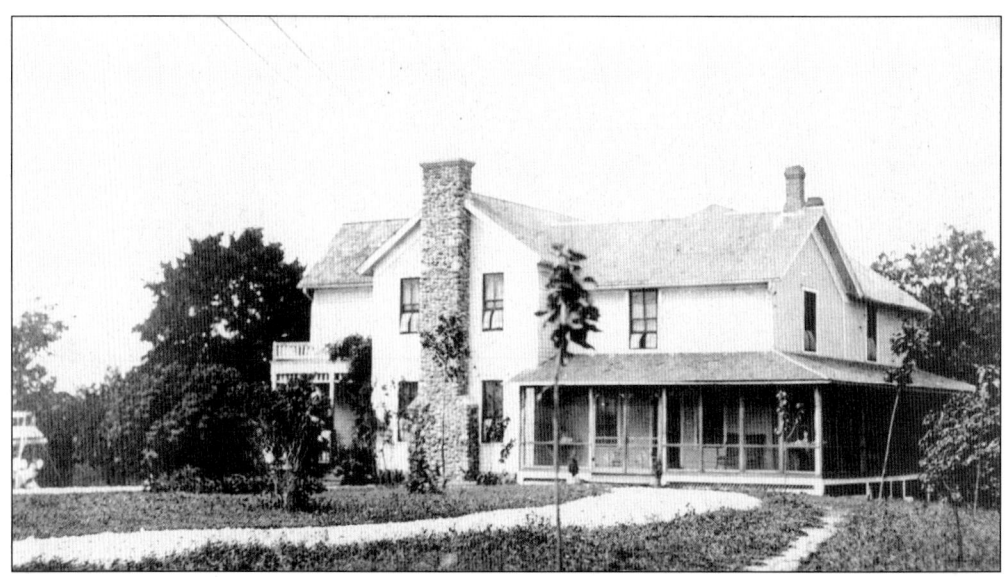

The summer residence of Charles M. MacFarlane, called Lilac Farm, was on the south shore of Taylor's Lake. He was an official with Wilson and Company in Chicago. MacFarlane is credited with changing the name of Taylor's Lake to Highland Lake about 1923. (Courtesy of Grayslake Historical Society)

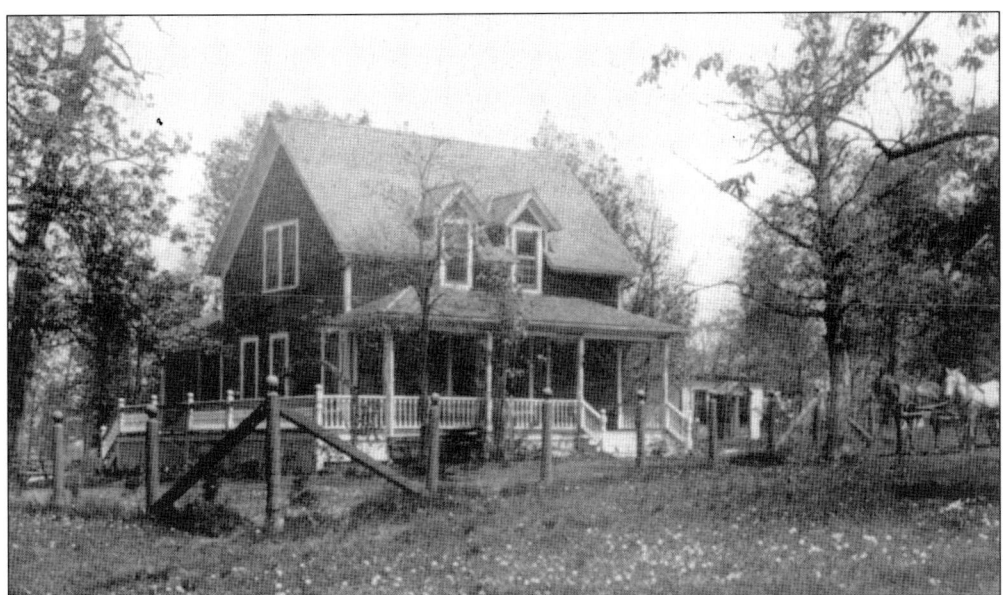

Rose Cottage was on the banks of Round Lake. Even though the houses are large, very often they were used only as summer homes or summer hotels. Vacationers traveled by train and then were transported by horse-drawn conveyances to their favorite vacation spot. This image is on a postcard postmarked 1909.

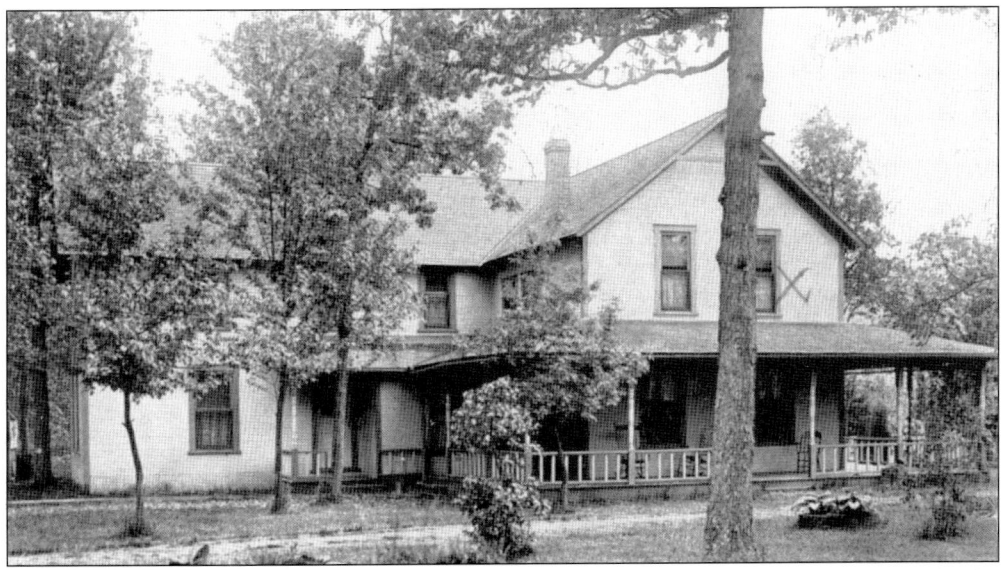

The Cedars Hotel was a summer resort in Edwards Subdivision on the east shore of Round Lake managed by Frank C. Sundwall. In 1919, Sundwall was one of the incorporators for the Round Lake Golf Club.

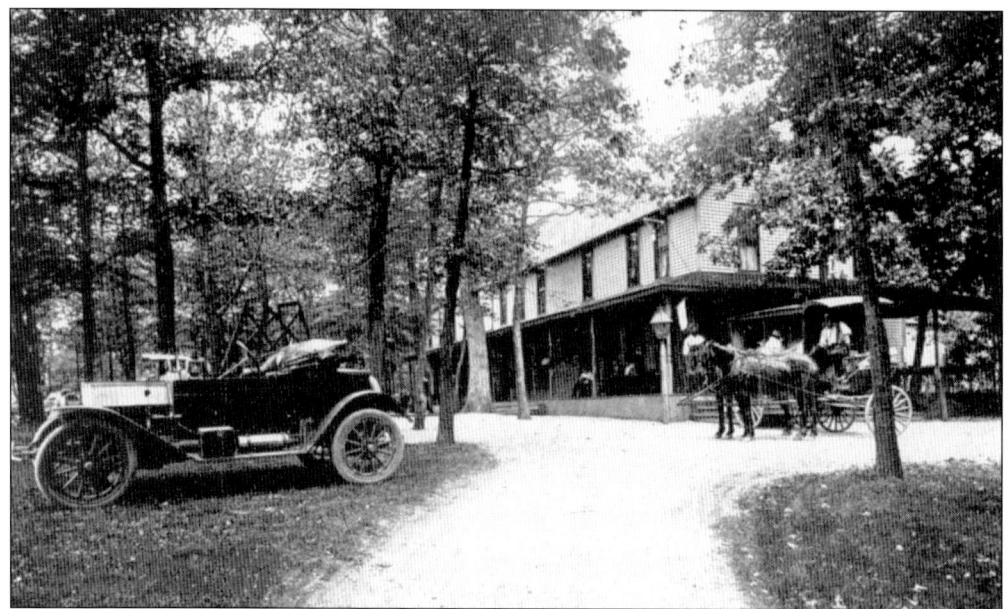

In 1900, George Renehan opened the Avon Park Hotel on the eastern shore of Round Lake. The summer hotel became locally known as Renehan's Resort. The hotel had a large veranda, 140 feet long and 14 feet wide. This postcard view is dated 1916.

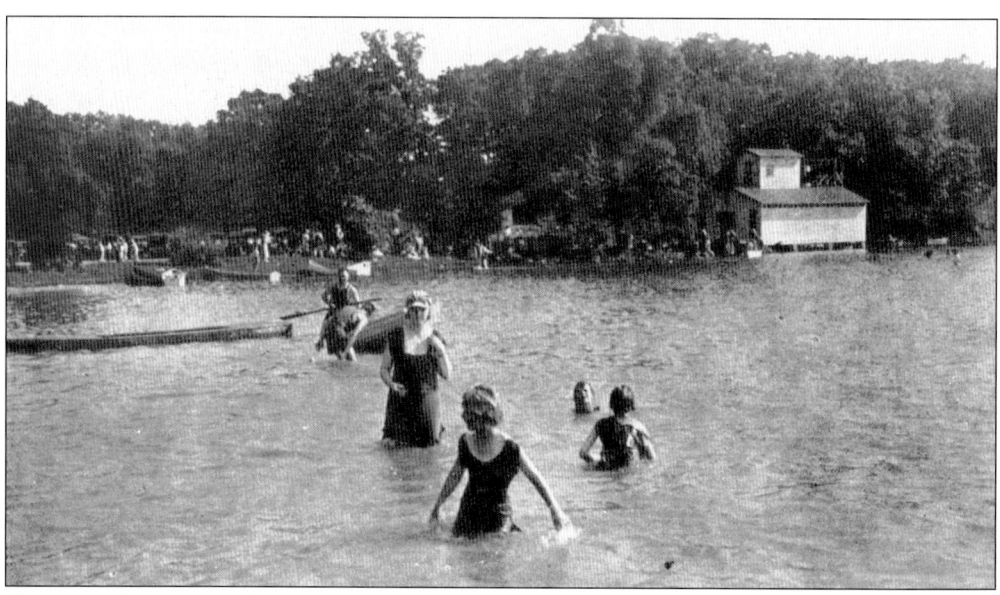

Guests at the Avon Park Hotel enjoyed swimming, boating, and fishing. Renehan hosted trap shoots, baseball games, company picnics, and wrestling shows. He also advertised having a museum, tennis courts, and croquet grounds.

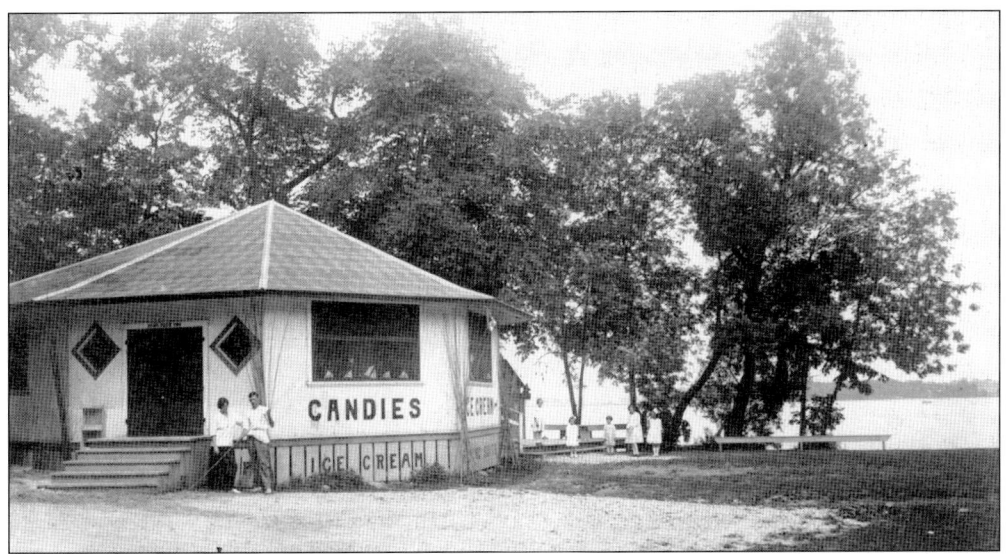

Day visitors to the Avon Park Hotel purchased refreshments and souvenirs at the inn, which is pictured in the photograph above. The picture below shows the interior of the inn.

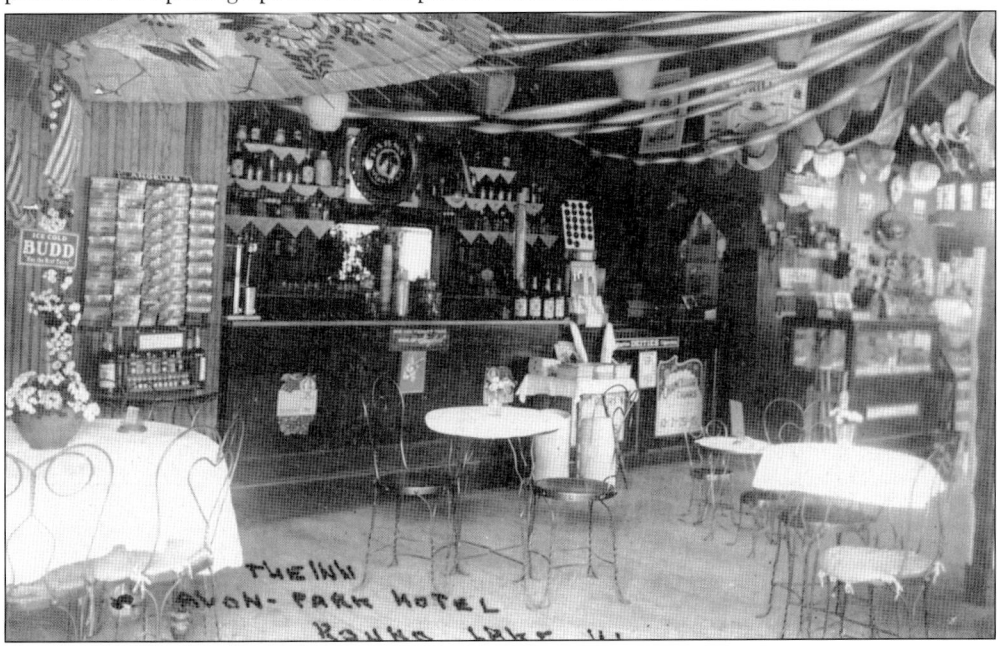

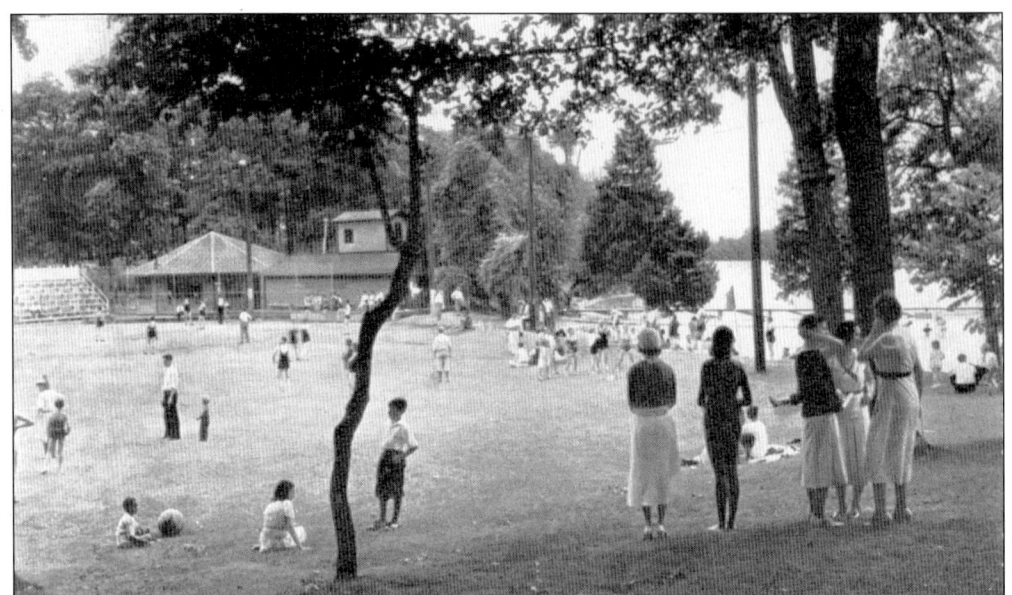

The Avon Park Hotel had spacious grounds. In addition to the hotel and inn, there were cottages and a dance pavilion. This postcard is dated 1942, but the picture was taken in the 1930s.

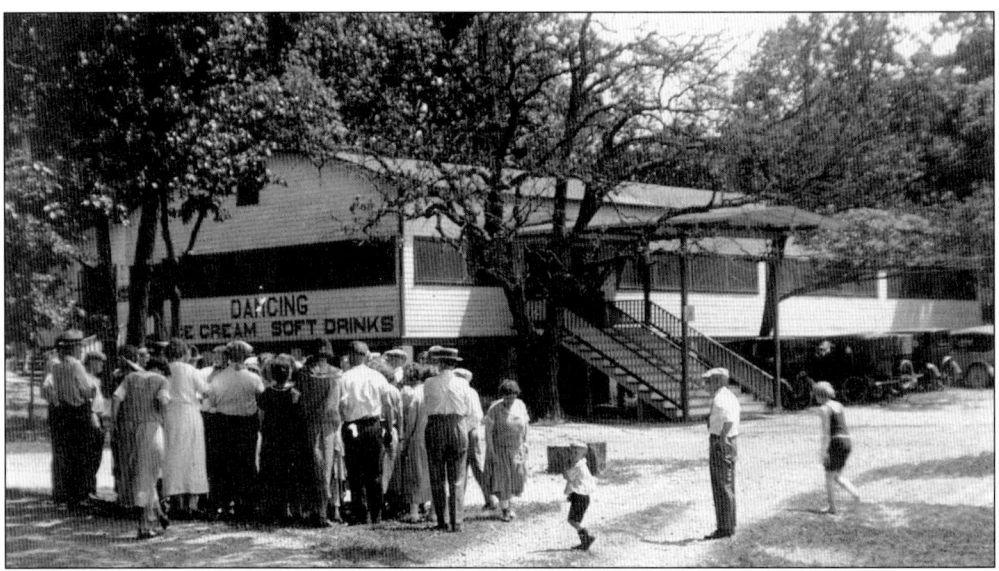

George Renehan built the dance pavilion in 1921. The Grayslake Volunteer Fire Department held St. Patrick's Day dances here. After the resort closed about 1941, the pavilion became known as Posh's Lakewood Park Pavilion. This photograph was taken in the 1920s.

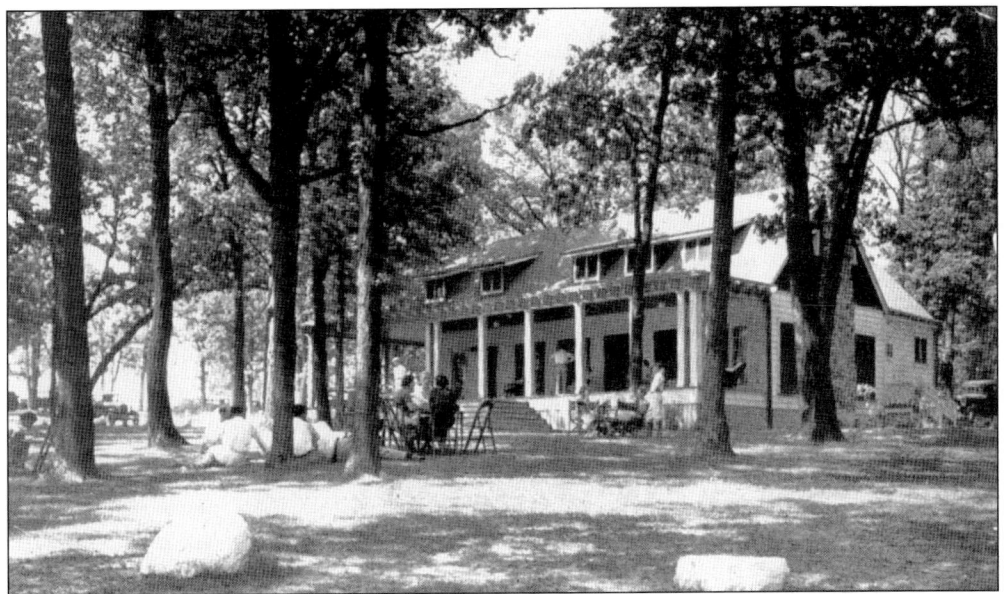

Porter Duell filed the plat of Shorewood Subdivision, located along the northern shore of Round Lake, in 1910. In addition, he constructed an 18-hole golf course and called it Shorewood Country Club. The clubhouse was moved to Cedar Lake Road and became the second village hall of Round Lake Beach. This scene dates to the 1930s.

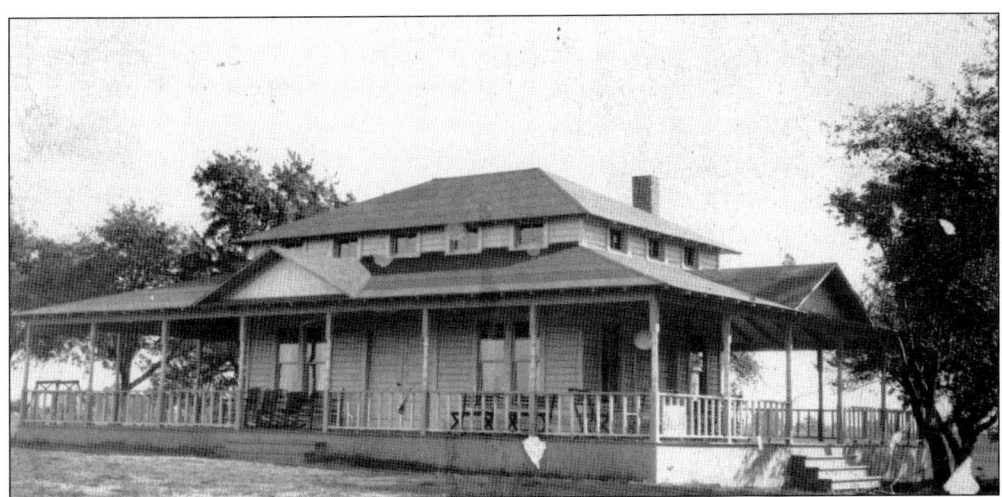

The Round Lake Golf Club was located on the east side of Hainesville Road between Rollins and Shorewood Roads. The Round Lake Golf Club incorporated in late 1919 and began acquiring property. In 1968, the golf course and clubhouse were sold with the name changed to Renwood Country Club. The land presently belongs to the Round Lake Park District. (Courtesy of Grayslake Historical Society.)

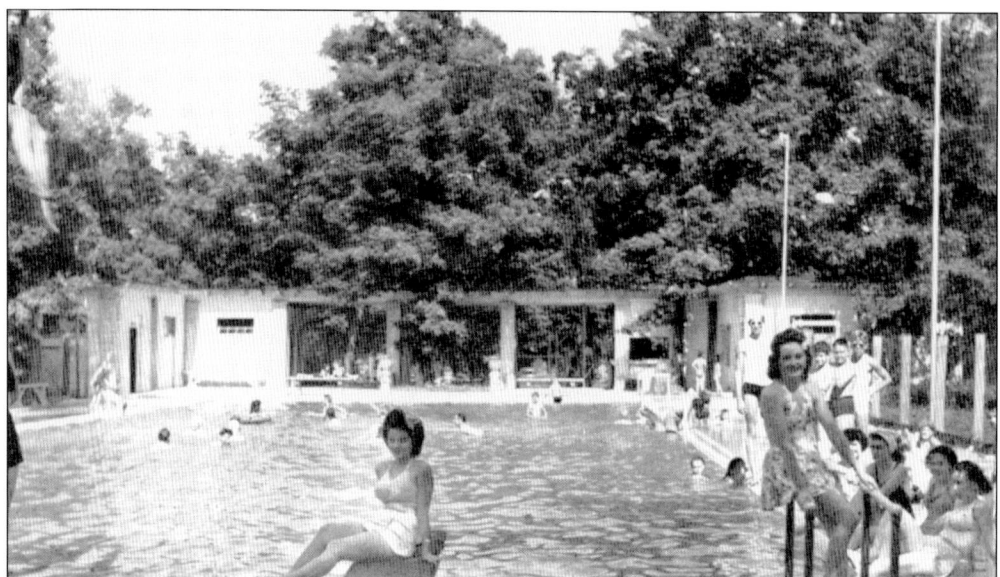

In 1932, on seven wooded acres, Carl F. Clausen opened a 115-by-42-foot swimming pool and named it Artemis for the goddess of woods and water. It was located on the west side of Hainesville Road, about a block north of present-day Washington Street. The pool had a diving tower and two springboards. The pool is seen in the image above. On the same property, Clausen also operated a roller rink, where a roller rink still operates. The first roller rink structure is seen in the photograph below. (Courtesy of Carl F. Clausen family.)

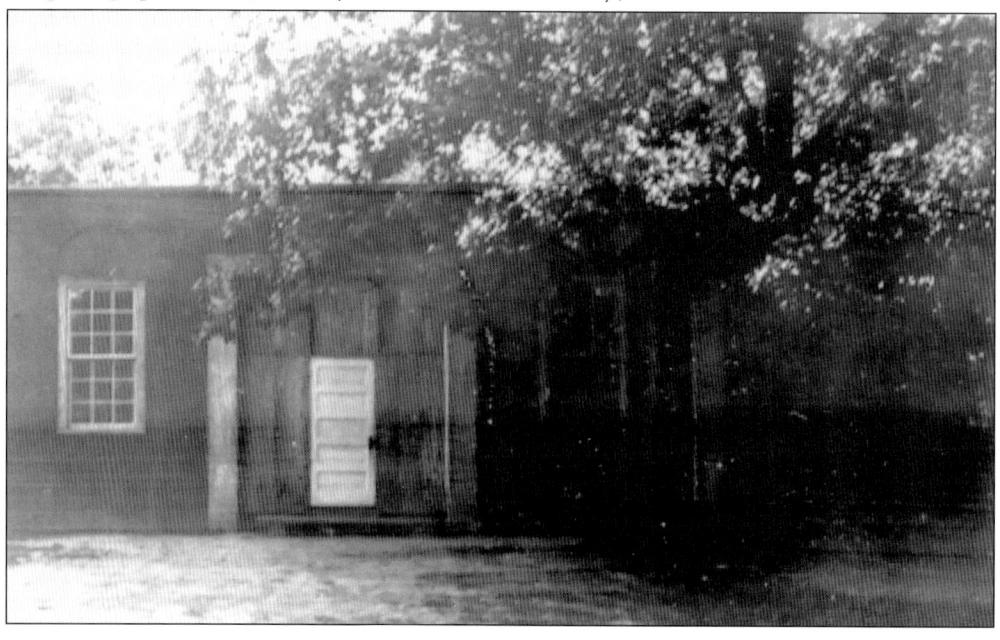

Five

THE LAND

When the early settlers arrived, they found not only lakes but also gently rolling land covered with prairie grass and groves of trees. Much of the land was swampland, later drained to make the fields tillable and buildable. The early farmers cleared the land and used the trees for lumber and fuel. On the newly tilled land, they planted crops to feed their families and animals. As their cropland produced more, they were able to sell their produce and commerce increased. The stores in these small communities sold essentials. As more people came, the land began to be used for other purposes. Gradually farms became subdivisions, and the subdivisions became part of the nearby villages. With the coming of the automobile, small-town businesses gradually disappeared. Shopping malls took away still more farmland. Former beaches were replaced with condominiums.

Forward-minded people saw the need to save land for environmental, recreational, and educational purposes. Villages and park districts acquired property for public use and forest preserves were created.

While farmland disappeared, land set aside for cemeteries continued with its intended use. Avon Township's cemeteries are varied. The smallest cemetery is the Druce Cemetery, a private family cemetery on Washington Street. Next in size is the Grayslake Cemetery, located on South Lake Street in Grayslake and maintained by the Village of Grayslake and the Grayslake Historical Society. The oldest cemetery is the Fort Hill Cemetery on Belvidere Road, just east of Fairfield Road. The east half of this burial ground is known as St. Joseph Catholic Cemetery, maintained by Ascension Cemetery of Libertyville. Avon Centre Cemetery, located on Shorewood Drive off Route 83, is the largest cemetery and is governed by a board of directors.

Two other early cemeteries, Sand Lake Cemetery and East Fox Lake Cemetery, dating from 1845, were once in Avon Township but have been in Lake Villa Township since the boundary change.

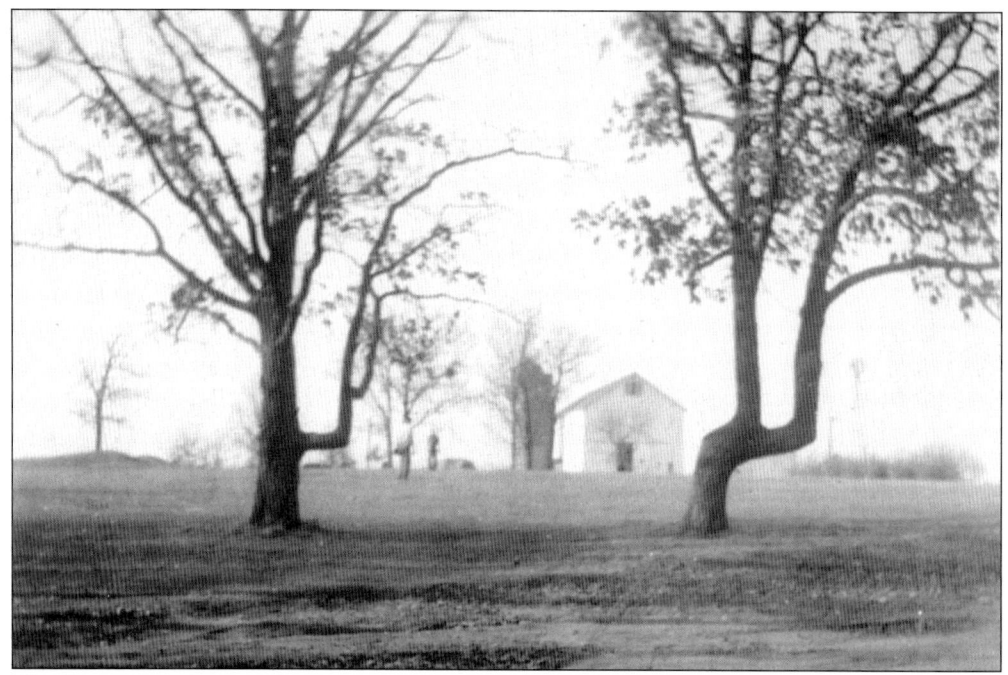

The Potawatomi Native Americans once roamed northern Illinois until they were required to leave as directed by the Black Hawk Treaty of 1832. To mark their trails, they created trail trees by shaping sapling trees. At one time, the trail trees seen here were near the Shorewood Subdivision north of Round Lake. (Courtesy of Lake County Discovery Museum.)

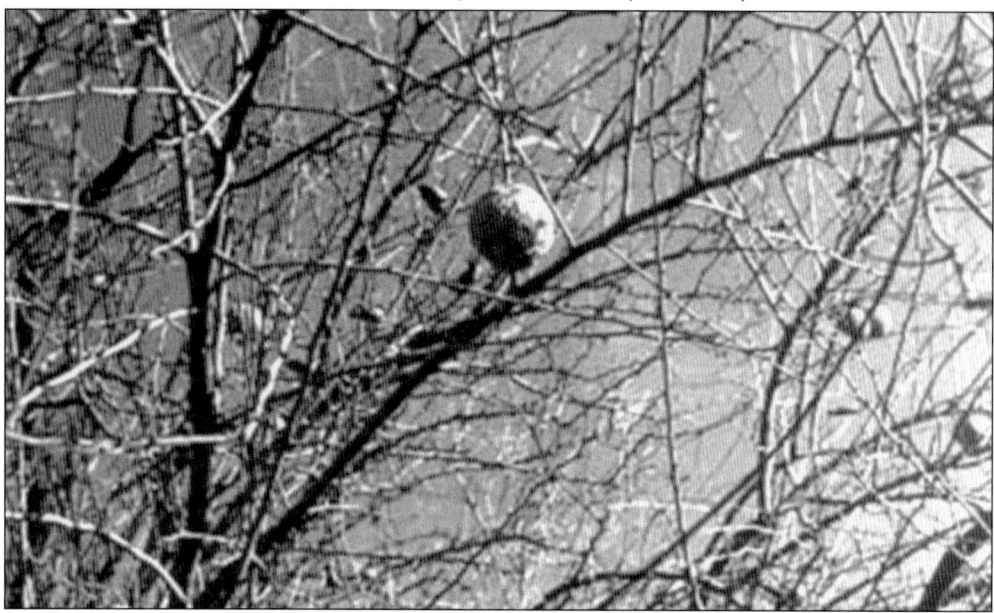

Early farmers marked the boundaries of their fields in various ways. Before the invention of barbed wire, wooden rails were used. Where stones were plentiful, they were stacked to form a fence. Many farmers in early Avon Township planted Osage orange trees, with fruit known as hedge apples. The pictured Osage orange trees were still found along Belvidere Road between Routes 83 and 45 in the early 1990s. (Courtesy of Grayslake Historical Society, Ruth Mogg Collection.)

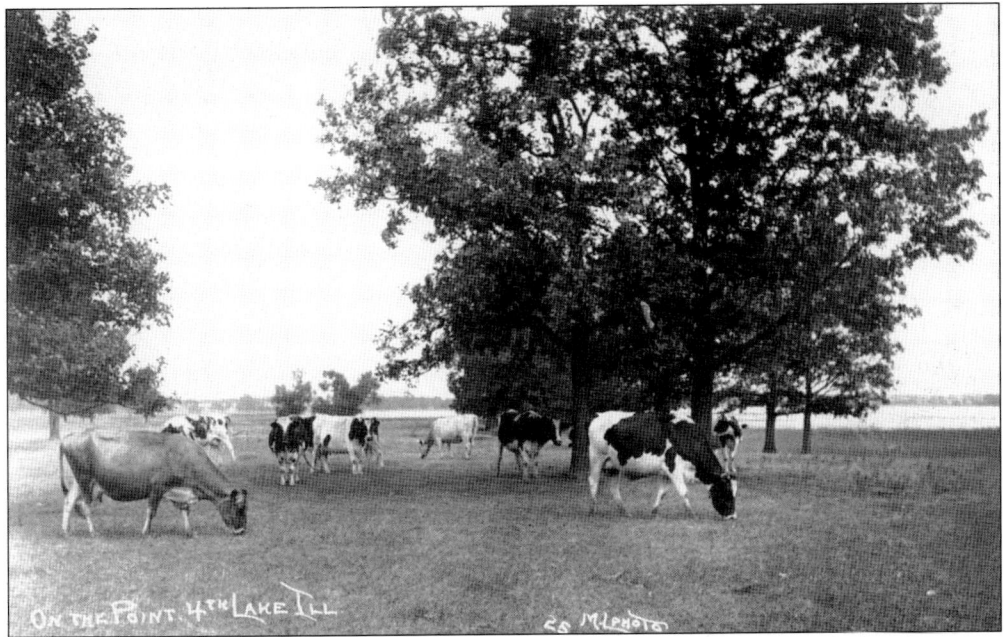

In addition to fields of corn, wheat, and oats, pastures with grazing cattle dotted the Avon Township landscape in its earlier years. The pictured cows are in a pasture adjacent to Fourth Lake on the former 84-acre George Sheldon farm.

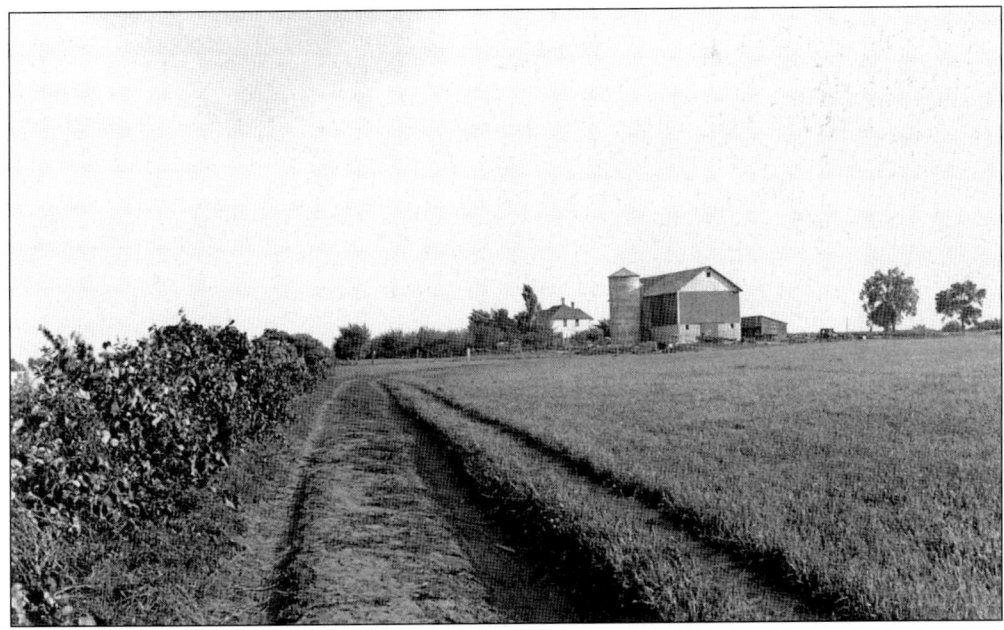

These cropped fields were on the George Sheldon farm at Fourth Lake. Before 1912, this farm was in Avon Township. Today his former property is in Lake Villa Township but has been annexed to the village of Grayslake as the Stoney Ridge subdivision.

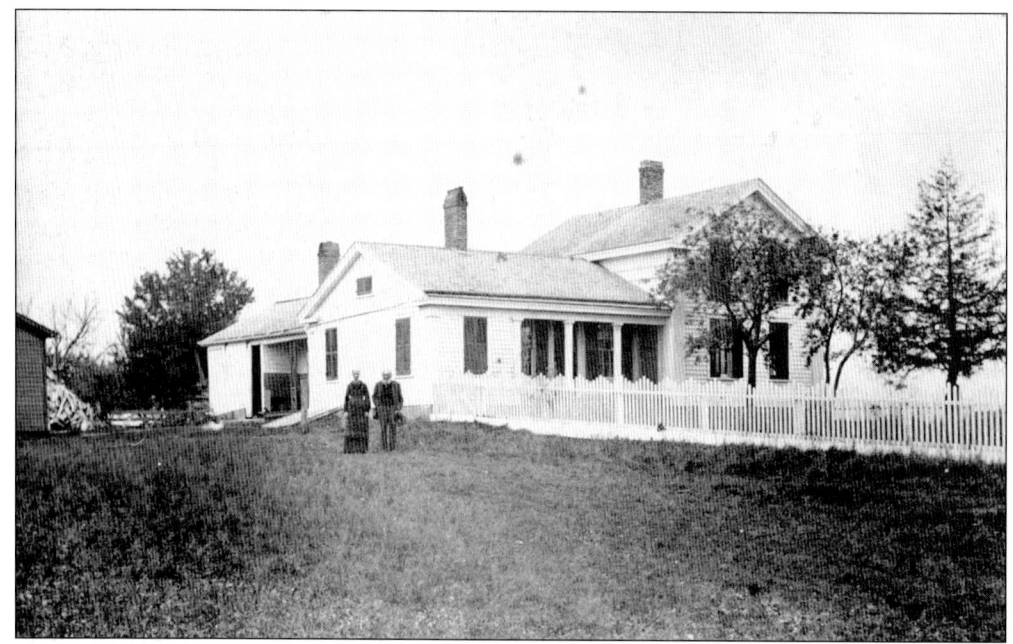

After coming to the area in 1837, Lawrence Forvor eventually owned 400 acres in the Grayslake area. Pictured here are his daughter Emma and her husband, John Wicks, at the family homestead. St. Gilbert Catholic Church on Belvidere Road is on the former Forvor farm. (Courtesy of Grayslake Historical Society.)

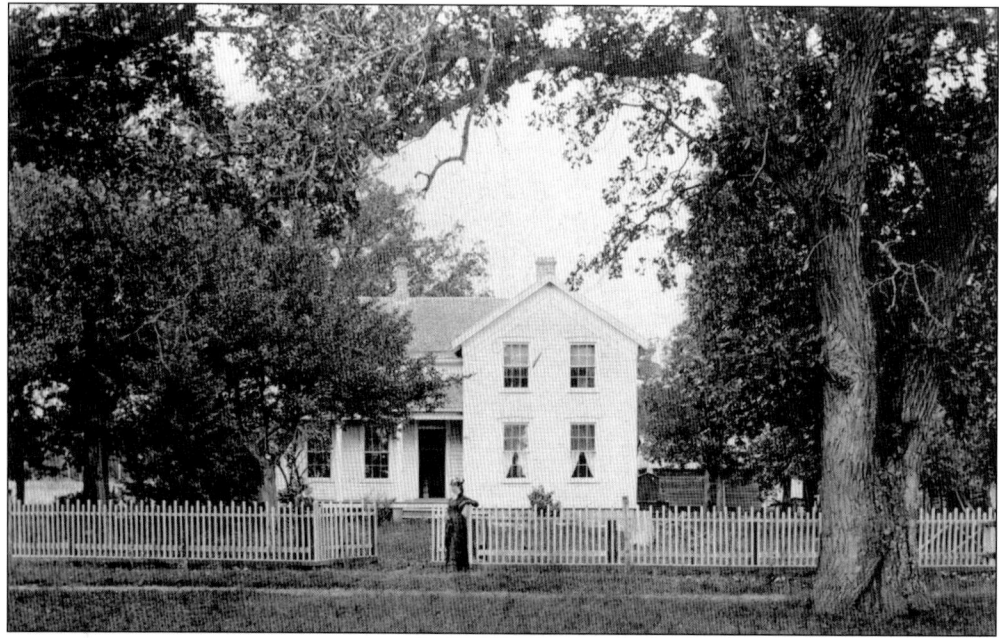

A member of the John Moore family is standing at the farm fence gate around 1900. The farm was on Route 83 east of North Lake Street and later owned by the Gooding brothers. The Grayslake Gelatin Company purchased it and had a farm manager oversee the farming operations of its Chesapeake Farm. Sold again, the Chesapeake Farms Subdivision started developing in 1991. (Courtesy of Grayslake Historical Society.)

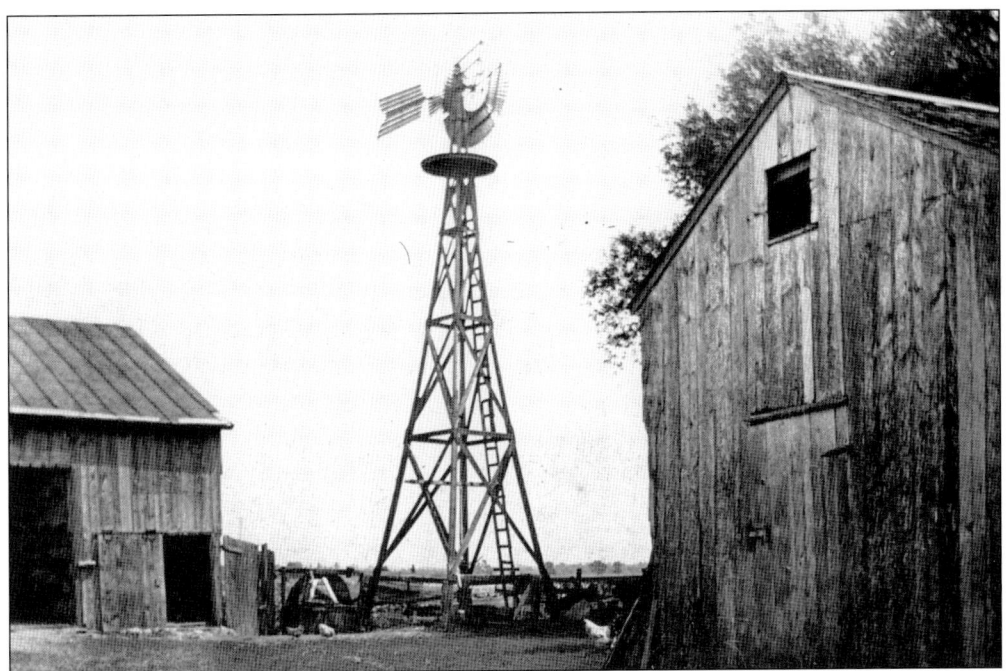

The children of Cassius Doolittle were born on the farm shown above. The farm was on the north side of Drury Lane, north of Route 83, and is now part of Rollins Savanna owned by the Lake County Forest Preserve. This image was taken around 1900. (Courtesy of Grayslake Historical Society.)

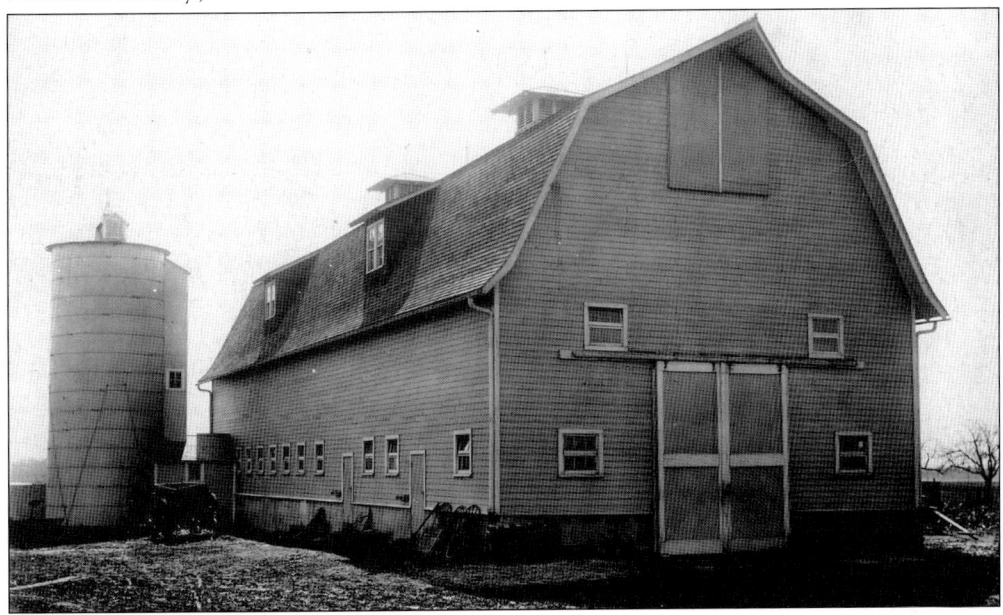

It is appropriate that the former William Doolittle farm, pictured here in 1918, is called English Meadows Subdivision. Many Avon Township early settlers emigrated from England. The Doolittle farm was sold in 1942 to the Rite-Way Products Company, which manufactured farm equipment, such as milking machines. The subdivision was platted in 1991. (Courtesy of Lake County Discovery Museum.)

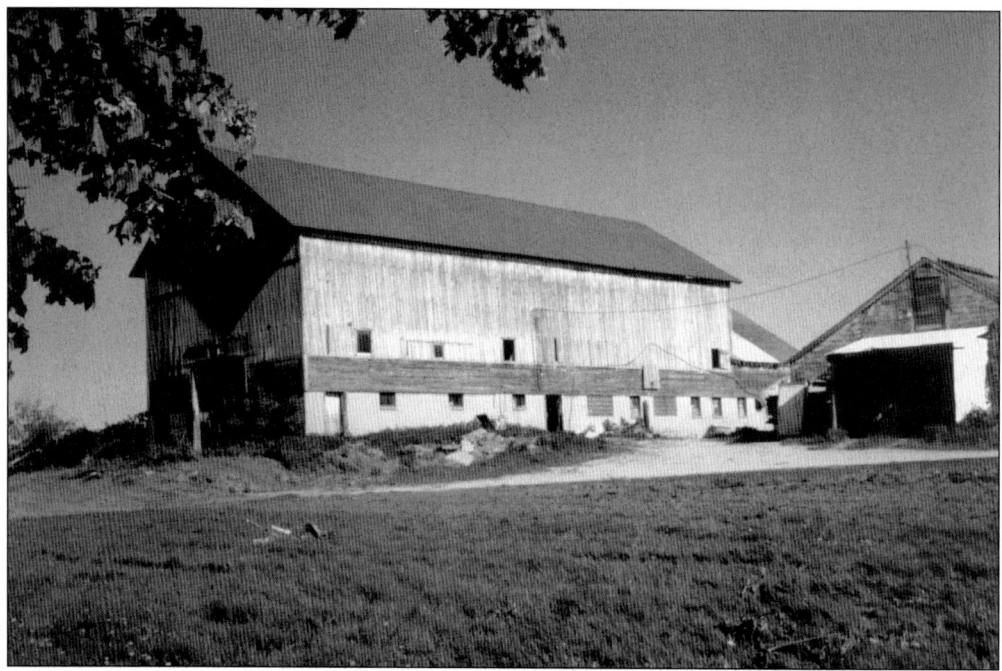

In England, William Hook had 11 children. Of these children, eight of them immigrated to the Avon Township area. Grandson John "Lou" Hook raised his family on a farm on Rollins Road. The Rollins Crossing shopping mall has replaced the family homestead. Hook Drive is nearby. (Courtesy of Karen Hook and Mary Hook.)

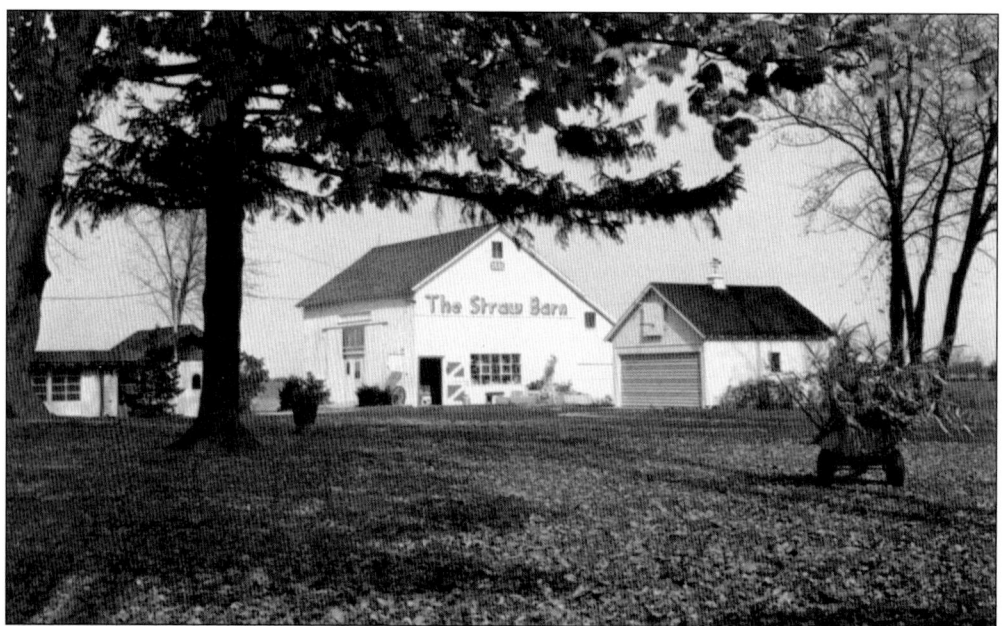

The Kapples came to Avon Township in the early 1840s and settled on land adjacent to Belvidere Road between Routes 83 and 45. For a period of time, a commercial venture, the Straw Barn, was housed here. Condell Acute Care Center is now on the former Albert Kapple farm.

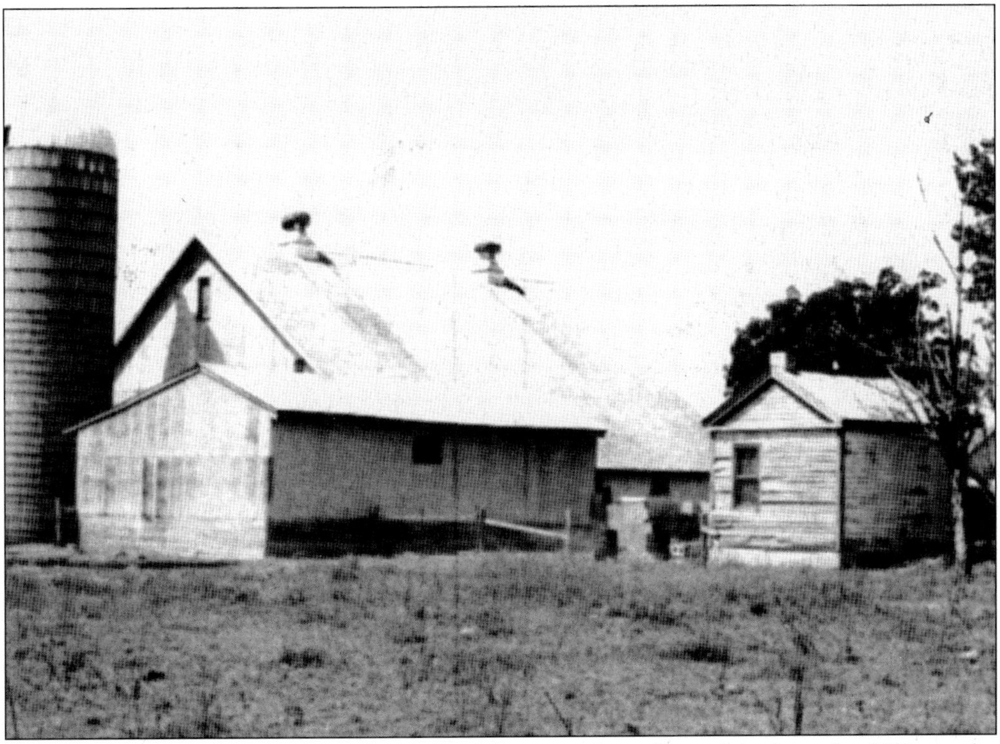

The Grayslake Gelatin Company has owned farms in Avon Township from the 1930s to the present. This is a 1976 view from Joanne Johnson's *Reflections of Hainesville, Past and Present* of the former farm, now lumberyard, at the junction of Belvidere and Hainesville Roads. The land was owned by the Haines family in the 1840s.

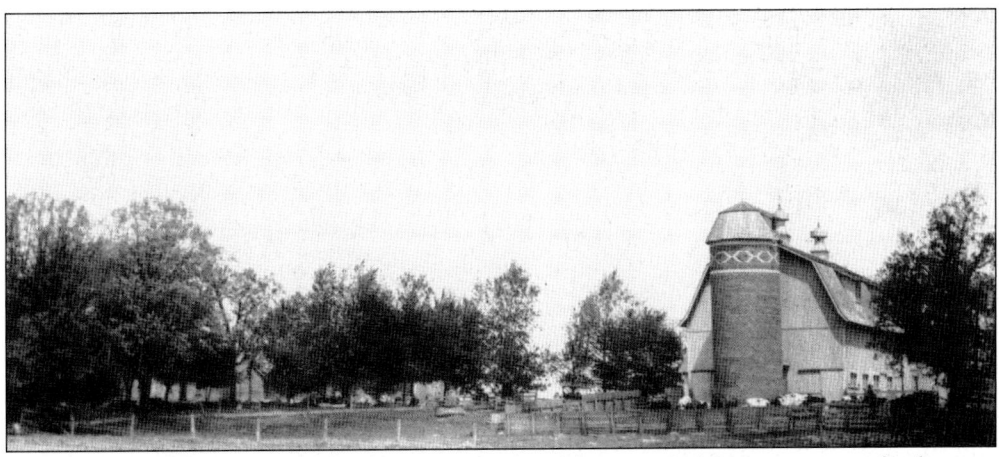

Charles F. Kuebker purchased the Charles Whitehead farm in 1895. His son operated a dairy on the farm for 10 years, beginning in 1925. The farm stayed in the family until 1967, when it was sold to the Grayslake Gelatin Company. The land presently comprises the middle school and library in addition to Grayslake's Central Park. This view is from the 1930s.

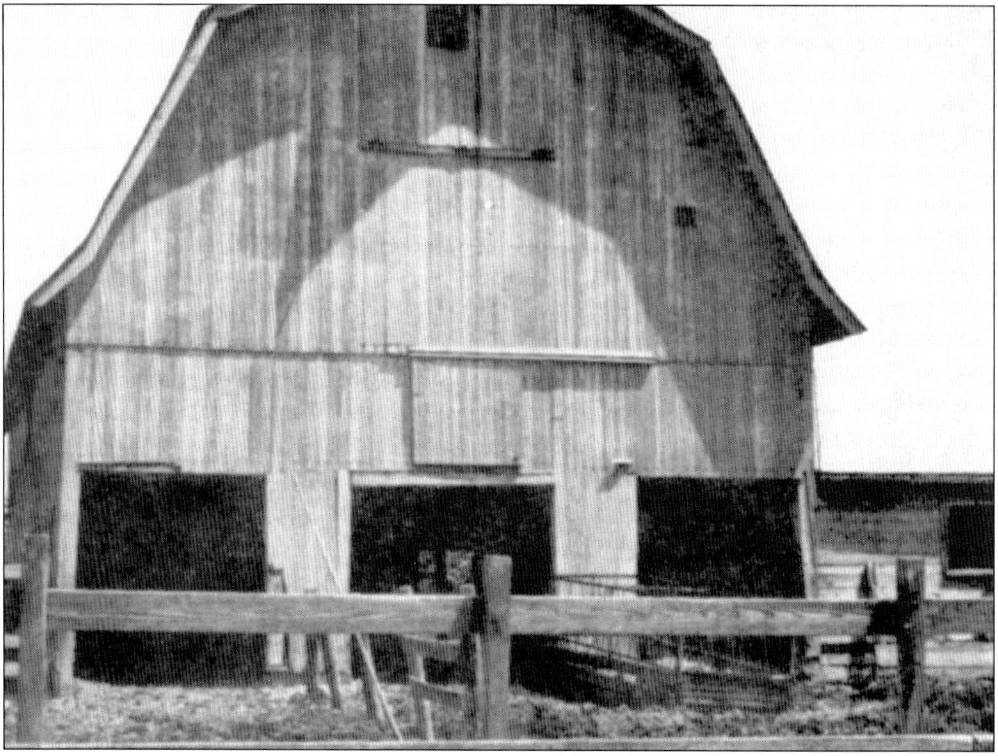

The barn, pictured here from Joanne Johnson's *Reflections of Hainesville, Past and Present*, was located on Route 134 about a half mile west of Hainesville Road on the former Grayslake Gelatin Company farm, purchased in 1935. This 1976 image recalls the farmer's castle of the past. The property has been developed as Cranberry Lake, a subdivision in Hainesville.

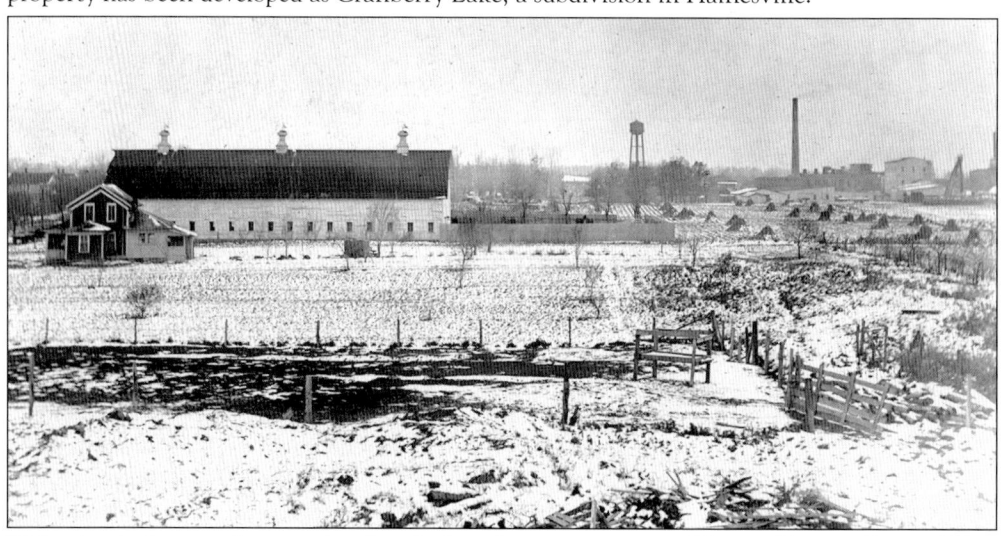

This view is from a photograph taken before the construction of Route 21, now Route 83, in 1922. The house to the left had been moved to this location and later became a restaurant. The barn was built in late 1917 or 1918 to stable mules for the canning factory. While the house and mule barn are gone, the water tower and smokestack in the horizon still dominate the Grayslake skyline. (Courtesy of Grayslake Historical Society.)

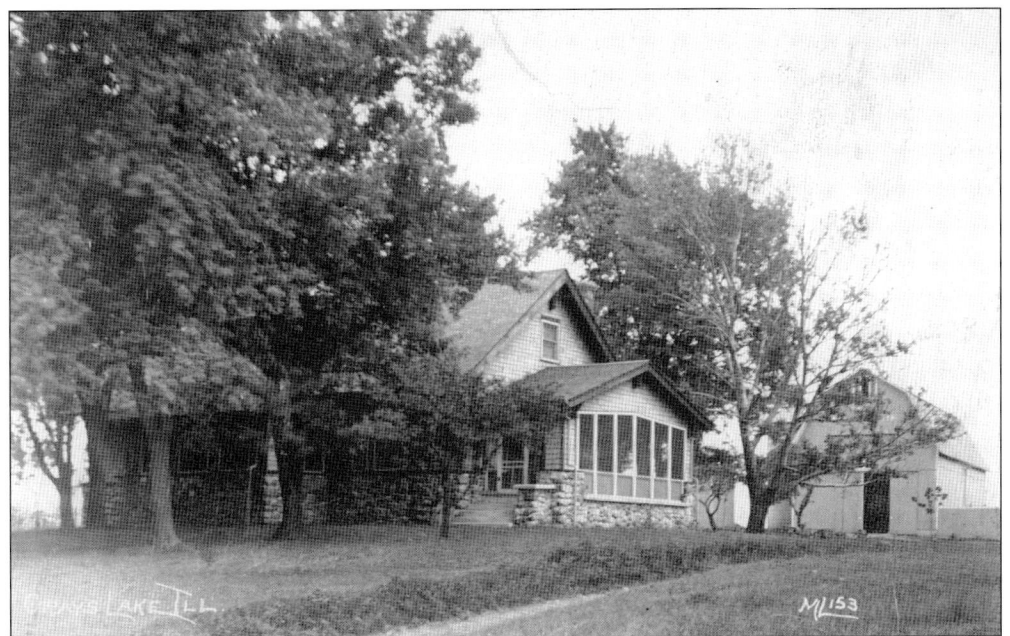

The former Raber Radke farm was located on Belvidere Road east of St. Gilbert Catholic Church, where the farmhouse remains as a residence. The property was annexed to the village in 1967, and the subdivisions of South Creek and Eastlake Farms were located on the former farm in 1989. (Courtesy of Grayslake Historical Society.)

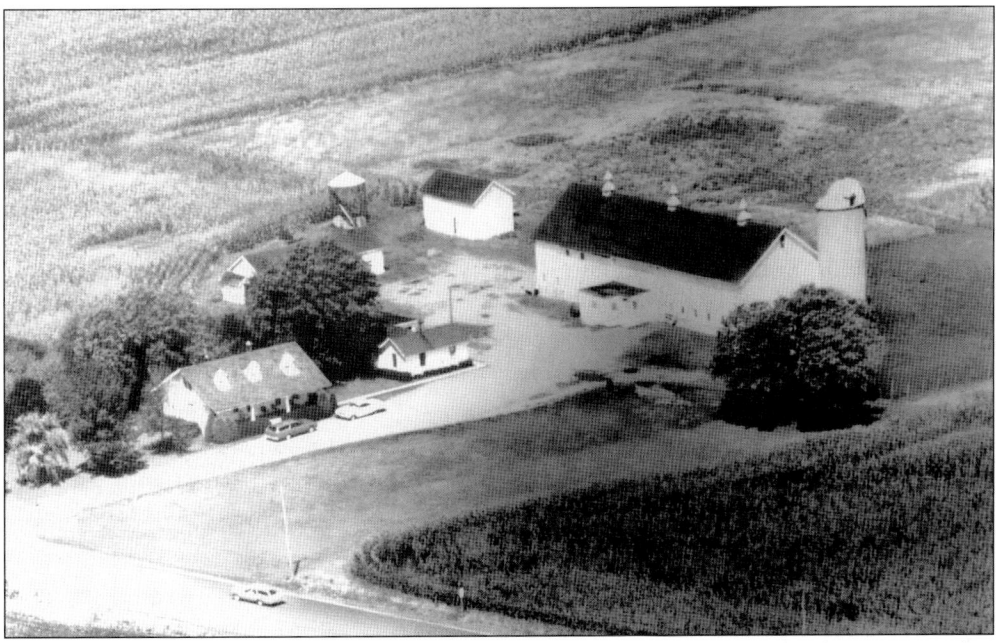

The Rosing name is associated with an early-20th century store in Round Lake. Later Archie Rosing had a farm on Route 120 east of Cedar Lake Road. This aerial view of the farm shows how each farm had a house, a barn, and several outbuildings, such as a machine shed, corncrib, and chicken coop. The former Rosing farm became Bright Meadows Subdivision in 1994. (Courtesy of Joe Lodesky.)

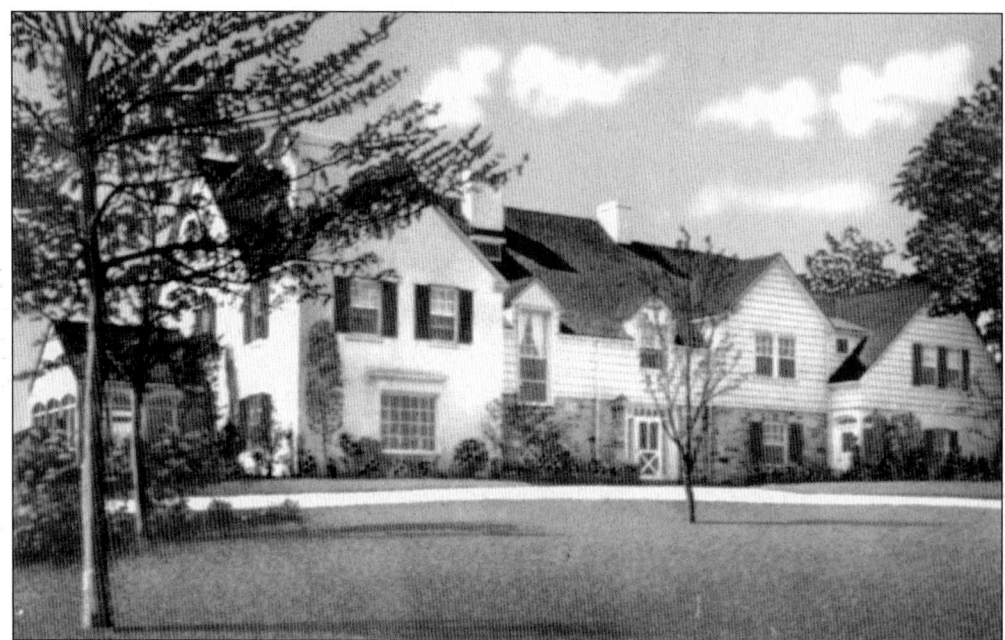

Wesley Sears, son of the founder of the Sears mail-order house, built this 17-room mansion in 1938 on 17 acres at the southwest corner of Routes 120 and 45. The mansion became the Country Squire Restaurant in 1954. (Courtesy of Grayslake Historical Society, Ruth Mogg Collection.)

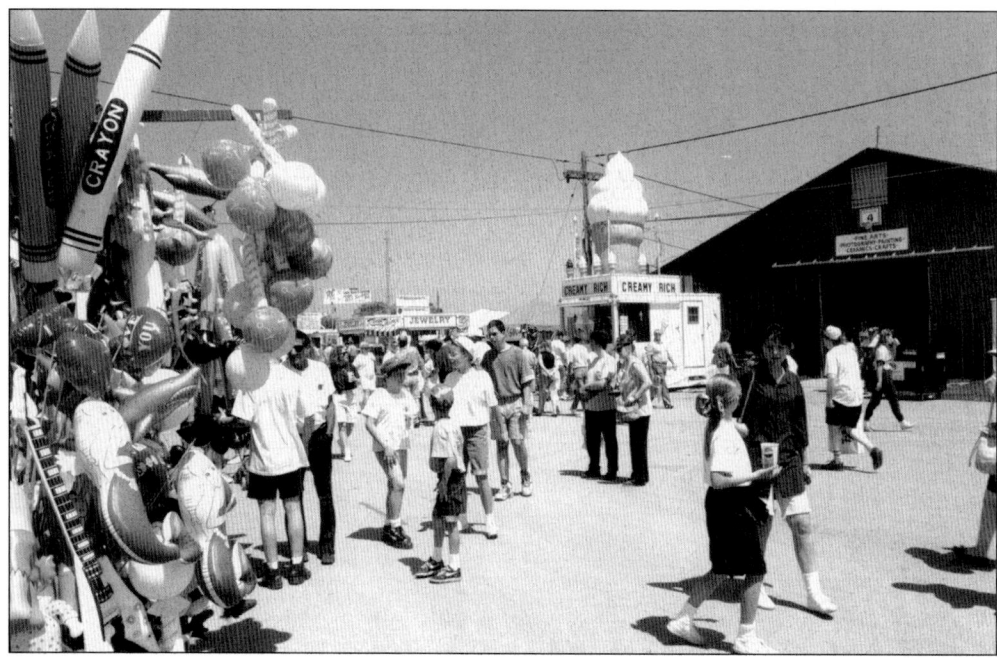

The Lake County Fair had been held in several locations before the purchase of 60 acres of farmland and its opening in 1956 near the northwest corner of Routes 45 and 120. The property was annexed to the village of Grayslake in 1984, and as of 2007, the Lake County Fair Association owns 106 acres. (Courtesy of Grayslake Historical Society.)

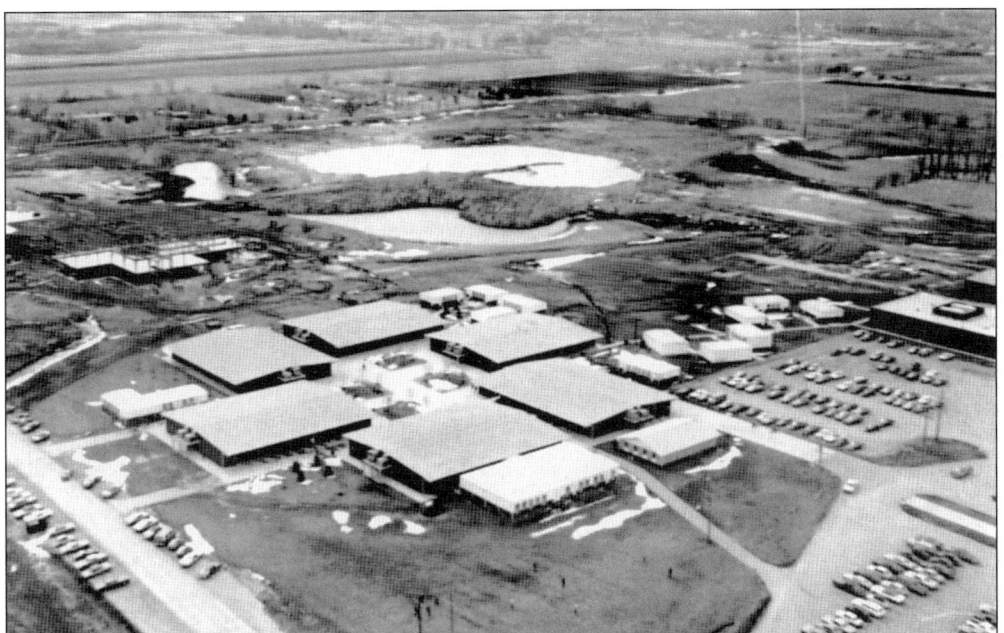

In 1968, A. Harold Anderson and Paul W. Brandel donated 181 acres to be used as the permanent home of the newly formed College of Lake County, which opened in 1969. This 1973 aerial view shows temporary buildings, which were used in the college's early years. (Courtesy of College of Lake County public relations.)

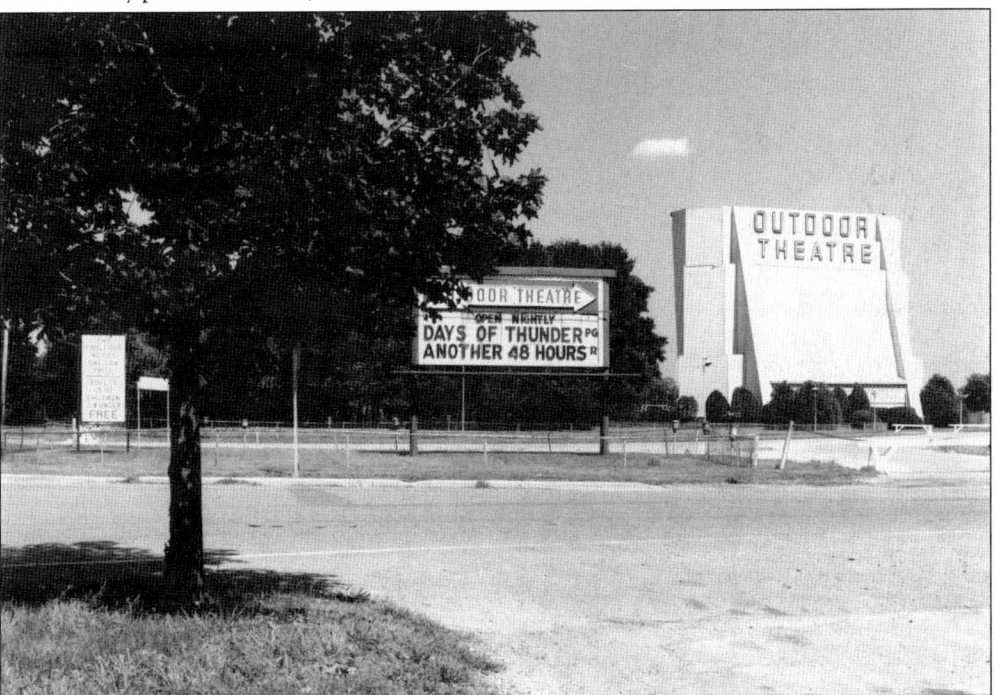

The Grayslake Family Outdoor Theatre opened in 1948 on a former Kapple farm at the corner of Belvidere and Ivanhoe Roads. The last show was in 1997. The property is now the site of Grayslake's Maple View shopping area. (Courtesy of Grayslake Historical Society.)

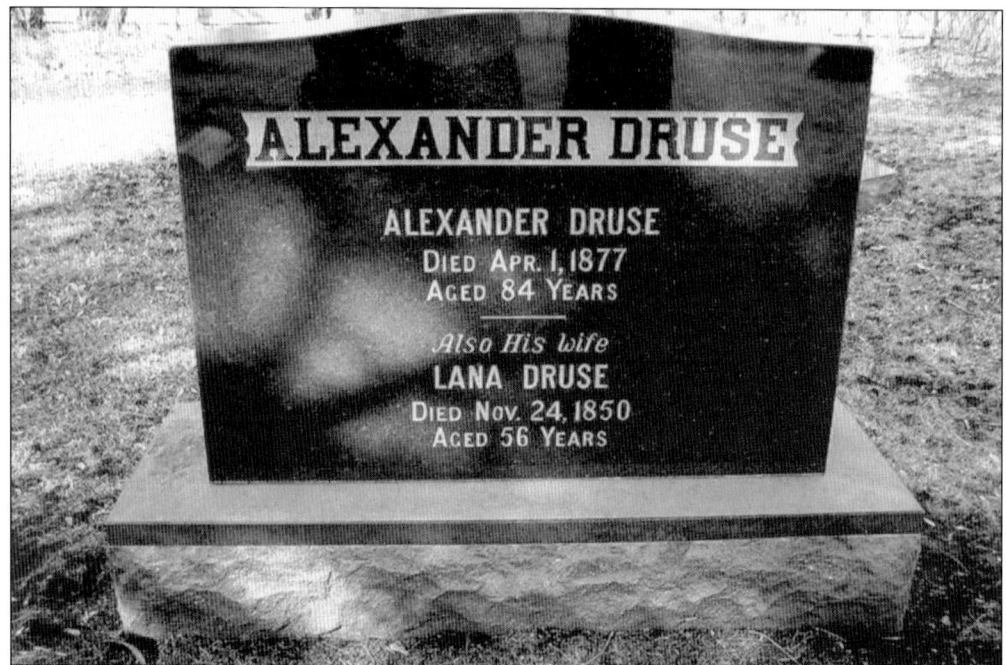

The original headstone for Alexander Druce/Druse has been replaced. It is located in the Druce family cemetery on Washington Street just west of Route 45. Druce was born in Massachusetts, came to this area by way of New York, and purchased a land patent in the early 1840s. He homesteaded on the south shore of what became Druce Lake. Washington Street between Routes 45 and 83 was known as Druce Lake Road until around 1968.

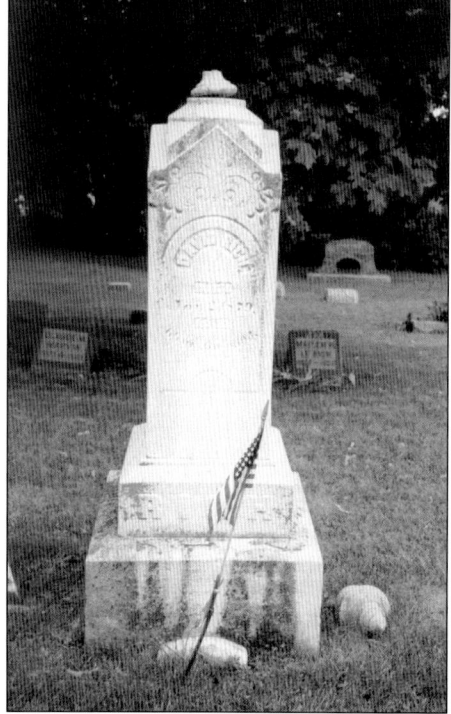

David Rich's tombstone is in the Grayslake Cemetery located on South Lake Street in Grayslake. Rich and his family came to the area from Allegany County, New York, in 1836 and settled about a half mile south of the lake. The road that led to the lake became Alleghany Road, which is spelled Grayslake's way. The land for the Grayslake Cemetery was deeded by Lawrence Forvor.

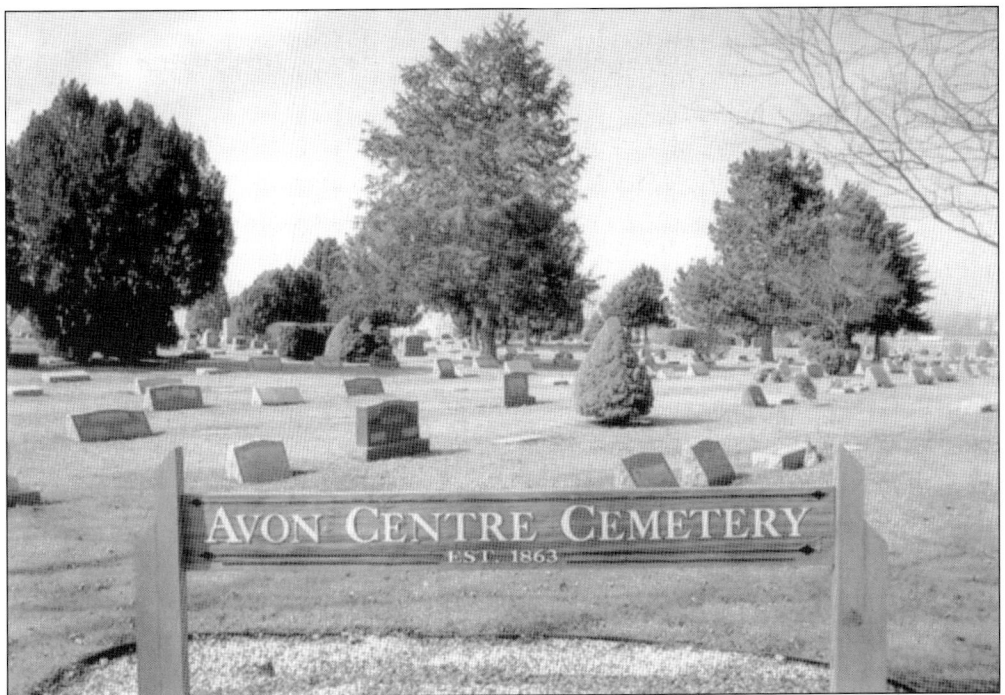

Avon Centre Cemetery is on property deeded in 1864 for $58 by the Edwards family. The cemetery was originally 1 acre and has enlarged to 15 acres. Located on Shorewood Road, it has burials dating back to 1847. Civil War veterans are among its entombments.

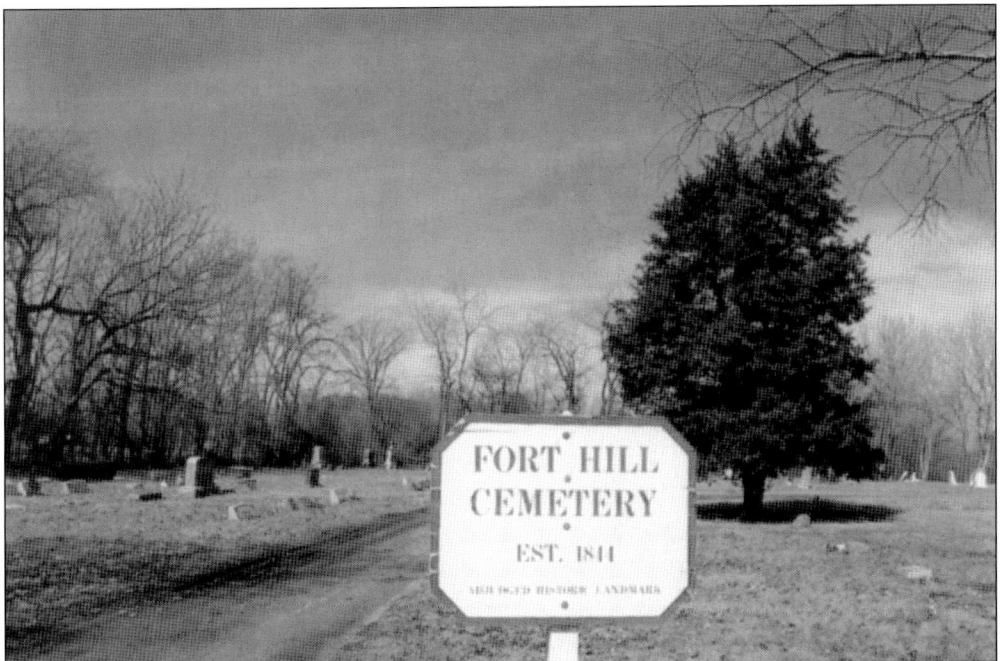

The Fort Hill Cemetery is on land deeded by George Thomson and Solomon Marble. The earliest burial in the Fort Hill Cemetery is 1844. The west side of the burial grounds is a public area while the east is St. Joseph Catholic Cemetery.

Across America, People are Discovering Something Wonderful. Their Heritage.

Arcadia Publishing is the leading local history publisher in the United States. With more than 3,000 titles in print and hundreds of new titles released every year, Arcadia has extensive specialized experience chronicling the history of communities and celebrating America's hidden stories, bringing to life the people, places, and events from the past. To discover the history of other communities across the nation, please visit:

www.arcadiapublishing.com

Customized search tools allow you to find regional history books about the town where you grew up, the cities where your friends and family live, the town where your parents met, or even that retirement spot you've been dreaming about.

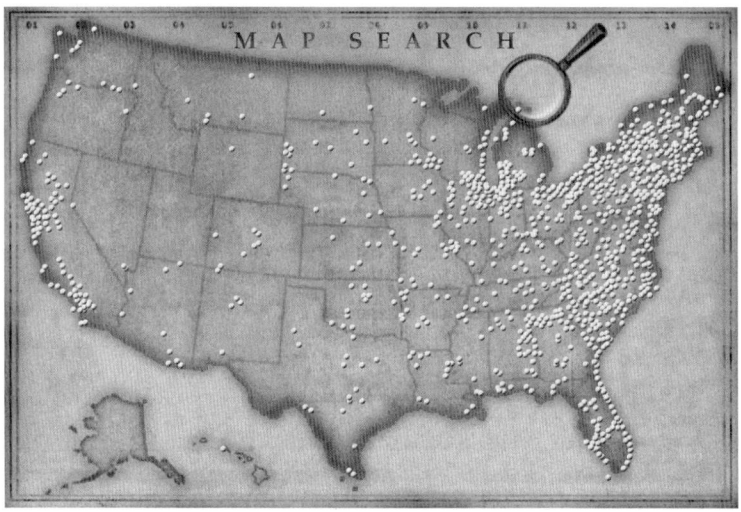